D0563885

AT WAR WITH TIME

AT WAR WITH TIME

The Wisdom of Western Thought
from
The Sages to a New Activism for Our Time

CRAIG EISENDRATH

HELIOS PRESS
NEW YORK

07   06   05   04   03
5   4   3   2   1

Published by Helios Press
An imprint of Allworth Communications, Inc.
10 East 23rd Street, New York, NY 10010

Cover and interior page design by Derek Bacchus
Cover photography by © Bilderberg/Photonica 2003
Page composition/typography by Rachel Reiss

LIBRARY OF CONGRESS CATALOGING-IN-PUBLICATION DATA
Eisendrath, Craig R.
  At war with time: the wisdom of Western thought from the
sages to a new activism for our age/Craig Eisendrath.
      p. cm.
Includes bibliographical references and index.
  ISBN 1-58115-307-4
1. Life. 2. Change. 3. Meaning (Philosophy) 4. Political
participation. 5. Life—History. 6. Meaning (Philosophy)—
History. I.Title.
  BD431.E42 2003
  190—dc22
                              2003014624

Printed in Canada

CONTE NTS

PART I The Permanence Complex

PART II Convergence

PREFACE

The Western world faces a time of crisis. Before us lie a continuing battle against terrorism, and the prospect of wars around the globe. Yet, even before September 11, the impact of massive social, economic, and technological changes had disrupted our sense of a stable, secure world.

In response to crisis, thoughtful people search inside themselves for confidence or security. For many, traditional beliefs, which provided comfort for earlier generations, no longer work. These beliefs include a faith in God, in the soul, and in eternal ideas; a belief that science can deliver sure answers; and confidence that history will inevitably have a favorable outcome. Together, these beliefs form what I call a "permanence complex." With these beliefs in question, many people are beset with the uncertainty which marks our age.

For over four thousand years, Western thinkers and religious leaders have used these beliefs to provide answers to many of life's problems and to develop the basis of our social institutions. The cataclysmic events of the last hundred years, such as the Holocaust and other human-rights horrors, have assaulted aspects of these beliefs, particularly in the essential goodness of the human soul and in the inevitability of historical progress.

In addition, massive technological and economic changes, begun at the very outset of the industrial revolution, have weakened our sense of community. Many people today feel lost and atomized by the media, economically at risk, and adrift in a sea of computerized information. Rather than seeking recourse in the political process, many here in the United States see politics dominated by moneyed interests, and so doubt their ability to effect change. Although there have been recent rounds of protest against war, economic globalization, and other perceived wrongs, the dominant political mode in the United States at the beginning of the twenty-first century is still one of declining civic engagement.

In the face of these uncertainties, large segments of the population have professed a return or continued adherence to traditional beliefs, particularly in God, in the immortal soul, and in the essential goodness of human beings. This is particularly true in the United States, as opposed to western Europe. Others, however, admit to genuine uncertainty, or, as I believe is often the case, are willing to hold contrasting views at the same time. As they question their basic beliefs, they find themselves increasingly distressed as they read the newspapers and watch CNN, raise their children, and face the contingencies of life.

No new philosophy has yet arisen to turn this situation around. The influential philosophic movement known as "deconstructionism," while attacking notions of permanence, has failed to provide an adequate basis for a sense of reality, personal identity, or social commitment. Despite a few celebrity "public intellectuals," the universities, for the most part, have abandoned their public role. Where is help to be found in our age?

As I review the history of the last 150 years, I find elements of a new basis of thought which I believe can help provide some answers. Starting with Charles Darwin and physical-field theory in the second half of the nineteenth century, advances in biology, physics, neuroscience, and artificial intelligence have prompted a new way of seeing the world as interrelated. These advances suggest a world that is responsible for its own laws and the increasing growth of complexity. This view offers a stark contrast to the notions of a static, permanent world which had dominated Western thought.

Parallel to this new direction in science, and influenced by it, developments in the social sciences and philosophy suggest a redemptive activism as the basis for a meaningful life. Rather than seeing human beings as passive creatures in a created world, we can now conceive of ourselves as active creators of a world which is interrelated and self-governing.

Unlike the idea of permanence, this new view does not offer total assurance. For one thing, it offers no promise of immortality. It also accepts the fact that living in the modern world means living with questions for which we have no final answers. This is a universe in process, and in which we are learning, and of which at this time, and probably forever, we will achieve only a partial understanding. What this new mode of thinking does make clear is that this uncertain, incompletely understood historical moment is ours to live in, and to improve if we can. It says that we live in a fertile, all-encompassing world which offers a rich invitation to understanding and commitment. It reassures us that even in a time of crisis, like today, we can grow as human beings into the responsibilities which the world demands.

Why the West?

This book focuses almost exclusively on the Western tradition, particularly as it has been advanced in western Europe and the United States. I am not arguing that this tradition has any monopoly on truth. Indeed, this book is not meant as a defense of the West as it increasingly comes into conflict with other cultures. Rather, I would hold that these other traditions offer parallel paths, and need to be understood in their own terms if nations are to interact peacefully with each other in an increasingly globalized economy and interconnected world.

Nevertheless, although many religions and cultures are having an increasing impact on the West, the Judeo-Christian tradition known as "Western civilization" is the foundation on which the United States and western Europe developed, and is still our nation's dominant culture. Its crisis, which began in the nineteenth century, is a personal crisis for many of us, and needs to be faced. This book is meant to address not only those readers who locate themselves within this tradition, but those who are rooted in other traditions as well. As Western culture increasingly encounters others, I hope this book will contribute to that understanding and empathy which, as our sages have told us for thousands of years, can only come through self-knowledge.

ACKNOWLEDGMENTS

It is impossible to thank everyone who has contributed to the writing of this book.

I am particularly grateful to these friends and colleagues: Rebecca Alpert, Christie Balka, Tad Crawford, Abraham Edel, Aaron Eisendrath, Rachel Eisendrath, Paul Elie, Melvin A. Goodman, Eric Hoffman, Anne Johnson, Stephen J. Kobrin, Michael Krausz, Jerome Lettvin, Joseph Margolis, and Gerald Marsh; and to my wife, Roberta Spivek, for her wise editing, substantive contributions, and boundless support.

This book is dedicated to my grandfather, Sam Newman, who was a blessing to my mother and, through her, to me.

PART I

The

Permanence

Complex

INTRODUCTION

O God, our help in ages past,
Our hope for years to come,
Our shelter from the stormy blast,
And our eternal home.

From the hymn "St. Anne" by Isaac Watts
(1674–1748)

In the West, a belief in permanence has taken a variety of forms. The most prominent has been the enduring existence of religious belief, including the idea of God, and God's role in the creation and maintenance of the universe. The need to believe in permanence has also been behind our conviction that we have souls, which, allied with God, can live forever. It is behind our notion that ideas are enshrined in a timeless realm that somehow forms the basis of the temporal world and of absolute truths. It is found in our beliefs in a permanent order of nature, in a fixed meaning in history, and in a belief that what we do or have done will survive our own death.

In part I, we will consider what influential Western thinkers have said about the idea of permanence, and how this idea has been embedded in Western civilization's structure of thought and belief, and its corresponding social institutions. The aim of part I is to present the main line of this tradition without being overly fastidious about its details. Our strategy is to take up the thoughts and beliefs of key religious movements in the West and a relative handful of important thinkers, rather than attempt anything like a comprehensive survey. Chapter 6, ending part I, shows how the ideas of permanence form a complex which, with variations, characterizes virtually all of Western thought until fairly recent times.

Many of us have grown up with some exposure to Judaism or Christianity. Some have studied the philosophers like Plato or Immanuel Kant.

What is important here is to consider how invested these belief systems are in the idea of permanence. Underneath their different terms and concepts, they share a desire to rescue humankind from its fear of death and the uncertainty of events, and to secure a permanent place for it in the world.

The Western tradition begins over four thousand years ago in Sumer, the first recorded civilization on the planet. Our study begins with *The Epic of Gilgamesh*, which dates from the third millennium B.C.E. (Before the Common Era). One of the first known works of written literature, the *Epic* is preoccupied with issues of permanence—the Sumerians' relation to the gods; their anxiety about death; and, above all, their quest for immortality. *The Epic of Gilgamesh* illustrates a view of the world as being controlled by the gods, that continues as the dominant belief of ancient peoples through Roman times.

More than a thousand years after the *Epic* was recorded, its themes are taken up in the Torah, the first five books of the Hebrew Bible, and then again in the Christian Gospels of the New Testament, and are provided new answers. In the Torah, the gods of nature described in *Gilgamesh* have been transformed into one God who is completely separate from the heavens and earth which he has created. This is the God who spells out the moral law; who has chosen his people and made a pact with them; and who intervenes in their history in a continuing, troubled, but caring relationship. While this God is depicted as permanent, human beings are mortal, as they were in Sumer, and only achieve permanence by virtue of their relation to him.

A radically different set of beliefs emerges out of Greek philosophy, which developed in relative independence of Hebraic thought. The Platonic dialogues are radiant with the promise that beyond our changing, sensible existence lies a permanent world of total purity and power, and that we have entrée into that world not primarily through experience, but through our minds. This other world, the world of the soul, of eternal ideas, and of God, Plato tells us, is the metaphysical ground for all being, including our present existence. In this sense, the world of experience can be seen as a set of hints, approximations, and clues to this higher reality. But it can also be viewed as essentially worthless, a mere stepping stone to something better. Aristotle departs from this view at key points, and yet offers considerable assurances of permanence in the unchanging, essential structure of the world and in the nature of God, its creator.

3

The New Testament is concerned with a central figure, Jesus, or the Christ, who provides a personal vehicle for an ultimate form of permanence—personal immortality. I strongly suspect that Christianity proved so immensely attractive because it offered a promise of permanence with which Judaism and other religions, including the official religion of the Roman state, could not compete. Indeed, point for point, the early Church shaped its doctrine in such a way that it became *the* guarantor of permanence in an age in which despair and instability left humankind anxious for precisely such a belief.

Since at least the end of the second century of the Common Era, the belief in permanence has been supported by a particularly powerful combination of religion and philosophy. One reason for that convergence is that religion and philosophy can take on separate but closely related functions, religion being the vehicle for fulfilling deeply felt emotional needs, and philosophy serving as the basis for a more intellectual understanding of the world.

But the distinction between religion and philosophy has frequently blurred in the West. Religion has itself carried its own worldview, and the histories of both Judaism and Christianity have been deeply influenced by their attempts to integrate philosophy. Even skeptical philosophers, such as the eighteenth century philosopher David Hume, have unconsciously worked within a framework of religious thought.

The philosophy with which Christianity merged was Greek, which deeply influenced its evolving theology. This philosophy was primarily Plato's or his followers, to be joined, particularly in the thirteenth century, when texts became more readily available, by the work of Aristotle. Christian theology, with these fundamental Greek components, seemed to provide an ultimate guarantee of permanence. In merging with classical thought, Christianity increasingly distanced itself from biblical Judaism, particularly with the doctrine of the Trinity. It also acquired elements from Hellenistic religion and from the structure of the Roman Empire which helped to insure its appeal and organizational effectiveness as the dominant religion of the West.

By the end of the Renaissance, voices other than those of Plato and Aristotle and their medieval scholastic commentators began to be heard, modifying the Christian message of permanence. Much of modern thought, like medieval scholasticism, however, is grounded in the notions of permanence that had been established in the earlier tradition.

Introduction

I have chosen five thinkers to represent the main line of modern Western thought from the Renaissance to the beginning of the nineteenth century—René Descartes, John Locke, David Hume, Immanuel Kant, and G.W.F. Hegel. Baruch Spinoza, Gottfried Leibnitz, and Friedrich Nietzsche also made major contributions to modern philosophy, but I have chosen these five thinkers who are, in my view, at the center of the Western tradition.

What we see in these masters of modern thought is an attempt to define a world which is constantly eluding their categories. It was one thing to define an essentially static world, quite another to define it in the very act of change. Yet the gulf they saw between the phenomenal world and the real world, between experience and reason, and between the physical world and mentality, was in many instances as deep as it had been viewed in the ancient tradition.

With inadequate assurances of permanence, and with a worldview still shaped by traditions based on it, these founders of modern philosophy left many adherents in the West both anxious and intellectually unsatisfied. The notions advanced by these creators of the modern philosophic mainstream were inadequate to explain change, and to help human beings understand their role in an evolving universe and dynamic culture. When the pace of change dramatically increased in the middle of the nineteenth century, a radically different model of thought would be necessary to give people a sense that they fully belonged to a new world.

Chapter One

Sumer: Gods and Humans

*There is no permanence. Do we build a house to
stand for ever, do we seal a contract to hold for all
time? Do brothers divide an inheritance to keep
for ever, does the flood-time of rivers endure? . . .
From the days of old there is no permanence. The
sleeping and the dead, how alike they are, they
are like a painted death. What is there between
the master and the servant when both have
fulfilled their doom?*

The Epic of Gilgamesh[1]

The West's romance with permanence begins with one of humankind's earliest
epic writings. *The Epic of Gilgamesh* connects with our human past almost
as far back as there are words to record more than the counting of sheep
or the site of a battle. This tale of thought and longing introduces most of
the ideas included in the notions of permanence which have continued to
preoccupy the West.

   Sumer was a full civilization which flourished in the valleys of the
Tigris and Euphrates rivers in what is now southern Iraq, in the third mil-
lennium B.C.E. The Sumerians developed city-states, the cuneiform system
of writing, irrigation canals, and a great literature which includes not only
The Epic of Gilgamesh, but also the first feminist epic, *The Descent of the
Goddess*, about the goddesses Inanna and Ereshkigal. Eventually, in the

next millennium, control of the country passed to the Babylonians, and Sumer disappeared, to be discovered, and its language translated, still not with total certainty, only in the twentieth century.[2]

Ancient Egypt might also have been a starting place for our inquiry. In many ways, its defenses against death are more dramatic than those of Sumer. With a fully developed technology for the preservation of bodies, and a full-blown theology of eternal life, the Egyptian civilization that flourished in the Nile Valley for over two thousand years before the birth of Christ offered a template for all subsequent efforts to try to ensure permanence. The evidence from Sumer, however, shows that our humanity's oldest civilization was not fully convinced that human beings can achieve permanence. Rather, in a strikingly modern way, the Sumerians questioned it, and so perhaps offer a richer resource with which to begin our discussion.

The World of Ancient Sumer

In looking at Sumerian religion, we are reconstructing possibly the first coherent worldview for which we have any written records, predating cultures in India and China. Pure philosophy, as we know it, would not appear in the West for at least another 1,500 years. As the great French sociologist Émile Durkheim once noted, "The first systems of representations with which men have pictured to themselves the world and themselves were of religious origin. There is no religion that is not a cosmology at the same time . . . Men owe to it not only a good part of the substance of their knowledge, but also the form in which this knowledge has been elaborated."[3]

At the heart of Sumerian religion is the belief that the world's natural forces are personified by gods and goddesses, who are modeled on human beings. These deities control everything which takes place in this world, and thus need constantly to be propitiated.[4] Behind even such commonplace objects as salt or flint is a deity who gives these things their particular qualities. It is the god who also chooses to cooperate or not to cooperate with humankind, and who chooses to do so in his or her special way. For example, salt lends its flavor to food, and flint chooses to flake so it can become a tool.

Some of these gods, indeed the most prominent in the Sumerian pantheon, are important for the *Gilgamesh* epic. These are Anu, the god of the sky; Enlil, the god of storms; Utu or Shamash, the sun god; Enki, the god of wisdom and of the waters of the earth; and Inanna or Ishtar, the moon goddess of love and war. It should be borne in mind, however, that a god like Utu or Shamash was considered to be both the sun and the personification of the sun. Other, less powerful gods were children, grandchildren, distant relations, and servant gods of these preeminent gods. The lesser gods held some power in their own right and some power by virtue of their relation to the greater gods. In comparison with the gods, human beings were considered to be relatively impotent or passive: gods held most of the power or the responsibility for what happened in the world. As we will see, this conception could move easily into the seventeenth century physics of Isaac Newton, in which passive matter is set in motion by an active and all-powerful God who prescribes the laws of nature.

The gods of the Sumerian pantheon explain how things come to be the way they are, or will be. They determine the stability of forms in the world, the order of nature, and the occurrence of particular events.[5]

The divine world of Sumer, and the earthly events derived from that world, were ordered by a council of powers whose leading figures wielded authority over lesser ones. The council of gods paralleled the councils of men who held power in the city-states, but it was the divine council which ultimately decided a person's fate and determined natural events.

The Epic of Gilgamesh hints at a still earlier stage of thought, in which every being is endowed with power and interacts with other beings which are similarly endowed. This earlier view of humankind participating in an interactive universe of powerful beings, a view held by most "primitive cultures," is worth pausing to consider. Despite its overlays of the awesome or magical, this view corresponds more closely to the world of contemporary physics than to any worldview between it and the present. We will be returning to this notion in part II.

As we have seen, Sumerian society reflected the divine order and served the deities. The chief landholdings in the cities were the temples of the gods. Grain grown for the priests and attendants, and thereby for offerings to the gods, took up a considerable amount of each city's foodstuffs. When it was said in Sumerian literature that man was created by the gods to relieve them of toil, this had, for Sumerians, a quite literal, although magical, truth.

Each early Sumerian city-state was considered to be an estate of its principal god, and was run by a manager or *ensi*, the most powerful of the priests. The *ensi* was often the city's chief judge, interpreting the god's decrees. The god communicated to the *ensi* through omens, the reading of the organs of sacrificed animals, or most directly through dreams. The dreams of the *ensi* were public news, a communication from the prevailing god about the city's future. The Sumerian chronicle books report that the god of a particular city has decided to make war on another city. When the city falls, it is because the god has withdrawn his or her power from it.

In general, common people had close ties not with the powerful gods, like Enlil and Anu, but with a personal god, usually a minor deity. This deity personified a person's luck or success. People were thought to do nothing on their own, and to achieve anything only through the work of their personal god, with whom they had a coaxing, sometimes hectoring, relation. They would pray to the god, bribe the god with sacrifices, or threaten to withdraw them. Sometimes the personal god was asked to write to a greater god, or petition him or her to influence a decision.

This conception of the world did not allow for the development of a self-conscious individual. If all power were in the hands of the gods, if the society were integrated around the notion of serving them, why should individuals refer matters to themselves? Even the most powerful individual, the *ensi*, was merely the capstone of a social order engaged in serving the gods. His task, and that of all other citizens, was in so acting that the gods might be induced to maintain the city-state.

Decisions were ultimately collective, for although the *ensi* was the most powerful person in the polity, he was merely a member of a council of men who cooperated to make things work. Kingship could be conferred on an individual, as in times of war, but when the emergency passed, power would revert back to the council.

The Epic of Gilgamesh represents a stage somewhat beyond this, when kingship had become permanent. This permanent concentration of power in one individual seriously affected the king's assessment of his own power in relation to the gods. A king could make decisions which seemed based on *his* will and *his* judgment. If power were some kind of common currency, the king's power could be compared to that of the gods, and their authority might be challenged.

Still another development which lent power to this challenge was that at this time in Sumerian history, people were beginning to control floods through communal dikes and dams; to resist famine through collectively maintained granaries; to devise and administer justice through courts; and to record history in language. Not only did human beings have an increasing capacity to control nature, they were also developing a social morality and a sense of themselves over time. Human beings were recognizing their *own* power to control events, and were just beginning to question the gods' responsibility for significant outcomes in this world.

Despite the Sumerians' increasing sense of their own power, the gods in the time of the *Epic* were still mostly in control, and were the repositories of permanence. While the gods created the forms of the world and intervened in its events, their nature was unchangeable.

The permanent nature of the gods, as conceived by the Sumerians, includes several aspects which still define the notion of deity most people hold today. First, the gods are immortal and incorruptible; they do not suffer permanent change or decay. Second, they are omniscient; that is, they do not learn, but already know everything that happens and will happen. Knowledge is not the result of a process, but a permanent state.[6] Third, the gods are omnipotent. The contingent nature of events and the obstruction of brute matter do not stop them from carrying out their intentions. What they will to happen happens, no matter what.

Because the Sumerian gods are modeled on human beings, they often seem less than purely divine. They learn things in ways which seem human, and their acts seem somewhat dependent upon the promptness of events and the receptivity and power of things. They are, as Friedrich Nietzsche would say, "human, all too human." At one level, we can see these lapses of the gods as weaknesses in the imagination of the Sumerian religious thinkers who conceived them. At another level, these weaknesses seem a concession to the Sumerians' truer understanding of the world. Nevertheless, in ways that far exceed human capacity, the gods embody these notions of permanence—immortality, incorruptibility, omnipotence, and omniscience.

These are, of course, all the qualities people want and cannot have. Mortal, vulnerable, and slowly dying, limited in knowledge and weak in strength, we dream of beings who live forever, who never change; who know the fall of every sparrow, our innermost longings, and the secrets of time; and have but to speak words in their hearts and the deeds are done.

Religion here can be seen as the desire to believe in and, if possible, become one with what one desperately wants to be. That is why, for one reason, the gods themselves are anthropomorphic. They seem present at the very birth of human desire—they are the fantasies we entertained for ourselves as infants. And yet they stay with us into adult life and through history, projected beyond our own clearly limited powers into the surreal and religious.

What gives *The Epic of Gilgamesh* its tension then is that its hero–king, Gilgamesh, is partially challenging the traditional notions of human passivity and the attribution of all power to the gods. This is the story of an adventurous king who seeks in vain to gain the power of the gods, but establishes himself instead as an epic hero.

The Epic of Gilgamesh

The *Epic* opens with Gilgamesh as the ruling king of the Sumerian city-state of Uruk (this is the city of Erech, mentioned in the Hebrew Bible). Gilgamesh is said to be two-thirds god and one-third man. His father, Lugalbanda, was a hero-king, and his mother, Ninsun, a goddess. Because Gilgamesh restlessly fights wars and asserts his first-night rights to sleep with the brides of Uruk, the gods find him troublesome. They create for him a man, named Enkidu, to be his companion and distraction. Gilgamesh represents an annoying disturbance of the divine order.

Enkidu is depicted as an animal-man, as natural rather than divine. The story of his creation, like most creation myths, describes the mixing of divinity with inert or brute matter to create human life. We read:

> So the goddess conceived an image in her mind, and it was of the
> stuff of Anu of the firmament. She dipped her hands in water and
> pinched off clay, she let it fall in the wilderness, and noble
> Enkidu was created.[7]

Right from the beginning, Gilgamesh's divine mother, Ninsun, interprets Gilgamesh's dreams, which predict that Enkidu is coming. Not only is Ninsun an example of divine omniscience, but of the idea that gods know truths which are denied to human beings.

After challenging Gilgamesh to a physical brawl, and losing, Enkidu becomes his first retainer. Together they fight battles against Humbaba, a monstrous, Caliban-like figure, who is the steward of a forest owned by Enlil, the powerful god of storms. They also fight the Bull of Heaven, an avenger sent by Inanna, the love goddess of the moon, whom Gilgamesh has insulted. Both of these divine servants suggest the dominant animal gods of an earlier period of Sumerian mythology. By fighting them,

Gilgamesh hopes to achieve heroic fame, a more attainable kind of immortality than that of the gods.

Both battles represent challenges to the gods' omnipotence, although, in his fight with Humbaba, Gilgamesh wins only because his mother's patron god, Shamash, the sun god, protects him. In this instance, Gilgamesh can apparently draw upon more divine power by virtue of his mother's relation to Shamash, than can Humbaba through his relation to Enlil.

During the battle with Humbaba, Enkidu is wounded, but Gilgamesh hardly pays any attention to his friend. He is too wrapped up in himself, in his own narcissistic power fantasies, to extend empathy to another person. Sumerian stories are clear, however, that attempting to become like a god brings one quickly to earth. Fantasy or belief is one thing, inflation another. For the challenge by Gilgamesh and Enkidu to their power, the gods decree that one of the pair must die. They choose Enkidu.

The death of Enkidu instigates the story's crisis. Gilgamesh, who has indulged himself in every pleasure, who has even challenged the gods and been oblivious to danger, including the injury suffered by his friend, has hardly thought that death applies to *him*. Now he feels vulnerable. He sets out on a journey which takes him all over the world, in search of Utnapishtim, a man who has survived the flood and been granted immortality by the gods. It is *he* who can tell Gilgamesh the secret of eternal life, and can provide Gilgamesh with the permanence he now desperately seeks.

At one point in his wanderings, Gilgamesh encounters Siduri, an attractive young woman, who is winemaker to the gods. Her message to Gilgamesh, not unmixed with seduction, is to give up his quest, and to enjoy his transitory existence:

> Gilgamesh, where are you hurrying to? You will never find that life for which you are looking. When the gods created man they allotted to him death, but life they retained in their own keeping. As for you, Gilgamesh, fill your belly with good things; day and night, night and day, dance and be merry, feast and rejoice. Let your clothes be fresh, bathe yourself in water, cherish the little child that holds your hand, and make your wife happy in your embrace; for this too is the lot of man.

But the lot of man, even including the attractive Siduri, is too transitory for Gilgamesh. He abruptly leaves her, and eventually crosses the Sea of

Death to find Utnapishtim. When he finds him at last, Gilgamesh asks Utnapishtim for the secret of eternal life. Utnapishtim replies, in the words which begin this section, that there is no permanence, at least, not for mankind. Instead, he relates the story of the flood by which the gods sought to destroy all human life.

The story, which anticipates the biblical tale of Noah point for point, ends with only Utnapishtim and his wife left alive. Enki, the god of wisdom and the waters of the earth, had intervened and advised Utnapishtim to build an ark. When the flood waters began to subside, Utnapishtim dutifully offered a sacrifice to the very gods who had sought, almost successfully, his species' destruction. He says bitterly, "When the gods smelled the sweet savour, they gathered [over the sacrifice] like flies."

What this section suggests is that there is a moral order which humans may know, and which the gods may ignore, which constitutes an autonomous area in which *humanity* may judge the gods. Just as the Sumerians' increasing physical capacity to control floods and store grain, and the growth of personal power through kingship, had prompted a tale in which a hero-king might physically challenge the gods, so too had their creation of a moral order, as represented by formal legal codes and law courts, set the stage for moral challenges.

In the moral sphere, the human challenge to the gods is exemplified when Enkidu asks the gods why he must die; when Gilgamesh insults Inanna by questioning her morals; and when Utnapishtim sniggers while the gods gather over his sacrifice. But, for the most part, the moral order is still thought to be primarily the creation of the gods, as is the physical order of the universe. The moral order is considered permanent or timeless, not the product of history or of a particular time. Much later, the God of the Hebrew Bible dictates the Mosaic law, and morality, to this day, is still thought by many conventionally religious people to be almost innocent of history or sociology, but rather to be given by God. The *Epic*, however, is concerned not primarily with morality, but with the hero's quest for immortality.

How does this quest unfold? After relating his tale, Utnapishtim questions Gilgamesh's worthiness to learn the secret of eternal life. He proposes a test: Gilgamesh must attempt to prevail against sleep for six days and seven nights. Implicit in this test is the notion that immortality has something to do with consciousness. The story goes no further than subtle suggestion, but later this connection will become the core of the philosophic idea of the eternal soul.

Gilgamesh boasts that the test will pose no problems, but then immediately falls asleep, as he does at other points of stress in the story. Wary that Gilgamesh will deny having slept, Utnapishtim tells his wife to bake a loaf of bread for every day that Gilgamesh is asleep, and to put the loaf behind his head. The loaves' mutable states—stale or rotten—convince Gilgamesh, when he finally awakens, that he, too, is mutable, like all material things. In despair, he prepares to return to Uruk and again take up his duties as king.

At the last moment, at his wife's urging—why do women have such sympathy for mortal men?—Utnapishtim relents and tells Gilgamesh of a plant at the bottom of the sea that will restore a man's lost youth. Elated, Gilgamesh boasts that he will grant immortality to all the men of Uruk, and thereby establish a society of permanent beings. Gilgamesh finds the spot, ties heavy stones to his feet, descends to the depths of the waters, and secures the magical plant. But before his triumphal return to Uruk, he stops to bathe in a pool. A serpent steals the plant, leaving, its sloughed-off skin as evidence—a symbol of its eternal life. The meaning of this may be that the order of nature is eternal, as Aristotle will later maintain, but that human life is not. The tale ends as a sobered but responsible Gilgamesh returns to rule his city.

What are the hero-king's final comments?

[C]limb up on the wall of Uruk, inspect its foundation terrace,
and examine well the brickwork; see if it is not of burnt bricks;
and did not the seven wise men lay these foundations?

The *Epic* relates no further adventures, but simply Gilgamesh's death, the city's lament, and its offerings to the gods. But the message is clear enough: The man Gilgamesh may die, and immortality for individuals cannot be achieved, but the city endures. Such endurance seems less satisfying than that of the gods' individual and collective immortality, but it is at least an edge into permanence, which otherwise, in this great epic, cannot be achieved. As Utnapishtim tells Gilgamesh, "There is no permanence," at least not for a man. Has Gilgamesh, by his heroic search, and by his extension of the possibilities for human beings, reached what measure of satisfaction is possible? Perhaps the *Epic* is wisely suggesting that being a hero rather than an immortal being, even in our fantasies, is a more fitting object of human aspiration. Ironically, the work which first describes many of the major elements of permanence in Western thought also suggests that for human beings, this more mundane, but more realizable role, may be more fitting.

Chapter Two

Judaism: Monotheism and the People

At the beginning of God's creating
of the heavens and the earth,
when the earth was wild and waste,
darkness over the face of Ocean,
rushing-spirit of God hovering over the face of the waters—
God said: Let there be light! And there was light.

The Book of Genesis[1]

As reported by Genesis, Judaism begins not with the many gods of nature, as in
The Epic of Gilgamesh, but with one all-powerful God who creates the
heavens and the earth. This God represents a concentration of divine energy in one source, and, reciprocally, the elimination of independent
power from the rest of the world, with the partial yet riddling exception of
human beings. This conception of God, I suggest, will pose severe limits on
the ability of human beings to achieve permanence, as had the many gods
of Sumer.

Whatever the historical accuracy of the text, or even of its reflection of
the society in which it was written,[2] the idea of God expressed in the Hebrew Bible is still at the core of religious thought for hundreds of millions
of people today. Without the contribution of Judaism, Western civilization
in its present form is simply inconceivable. Curiously, even within the text
of the monotheistic Genesis, we find more than a few references to other
gods, angels, and demonic or monstrous beings.[3] There are also inconsistencies, which scholars tell us are based on the fusion of several sources.[4]

But the message of a single, all-powerful Creator is clearly the emergent idea overshadowing everything else in the text.[5]

Although the idea of God which emerges from the Hebrew Bible and the religion based on it undergo numerous permutations throughout Jewish history, I want to focus on what I think is its essence, the idea of divine majesty. This idea, which permeates the entire work, perhaps achieves its acme when God speaks in this passage from the Book of Job:

> Where were you when I laid the earth's foundations?
> Speak if you have understanding.
> Do you know who fixed its dimensions
> Or who measured it with a line?
> Onto what were its bases sunk?
> Who set its cornerstone
> When the morning stars sang together
> And all the divine beings shouted for joy?[6]

Such a god can be compared to a blinding white light which contains all the colors of the rainbow and which effaces every other visual object, or a noise so loud that nothing else can be heard. An intuition of God's power, or of God as an ultimate resource, lies behind every biblical story.

The Hebrew Bible makes clear that elaborate caution must be taken in evoking the name of God, and that the sight and presence of God can be dangerous or fatal. This God, or Yahweh, is a jealous god, demanding worship and punishing those "unto the third or fourth generation" who would disobey his commandments or invidiously compare him to any other entity in the universe. This means not only dismissing other gods, but denying that human beings can possess divine attributes, such as immortality or omniscience or any powers which are the special prerogatives of the Divine. The very differences between God and human beings, the very reasons why God compels worship, place fairly strict limits on the human pursuit of permanence and create seemingly unbridgeable distances between human beings and God.

First of all, God is reported to have created the world, an act of stunning power and complexity which puts God totally out of humankind's class. What God did specifically was create all the *forms* of the world, from the astronomical bodies to its living creatures. Matter, which is seemingly independent of God, is permanent, as it is in Sumerian and Greek thought.

In its original state of chaos, it lacks the interest and dynamism of either shape or life. These are the creations of the all-powerful God who functioned as the world's single artist, shaping its materials to their final forms, imparting such order and regular motions as the world exhibits, and engendering life, including human beings. As the single creator, God unifies all the essences personified by the gods of the ancient world into one generative agent.

Genesis says that humans resemble God, who created them "in our image." Yet, in the Torah, or the first five books of the Hebrew Bible, despite undefined similarities in form and nature, humans are not God, and they do not seem to have God or divinity in them. There is God, and there are human beings. Any attribution of divinity to a human being, as Christianity would later seem to make, would be considered sacrilegious.

The God in the Torah is a being apart. To begin with, God has no mythology or history. The Sumerian goddess Inanna, by contrast, is the daughter of the god Nanna and the goddess Ningal, and the mother of the deities, Shara and Lulal. Greek mythology is full of the genealogies of its gods, their ancestors, spouses, and progeny. But the Hebrew God is not the son or daughter of a god, nor a father or mother of gods; nor does this God have intimate relations with anything like himself. Nor, for the most part, is this God at the apex of any hierarchy of divine beings, despite some allusions to angels or demons.

Again, unlike the other gods of the ancient world, and unlike human beings, the God of Genesis, or Yahweh, does not possess the condition or qualification of being made of the same stuff as the universe, or, at least, the Torah says nothing about this. Nor, unlike the Sumerian gods, is Yahweh a part of nature. He is not the god of the winds, nor the divine embodiment of the sky, the waters of the earth, the moon, or any of the natural forces, as were Enlil, Enki, and Inanna. He is utterly distinct from the world.

Nor, for the most part, is God acted upon by anything, or in any way dependent on anything, as are the gods of the ancient world. Yahweh does not need worship or the food of sacrifices; nor does he need sex, companionship, or perhaps even information. Although Yahweh interacts with human beings, it is clear that all the power is in his hands.

Of course, as are the Sumerian gods, Yahweh would seem to be modeled on human beings, and never achieves the purity of those absolute notions of divinity which more philosophical ages would ascribe to him. For example, the Hebrew leader Moses argues with God and convinces God that he is in error. At times, God seems to have a distinct physical shape. His intense involvement with human beings also suggests an attraction or need for companionship or information. The Hebrew Bible also suggests that God may need human beings to complete the Creation. But, in any case, within Judaism, God is as immortal, omniscient, and omnipotent, and as utterly distinct from the rest of the universe, including human beings, as it was possible for the writers of the Torah to conceive.

Precisely for this reason, there seems to be no completely sure way humans can make contact with this primary, potential source of permanence. They cannot conjure this God, evoke him with magic, or manipulate him with ritual so that he does their bidding, as they might the other gods of the ancient world. There is, however, some sense that people will be rewarded by following God's commandments. People can pray to this God, but it is entirely in God's power if their prayers are answered, or even heard. No, God appears to humans when and where he wishes, whether that be in a burning bush, in an angel, through a prophet, or through the majesty of his acts. Although God often appears to the early figures in the Torah, God grows increasingly remote as history passes, becoming, in the words of the twentieth century French poet Pierre Emmanuel, "infinitely elsewhere."[7]

If, in biblical Judaism, humans cannot reach God with any surety while they are alive, in death there seems no possibility at all of union with this source of permanence. At death, humans are simply buried in the earth.[8] The dead do not return to God, dwell with God, or in any way directly participate in God's nature, although this doctrine is considerably softened, and even radically changed in later teachings of Judaism.

The Torah does not make at all clear how a being like God, so distinct in type from the world, can yet interact with it. This distressing distance between humankind and God, in life and in death, would indeed seem unbridgeable in biblical Judaism but for the fact that this God, for reasons best known to himself, seems deeply concerned with our fate. Although God has no need of us, he is driven by some fathomless concern, which at times makes God appear like a parent, worrying and sometimes exasperated or petulant, and yet deeply caring.

God's concern for us goes beyond humankind's merits, and, in any case, as God is depicted, our merits could not possibly have any compelling power with him. In later developments of Judaism, performing good deeds will inscribe the doer in God's "Book of Life," but in the Torah good deeds do not seem to have any metaphysical hold on God. Rather, God's regard is what the British psychiatrist R.D. Laing once called "ontological concern," that is, an unconditioned love not based on accomplishment but on humankind's mere being. He loves us in the way that parents love a child because of his or her very existence as *their* child, and not because the child is beautiful, or clever, or athletic.[9] While the gods of Sumer or Greece seem egocentric and almost entirely self-concerned, Yahweh is touchingly taken with humans, who can use protection and the love of an all-powerful parent in this frightening world. The Torah certainly suggests that God demands praise or honor, and particularly obedience, and is upset and vengeful if they are not given, but God's dominant mode, is, I think, parental care. That is perhaps the supreme mystery of the Torah, why God cares for us at all.

But he does. It is God who tells the Hebrew people how to act; it is God who reproves them, and coaxes them, and bargains with them to obey, and who forgives them time and time again when they lapse; and it is God who saves them when they are in danger. The tense and touching relationship between God and humankind becomes the key to human history, and then specifically to Jewish history, as the story of how the Jews relate to the other peoples of their region unfolds in the Torah and continues into the later books of the Bible.

Although God desists more and more from direct contact in these writings, God is still a tangible presence, speaking to the people through the prophets, judging their effort by his moral standards, and punishing and rewarding them through historical events which are presumably under his control. In the Torah, it is not humankind who creates the moral law from the historical development of human society, but God. This leaves human beings no other primary role except to choose between obedience and rebellion in his presence.

This continuous sense of the God-presence who orders and cares and remonstrates with every individual is the very core of Jewish religion. A sense of permanence is perhaps garnered from the very idea of God's continuing and watchful presence, the sense of being in conformity with God, and from the absolutely dependable purity of God's judgment.

God's strictly unqualified concern, however, changes early in Genesis when humankind disobeys him.[10] From then on, human beings relate to God not as animals or innocent children playing naïvely in the garden of Eden, but as adolescents or even adults freely responsible for themselves in the world. After they disobey God, people find themselves in the uneasy relationship of testing their freedom and autonomy before an ever-watchful, divine parent. Implicit in this story is the idea that humans have the independent power or free will to disobey—indeed, that this is the primal way in which they manifest this freedom.[11]

But the compensating idea is stated over and over, that God will bless the People of Israel and they will prosper, if only, now by their free choice, they obey God's commandments. The prophet Isaiah says:

Come, let us reach an understanding—says the Lord.
Be your sins like crimson,
They can turn snow-white;
Be they red as dyed wool,
They can become like fleece.
If, then, you agree and give heed,
You will eat the good things of the earth;
But if you refuse and disobey,
You will be devoured [by] the sword.[12]

God makes a series of such covenants with humankind, and then specifically with the People, the most solemn of which is the giving of the law at Mount Sinai.[13] To be sure, the agreement is negotiable, and God can be bargained out of destroying the People, as Moses, in one instance, persuades God to relent, but the bargain has the look of an unbreakable contract, the look of permanence. This Covenant, in which the People can receive prosperity in this world by obeying God's eternal commandments, offers the ultimate security or sense of permanence that the Hebrew Bible offers. This security adds to an initial, however secondary, status humans enjoy as God's creatures and being made in God's image, and the emotional security of God's continuing presence and regard.

The creation of a society devoted to God's service, and the maintenance of the Covenant, gives God's continuing presence institutional stability. Originally, the Torah is concerned with a federation of tribal groups, and indeed its language, as Frank Moore Cross points out, carries strong tribal references. Thus, God is seen as a tribal deity:

The Divine Kinsman, it is assumed, fulfills the mutual obligations and receives the privileges of kinship. He leads in battle, redeems from slavery, loves his family, shares the lands of his heritage..., provides and protects. He blesses those who bless his kindred, curses those who curse his kindred. The family of the deity rallies to his call to holy war, "the wars of Yahweh," keeps his cultus, obeys his patriarchal commands, maintains familial loyalty..., loves him with all their soul, calls on his name.[14]

Later, in the Hebrew Bible, when the monarchy is established under David and Solomon, the social counterpart of Jewish religious belief becomes the theocratic state, that is, a nation that is committed to carrying out God's will and commandments. This nation has three principal components, in addition to the People themselves. The first is a hereditary priesthood, a special segment of Jewish society committed to facilitating interaction with God. This group, sometimes divided in Jewish history between competing bodies, operates sanctuaries and special places of worship, and enforces behavior according to revealed or traditional laws. It also operates the Temple in Jerusalem, with an attendant high priest and bureaucracy. The second is a series of prophets who serve as spokespeople for God, and who operate as an independent moral force in relation to the priesthood and the secular rulers. The third component is the king, palace, court, and national or imperial government, which act in God's name and seek his blessing. Jewish history, as depicted in the Hebrew Bible, shows how these elements arose, and how they and the People they served either hewed to the line of divine commandment, or fell away into evil or self-serving behavior, and the consequences of such declension.

The moral burden of the Hebrew Bible is that the Covenant, the legalistic aspect of the Jewish sense of permanence, can only be upset by the failure of the People or their rulers to keep their end of the bargain. Biblical writers take infinite pains to show how adverse historical events, such as military defeats and famines, result from such human lapses. When the People do act in conformity to divine law, they form a part of an eternal order, and in this way achieve a form of permanence.

Needless to say, despite the Bible's most strenuous efforts to show that ill fortune is deserved, it is not possible to correlate ethical behavior and material prosperity. Thus, this seemingly secure source of permanence becomes increasingly shaky, as the Jews suffer their relentless three-thousand-year history of exile and persecution. Destruction and massacres abound, as the Jews become the pawns of larger powers. The book of

Lamentations, for example, expresses the grief of a conquered and despoiled people.

Equally dramatic, beyond the historical events depicted in the Hebrew Bible, are the depredations of the Roman Empire's Jewish War in the first century of the Common Era, culminating in the destruction of Jerusalem in 70 B.C.E. The horrors of Jewish history, which include the Crusades and the Inquisition, continue, as this small, determined people becomes an object of unspeakable persecutions. Each time, God apparently fails to intervene. The evildoers appear ever more powerful and unpunished; piety and obedience to God's commandments seem to earn nothing. Yet the People continue to believe. Even the twentieth-century Holocaust, the nearly successful "final solution," in which most of European Jewry perished in the Nazi gas chambers and killing fields, failed to destroy the faith of many Jews.

Perhaps one reason faith in the abiding Covenant has proven so strong, in addition to the awesome yet comforting concept of God itself, is that the Torah teaches that God, the creator of the entire universe, has chosen to focus concern on one people, and a not very powerful one at that.[15] The idea of being a "chosen people" is inherently challenging, as this people can see itself not just as an insignificant fraction of the world's population, but as a "beacon of righteousness" and example for all humankind. The idea of being chosen can thus induce a suspension of disbelief, even faced with the clear evidence of history.

The idea of a chosen people with whom God has an eternal covenant contains its own contribution to an assurance of permanence, that God is committed to the ultimate salvation and prosperity of this people, this kingdom of priests, this holy nation. Then one can suffer unjustly and die, but still take comfort in knowing that *ultimately* the People will come into their own under God's watchful eye. Not only are the People redeemed, but they play their crucial role in the redemption of the entire world, and the establishment of a permanent reign of peace and justice. Isaiah writes:

In the days to come,
The Mount of the Lord's House
Shall stand firm above the mountains
And tower above the hills;
And all the nations
Shall gaze on it with joy.

And the many peoples shall go and shall say:
"Come,
Let us go up on the Mount of the Lord,
To the House of the God of Jacob;
That He may instruct us in His ways,
And that we may walk in His paths."
For instruction shall come forth from Zion,
The word of the Lord from Jerusalem.[16]

Here again, as in *The Epic of Gilgamesh*, death is real, suffering is real, and the idea permanence through immortality is achieved only in the future and through membership in a collective which succeeds an individual's personal death.

In the centuries which followed the codification of the Hebrew Bible, particularly the Torah, its interpretation became the great task of the Jewish people, beginning with the rabbinic writings in the first centuries of the Common Era, and continuing through the medieval commentators and into contemporary criticism.[17] This task of interpretation rests on the idea that if God is spirit, the Torah can be considered not only a representation of God's thoughts, but God's very essence. In this sense, it becomes both a living and a permanent text. The world's meaning, and so the intention of the God who created it, can be distilled through interpreting the Torah. History is the ebb and flow of events, whose basic insignificance is defined by their impermanence, but the text endures. Each story, each admonition, each regulation, however trivial it might appear, holds the promise of insight into the permanent source of all wisdom before which history is but a passing moment.

During the Common Era, Jewish thought, like its progeny, Christianity, expanded to reconcile Scripture with the philosophies of Plato and Aristotle, for example, in the writings of Philo of Alexandria (d. circa 50 B.C.E.) and Moses Maimonides (d. 1204 B.C.E.). It also expanded to claim both some measure of divinity of the human soul, and union with the divine in the mysticism of Kabbalism and in Hasidism.[18]

Despite the growth among some Jews of a belief in existence after death, or personal resurrection, the belief in a collective, rather than individual, possibility of permanence was the primary message which Judaism had for the world at the time of Jesus. The growing Jesus movement, which appropriated much of its initial beliefs from Judaism, went far beyond it in holding belief in Jesus as savior and eventually as God, as the condition for personal salvation. As Christian theology developed, it moved from being a Jewish sect to a separate religion. In the name of Jesus and the Christ, this new religion expanded to embrace the gentile (non-Jewish) world, capturing the imagination and longings of a civilization which was at the very edge of despair. To many Jews, Christianity's message compromised the monotheistic basis of Judaism, and could not be accepted.

As Christianity developed as an independent religion, it also incorporated major elements of Hellenistic thought. Under Greek influence, Christian theology increasingly departed from its historical Jewish origins, reaching its fulfillment about the time the Roman Empire in the West began to dissolve. To understand Greek thought, and its establishment of those doctrines of permanence which would be amalgamated into Christianity, let us turn to chapter 3.

Chapter Three

Classical Philosophy: Ideas and Essences

"And what do we call that which does not admit death?"
"Immortal."
"And soul does not admit death?"
"No."
"So soul is immortal."
"Yes, it is immortal."

The *Phaedo* of Plato[1]

In the formation of Western thought, with its endorsement of the idea of permanence, the next decisive element was Greek philosophy. Outstanding examples, offered by Plato and Aristotle, present a vision of permanence which has beguiled people in the West for over two thousand years.

As early as the sixth century B.C.E., Greek philosophers began to speculate about the world in ways that moved thought from gods to essences, and from religion to philosophy. The integration of this philosophy into Christianity in the centuries following the death of Jesus produced a complex theology which could satisfy the sophisticated intellectual needs of the Greco-Roman world. The simpler and more humane stories of Jesus and the Holy Family, and a more understandable theology, which, despite basic modifications, remained closer to biblical Judaism, continued to satisfy the needs of Christianity's growing millions of believers.

Although the thousand-year hold of scholasticism diminished with the Protestant Reformation, initiated in 1517, Greek philosophy had permeated the entire structure of Western thought and language. Even today, our basic categories of existence and philosophic terms are still predominantly the thoughts of men who lived well over two millennia ago in a small country on the edge of Europe, and who took into their broad gaze a dazzling universe.

The freedom Greek philosophers felt to speculate about the nature of the world liberated enormous energy, and eventually created an unsurpassed standard for mind in the West. Socrates, one of the first philosophers to inquire into political and social problems, used the dialectical form, in which he and others pursued the connections between the truth of a statement and its consequences. Here Socrates assumed that if a statement were indeed true, its consequences could not be false. The dialectical form also meant engaging people at their initial point of understanding, and then widening their vision by progressively increasing the generality of the discussion, or moving it from opinions and impressions, to truth and ideas. Socrates pursued this method wherever it led him, even if his conclusions should run counter to prevailing religious beliefs.

In general, the people Socrates engaged in this process were the wealthy young men of Athens with plenty of time on their hands. The Athenian city was a limited democracy, granting full citizenship rights, for the most part, only to land-owning men. Just as its citizens were free to speculate about the nature of the world, they were free to govern their city through a free exchange of ideas. However, in times of war and social stress, as during the extended Peloponnesian War with Sparta (431–404 B.C.E.), these citizens acted with the same brutality as any dictatorship, and also subjected themselves to oligarchs and tyrants.

In the aftermath of Athens' defeat, Socrates was brought to trial for corrupting the youth of the city and for espousing heresies. After a moving defense, which appears in the *Apology*, he was found guilty and died by drinking poison in 399 B.C.E. He left us no direct writing, and is known chiefly through the works of his disciple, Plato (d. 347 B.C.E.). Plato founded a school in Athens, the Academy, where he taught philosophy and mathematics until his death. Aristotle (d. 322 B.C.E.), Plato's most famous student, opened his own school, the Lyceum, and also tutored the young Alexander the Great.

In the period following the birth of Jesus, Platonic thought most prominently represented Greek philosophy, and, as we will see, strongly influenced the development of Christian theology. As Aristotle's works became more available in the Middle Ages, scholastic thought moved away from its Platonic base until Aristotelean thought, imbedded in the work of St. Thomas Aquinas (1225–1274), became official Catholic doctrine.[2]

Plato

In Plato we have one of the finest writers of any age, a stylist of grace, power, and humor, who effortlessly transports the reader from idea to idea. His philosophy is compounded of four notions, which are closely related: God, the soul, the world of eternal ideas, and the world of experience. Most of Western philosophy has been an attempt to fit these notions into believable systems, generally representing variants which Plato himself suggested.

Platonic philosophy achieves its supreme power because it repudiates the world people inhabit, while holding up a higher, permanent world of the mind. The first world is life's transitory enmeshment in sense impressions, emotions, things, and movements. The second is the world of ideas, a world unassailable by time and corruption, which eternally stands behind the first, transitory world, and offers a stirring promise of permanence.

For Plato, the world of sense, emotion, action, and physical things is the world of the body, which "fills us with love and desires and fears and all sorts of fancies and a great deal of nonsense..."[3] Plato likens this world to the shadows on the walls of a cave which, by virtue of the fetters on our minds, we are condemned to see all our life. This world is not only despicable, Plato says, but, what is most shocking, unreal.

When, through philosophy, one is finally released from this world of illusion, Plato tells us, the experience is at first painful but eventually totally illuminating, as it allies the mind with what is truly real—the eternal world of ideas. This is the timeless, intelligible world which supplies the prototypes of all the things in the world of process, which are just variants or shadows of these eternal ideas. This timeless world, which the soul apprehends, is curiously much *like* the soul. Plato writes, "The soul is most like that which is divine, immortal, intelligible, uniform, indissoluble, and ever self-consistent and invariable, whereas the body is most like that which is human, mortal, multiform, unintelligible, dissoluble, and never self-consistent."[4] Plato argues that it is this soul, or mind, which animates the body into life, and departs from it at death. The purpose of philosophy, then, should be to allow the soul to purify itself from its attachments to day-to-day process by its contemplation of the world of ideas, and so free itself for its eventual union with God.

The soul, in turn, is sensitive to the persuasive power of ideas. One vehicle for ideas to manifest themselves in is the daily world of process in which they participate. Here the soul, or mind, will discern the regularities of, say, proportion in beautiful bodies, and will see behind them the beauty of their true exemplars, the eternal ideas themselves.[5]

Rhetoric, or the art of persuasion, is the means by which one soul awakens another to the world of ideas. This notion is developed in Plato's dialogue, the *Phaedrus*, where Socrates charms a handsome youth with his ideas, as he would charm centuries of youth from the medieval academies to the English public schools. In the *Phaedrus*, rhetoric, the rhetoric of the physically ugly but intellectually beautiful Socrates, persuades, even seduces, the soul of Phaedrus, through ideas, and so creates a tremulous resonance.

Plato argues that because the world of ideas seems to be remembered, rather than learned from the world of experience, the soul must have existed before birth. To prove his point, he "demonstrates" in the *Meno* that an uneducated slave boy, with no prior understanding of mathematics, already "knows" or "discovers" in himself the Pythagorean theorem from the previous and eternal life of his own soul. Where could this knowledge have come from, Plato argues, if it did not already exist in the soul? Or where could the soul, with this idea, have come from, if it did not already exist before birth? What Plato contends is that ideas are of the very *nature* of the soul, and so reside there, because they are manifestations of the same timeless, intelligible world.

This world of ideas and of the soul not only animates bodies, and so creates life, but shapes everything else in the daily world of experience and physical processes, by lending this world its particular forms. In the dialogue *Phaedo*, Plato states that there is "no other way in which any given object can come into being except by participation in the reality peculiar to its appropriate universal."[6] This power of ideas to shape the world of process represents philosophy's expropriation of the power of the eternal gods to lend shape, definition, and, in some cases, life, to matter. This notion, whose beginnings we saw in ancient Sumer, ends up in the Platonic philosophy of eternal ideas.[7] "It seems to me," Plato writes, "that whatever else is beautiful apart from absolute beauty is beautiful because it partakes of that absolute beauty, and for no other reason."[8] Here, the notion only hinted at in *The Epic of Gilgamesh* reaches its fruition.

Ideas not only inform all the world's particulars, but their interrelation in the world of ideas is the basis for their interrelation in the laws of *nature*, as well. Mathematics is the model, for Plato, of the unification of ideas, and their involvement in the daily world. In geometry, for example, which Euclid would codify a few generations later, a relatively small number of ideas, expressed as axioms, forms the basis for a vast system that covers an infinite range of spatial relations in the world of ideas, and, parallel to it, in the experiential world of things.

Unification of ideas proceeds as one ascends the ladder of abstraction and generalization—as one goes, say, from the beauty of a flower to the idea of beauty itself. For Plato, reason, ideas, beauty, and virtue all achieve integration at the highest level, as separate categories fall away to become the essence of all being. Plato writes:

> [I]t is when he looks upon beauty's visible presentment, and only
> then, that a man will be quickened with the true, and not the
> seeming, virtue—for it is virtue's self that quickens him, not
> virtue's semblance. And when he has brought forth and reared
> this perfect virtue, he shall be called the friend of god, and if ever
> it is given to man to put on immortality, it shall be given to him.[9]

Plato suggests, but never argues, that the integration of all ideas, including beauty and virtue, is in the nature of God, or the Good. The purpose of philosophy is to cleanse the soul for its reintegation with God at death. Like the soul, God is a self-moved mover. It is God who creates the world, by endowing chaos with form, just as it is ideas which animate matter and give it form; and it is the soul which animates the body, giving it life, reason, ideas, and thereby philosophy.

The imperfection of the transitory world is due not to God, the creator, but to the stubbornness of brute matter.[10] It is God who imposes the order; the order does not arise from matter itself. Nor does Plato make any attempt to show how complex forms arise or evolve from simpler ones, either in the world of ideas or in the world of physics and biology. The first world, of ideas, is timeless and complete; the second, of physics and biology, is completed at creation or is eternally infused into creation by the mind of God.

Plato's description of the creation gives the physical world all the appearance of substantive reality. Although this notion seems incompatible with his belief that the physical world is deficiently real, illusory, or despicable, it is the best he can do. Timaeus, the apparent mouthpiece for Plato, modestly declares, "If then, Socrates, amidst the many opinions about the gods and the generation of the universe, we are not able to give notions which are altogether and in every respect exact and consistent with one another, do not be surprised. Enough if we adduce probabilities as likely as any others..."[11]

When Plato comes to politics, he is clear that those extraordinary beings who have achieved wisdom, including the knowledge of the Good, should rule the state. These people, as Plato maintains in *The Republic* and *The Laws*, are the philosopher-kings. After their enlightenment, Plato acknowledges, they will be so dazzled by the Good, and so unfamiliar with the lowly world of the senses and of human affairs, that initially they will rule awkwardly. A period of transition will be necessary, but eventually these kings will become effective. Alternatively, those who have not achieved enlightenment should have no role in governance, either as rulers or electors. To enforce their laws, fight wars, and fend off any challenge to their rule, Plato maintains that the philosopher kings should be supported by an armed group called "guardians," or what the Church would later call the "secular arm." Democracy is a dirty word for Plato, as the people, lacking philosophy, cannot understand what is best for them. Conflict will not occur in the state because the people are simply incompetent to argue with their rulers, and will be prevented from doing so by the guardians. Conflict will not occur between rulers because the Good is absolute and unitary, and therefore will be perceived as one by all who have achieved enlightenment.

For Plato, the three components of the state—the philosophers, the guardians, and the artisans—correspond to elements in the soul, the intellect, the spirit, and the desires, and create an organic unity. The purpose of the state, what Plato calls justice, seems based on having each layer of society do what it does best: the wise to govern, the spirit or brave to police and fight wars, and the people to pursue their material desires. The result, however, of this organic theory is authoritarian rule.

Taken as a whole, Plato's vision, whatever its inconsistencies, promises permanence at a variety of levels:

- It proclaims the immortality of the soul, and suggests a route—philosophy—by which the soul can regain its purity and avoid anxiety on earth, and dwell permanently with God after death
- It establishes the invariance of human reason, and its similarity to the invariant, eternal realm of ideas

- It suggests that reason, ideas, beauty, and virtue are highly interrelated, and at the highest level may be the same

Plato incidentally suggests that, to the extent the world is intelligible, that is, to the extent it is guided by the eternal relations of ideas which lend it form and organize it, the world will also show invariant or eternal relations—that is, the fixed laws of nature. By inference, similar conclusions can be drawn for human history, which will, in part, be guided by eternal, invariant laws.

- Everything in the world of process, which exhibits these ideal forms, thereby participates in what is permanent, even if the phenomena themselves are transitory. Effort in the transitory world will also take place, or be registered, in the eternal world of ideas, and thus will not be totally wasted. The song is ended in the real world, but "the melody lingers on" in the eternal realm of ideas. Every thing of beauty, every moral action, has its eternal counterpart in the world of ideas, and so lives forever.

- Plato's philosophy suggests the integration of all ideational categories—ideas, reason, beauty, virtue, and the soul—in the nature of God, the Creator, who lends his likeness through creation to the world. Rather than the Greek panoply of gods, such as Zeus, Hera, and Athena, Plato, as did the Hebrews, unifies divinity in one comprehensive nature, which he calls the Good. But this is a God, unlike the God of the Hebrews, who directly participates in the world, and who forms its basic metaphysical structure. By their participation in God's nature, Plato says that the forms of the world—indeed, all beings—participate in divinity, which is timeless and permanent.

- Finally, Plato outlines a political system which is based on the highest truth, the Good, and on rulers, the philosopher kings, who have discarded any shred of personal interest and are concerned only with the translation of an absolute philosophy into secular rule.

As we will see in chapter 4, Platonic thought provides an extraordinary set of assurances, which would radically transform Christian theology from its Judaic base:[12]

- Here is the creation of the world by God or the Good, who endows it with all its shapes and forms, and is the source of animation and the soul. Plato's doctrine can easily be integrated into the creation story from Genesis, or, in Christian theology, in the doctrine of the Trinity.

- Here is the entire drama of the soul's passage into the body; the soul's disdain for the goods of this world in its quest for purity; its search for guidance in religion; and its return to God with whom it is allied. The entire Christian drama of salvation is played out.

- Here is the rationale for the moral life, not because such a life creates desirable effects in this world, but because it is godlike and efficacious for salvation in the *next*. The basis of this morality is eternal and divinely inspired, rather than historical or sociological.

- Here is the idea of a special group of people who have reached a higher order of wisdom, and who therefore should take responsibility for governing the state. These are Plato's philosopher kings, who, in the writings of Saint Augustine, become the hierarchy and priests of the Church.[13]

Plato's politics is governed by his epistemology. Plato's disparagement of the daily world of process dictates that those who inhabit the world of ideas alone are worthy to rule the lower world. Such thinking easily translated into the idea that the hierarchy of the Catholic Church, with its special knowledge, and aided by princes as the secular "vicars" of God, should govern the Christian Commonwealth.

- Here is an eternal order which is independent of process, and which, like the Kingdom of Heaven, receives the soul. The world of ideas forms the ultimate contrast with the world of process, later the scene of Christ's passion. Such thinking undergirds the abandonment of the concerns of this world which is manifest in Christianity's preoccupation with salvation as opposed to social reform, and in a theology which progressively relies less and less on the life and teachings of Jesus, and more on his metaphysical role.

- Finally, here is a description of the individual's ultimate unification with God, which lies at the heart of Christian mysticism.

The merger of Platonic thought and Christianity laid the basis for the full development of permanence in Western thought, that is, for the realization of an ultimate ideal of security against the contingencies of life. Everything would be preserved, nothing would be lost. Every idea in this world would have its eternal prototype in the other; every soul could live forever with God, the world's creator and sustainer. The dream of Gilgamesh could be realized: Yes, there *is* permanence, and death is but a temporary illusion.

But Plato's splitting of the two worlds, the world of ideas and the experiential world of physics and biology, leaves questions for epistemology which are simply unanswerable. For instance, why are mental experiences metaphysically different from sensory or emotional experiences? If God, ideas, and reason are not in the world of experience, where are they? How do entities which are so fundamentally different and separable from each other, such as the body and the soul, or ideas and matter, interact to create the daily world we know? Or how can we believe in freedom if process, or even intelligible process, is ultimately controlled by the eternal relations of ideas? These problems, in addition to those involved in Plato's politics, would remain as major questions for philosophy in the future.

Plato presents a glittering world of ideas. That his work influenced Western thought for so long is a testimony to its beauty and the longing of human beings for its vision. Imbued with Platonic thought, no human being need fear any of life's contingencies. Here in Plato's world of ideas, of the soul, and of God, would seem to lie the ultimate security.

Aristotle

Aristotle poses an alternative to Plato which has established a dialogue in Western thought down to the present.[14] Although Aristotle based his thinking in part on his teacher, the differences in their work are fundamental.[15]

Where Plato is preoccupied with ideas and discounts the world of experience, Aristotle credits experience with depicting reality and providing true knowledge. Where Plato is drawn toward mathematics and the formal relations which lie behind observable facts, Aristotle focuses on organisms, which he closely observed, experimented upon, and seems to have dissected.

Aristotle describes in detail what true knowledge consists of. This description is at the heart of his system, and is the basis of its mode of permanence. It is also the major source of that system's difficulties.

Aristotle believed that things, such as axes, animals, human beings, and societies, may be thought of as "this such-es." They are combinations of matter (the "this-es"), essences (the "such-es"), and accidents.[16]

A thing's essence is what it is typically. In this sense, it is close to what we think of as its species' characteristics, rather than an individual's characteristics—for example, the characteristics of raccoons, rather than of a specific raccoon.[17] The essence determines not only the thing's form, but also its typical actions. For an acorn, such an action involves growing into an oak tree; for a body, it is falling to the earth; for a man, it is the Good; and for a state, it is the good life of its members. The end toward which a thing normatively or typically tends is Aristotle's "final cause."

But things may also suffer changes which mar their essences, including their characteristic ends. For example, a pig may eat the acorn, a body's fall may be stopped, a man may be enslaved, and the city-state may be destroyed by war. This diversion from the thing's characteristic form or end is accidental, Aristotle tells us. It is not really in the essence of these things to suffer this kind of change, but the agent of such change—an accident—is effective.

For Aristotle, the soul is the life or life-spirit of the body, and mind is the soul's activity. Here, the soul is not immortal, as Plato says it is. Although individual plants and animals, including human beings, are born and die, species, Aristotle believes, are immortal, because their *essences* are invariant. The species that are here now, he says, were here at the moment of the world's creation. Interactions occur in this world because of the essences of things, but also because of accidents. Nevertheless, essences, which are eternal, as opposed to incidental accidents, persist in controlling most process, and the world is generally as it has always been.

Aristotle believed that we can know the physical world through investigation. Such investigation mainly concerns learning the eternal essences of things, and the characteristic actions which they control. This Aristotelean science would be discredited in the late sixteenth and seventeenth century because it was thought to be anti-empirical, although Aristotle differs from Plato precisely by his recourse to direct observation, which he believed is required to learn the true essences of things.[18]

For Aristotle, the source of essences, which includes final causes, is God, who is eternal and immanent, that is, indwelling or intrinsic, in the world (although Aristotle is not entirely clear in discussing God's nature). It is God who, through thought, puts the world into motion and endows it with its essences, including its final causes.

As God is responsible for final causes, which means, in the moral sphere, for the Good or goods which men seek, he is the final source of ethics and politics. An important issue for Aristotle, as for Plato, is to clarify what comprises the Good for man's essential nature, which is the source of his true happiness or satisfaction.[19]

Where Plato discusses politics mainly from an idealistic perspective, Aristotle's writing in both the *Nicomachean Ethics* and *Politics* seems to be empirically based. Here he cites numerous examples of political behavior from Greek city-states and other countries, and often seems more concerned with what can actually be achieved than with the ideal. Yet Aristotle deals with the political state as if he were observing an organism, and finds it subject to the same essentialist analysis as are human beings, plants, or animals. Thus Aristotle believes that the city-state tends toward the Good or happiness of its citizens as a final cause, just as the Good or happiness is the end of man. Accordingly, the science of the Good for men is politics, but like all sciences, for Aristotle, it is concerned with gaining knowledge of the necessary, ideal, and permanent, that is, with what concerns man's *essential* nature.

Where Plato sees the philosopher as the ultimate ruler, Aristotle says that the philosopher, rather than rule, will achieve happiness by exercising that part of himself which is most unchangeable and godlike—his reason. Accordingly, his highest form of activity, and so his greatest happiness, is contemplation.[20]

But if the highest good of man, and his greatest happiness, is contemplation, it is the state's duty to support it. With Plato, Aristotle believes that the rulers of states should be virtuous, and that politics is the highest activity of a citizen as citizen, but it is not the highest activity of man, which is contemplation. Rulers must be wise, while subjects need not have such virtue; they need only be obedient and have "true opinion," not wisdom. Politics, of course, is also concerned with fulfilling lower needs, such as sustenance and security, which create the necessary conditions for contemplation.

In choosing rulers, one must look not for birth or wealth, but for virtue. Depending on whether that virtue is exercised by an individual, a small group, or the larger body of citizens, the government will be a monarchy, aristocracy, or polity. Each form of government, in turn, is capable of perversion if the governors work for their own interests as opposed to those of the citizens. This perversion is the basis of tyranny, oligarchy, and extreme democracy.

Aristotle, like Plato, deeply distrusts the mass of people, believing they will overthrow all law and simply use the government to enrich themselves at the expense of the wealthy. Like Plato, he rigorously denies women any role in the polity, as he considers them inferior beings. Universal male suffrage is also an anathema; the furthest Aristotle will go is to allow rulers, priests, and warriors to be citizens. Mechanics, tradesmen, and husbandmen, that is, the vast majority of people in a state, should be excluded. ("No man can practice virtue who is living the life of a mechanic or labourer.")[21]

Like Plato, Aristotle suggests that the classes of men are or should be genetically determined by the scope of their intellects.[22] He, like Plato, proposes giving the rulers drastic powers over education and the regulation of morals, to ensure civic virtue and strong and healthy citizens. Thus, despite differences, Aristotle, like Plato, lays out the basis of rulership based on intellectual acumen, and justifies its use in creating what today would be considered authoritarian power. Here again, absolutism in the theory of knowledge justifies absolute rule. The politics of both Plato and Aristotle later would fit in well with the medieval system of Church and secular ruler.

Where is the idea of permanence in Aristotelean thought? Permanence is not found in the soul's existence, as in Plato; for Aristotle, the soul dies with the body. Rather, permanence is found in the soul's God-given nature, as it is found also in the fixed natures or essences of all created things, which are supplied eternally by God. Because the world is a constantly replenishing system of things with fixed natures, it is fundamentally without changes beyond those introduced by accident.

Permanence is thereby also established by the eternity of nature. When, at death, one is "received" into the earth, one simply becomes a part, although a simpler one, of eternal nature. As simple matter, a person becomes a group of efficient causes in the endless flow of motion which constitutes the processes of the eternal, natural world.

According to Aristotle, reason is part of the essential nature of the human soul; thus, it is permanent and invariant. Science tends toward final or perfect knowledge as observation becomes more precise, and logic, whose rules are equally fixed, becomes more expertly applied.

Because a person's essence, including his or her final causes, is fixed by God, human history contains this element of invariance as well. The world, therefore, represents a stage on which, over and over again, the performance of our essential nature can be played. Intelligence is necessary to understand one's part, and will is necessary to play it, but the part is written in our eternal nature, and is played out in a world whose essential character is also changeless. In this sense, the play has the timelessness of ritual. We gain eternity by repeating our roles, just as Byzantine artists sought eternity by depicting the Christ or the Virgin in a style which was indifferent to the actual time in which the artists lived.

For Aristotle, the world is rather like a garden, with each plant and flower waiting to be identified, its characteristics to be known. The wise gardener cultivates the garden, learning the essences of each plant, including its need for water and sun, and controlling against the accidents of animals or bugs, or insufficient or excessive rain. Each year, the garden grows, flowers, and dies, only to be reborn the following year. From the practical side, the gardener's task is to cultivate the garden; from the philosophic side, the task is to contemplate the garden's intricacy and beauty, and the display of ideas in the essences of each of its plants, and in the garden as a whole. The science of gardening, then, moves steadily toward true, invariant knowledge. It may not be too great a leap to suggest that the charm of gardening, particularly for contemplative monks, might have been due to its approximation to this Aristotelean model.

Darwinian evolution, which we will address in chapters 7 and 8, would represent a direct attack upon the Aristotelean system, by showing that species develop through time, rather than, as Aristotle believed, that they originate at one moment, to remain fixed forever. Ironically, random variation of genetic material, the driving force of the Darwinian theory of evolution,[23] would have represented for Aristotle the introduction of accident into a world controlled by essences, the otherwise stable genetic materials. But the cumulative result of evolution, the development of species, runs precisely counter to the picture of a static world which Aristotle describes.

Indeed, the Aristotelean system is fundamentally opposed to what might be called progress, either in biological evolution or in political affairs. It thus stands at some distance from the modern world, with our preoccupation with change. That distance may, in part, account for why Aristotle began to lose some of his immense authority in the centuries following the Renaissance.

For Aristotle, permanence is also achieved by the human relationship to God. This relationship is far less direct than for Plato. Aristotle maintains that the aims which drive the world, its final causes, including the Good for man, are part of its reality. They are not a gloss on the text of being, but its essential nature. These aims come from God. Thus, in pursuing his highest nature, man is in harmony with an eternal order and with God.

But unlike Plato, Aristotle offers little suggestion that the human soul, directly and immediately, forms part of God's nature. Nor, unlike Plato, does he propose any ultimate unification of final causes or essences *in* God's nature. As for the world we live in, it remains pluralistic, atomistic, and temporal. But such value as we can realize is divine and permanent, by virtue of its derivation from God and its harmony with his nature. This is probably the strongest guarantor of permanence Aristotle can provide.

Finally, in the political sphere, the state is designed to achieve the Good for man which is the permanent final cause of his nature. This Good is realized in activity, that of contemplation of what again is permanent in the world, the essences of things, and how they relate to each other in timeless ways. Politics, then, is the realization of the permanent through a system supporting intellectual activity.

Aristotelean thought left huge difficulties:
- Despite his empiricism, Aristotle created a two-class description of the world of things, one based on matter and essence, and the other based on matter and accident. This is a distinction which modern science would destroy. As for matter and essence, Aristotle holds that the essential natures of the things of the world are the creation of God. He thereby puts out of the reach of causal explanation what might be called the essential state of the entire world, including the basic forms of the world, their characteristic motions, and their final causes or ends.
- Because Aristotle's system of essences is static, the world cannot develop in any fundamental way; it can only fulfill its nature. Some more basic explanation needs to be available for the origins of complexity, for evolution, and for novelty.
- Aristotle integrates reason and ideas in the things of the real world perhaps more than does Plato. In Aristotle, reason is part of the essential nature of the human soul, which is its life-spirit, as opposed to its role in Plato as the body's inhabitor. Nevertheless, such integration is not sufficient to avoid the enormous problems which arise from proposing two metaphysically different classes of things in apparent interaction. The idea of reason as a permanent aspect of human nature, divorced from biological or historical process, would haunt modern thought from Descartes to Hegel (see chapter 5).
- For Aristotle, since neither man's nature, nor the nature of the world, changes, history can only play out these essential natures, or their relations to accident, and cannot achieve anything of fundamental importance.
- As God is separate from the essential nature of the things of this

world and of souls, Aristotle's God is perhaps even less integrated into the nature of the world than in Plato, for whom the forms of the world and souls directly participate in God's nature.

- Finally, at the practical level, Aristotle, like Plato, deeply distrusted the common man and democracy, and discounted women as secondary beings. Aristotelean thought easily lends itself to an organization like the Church which, through its special knowledge, can define a static social and political structure by which human beings may be governed by their "betters" and their souls saved by specially ordained mentors. This is not a governing structure which would survive the democratic revolutions of the modern world.

This, then, was the dual legacy which Christianity inherited: Judaism, the religion of Jesus; and classical thought, the philosophy of the Roman Empire's Hellenized world, provided initially by Plato and then by Aristotle. Both Judaism and Greek thought would combine to produce the mature theology of Christianity, which would also borrow aspects of pagan religion and the forms of Roman governance. The combination would present the most solid edifice for permanence ever erected in the West.

Chapter Four

The Good News:
The Alternative of Personal Salvation

I believe in God, the Father almighty,
maker of heaven and earth;
And in Jesus Christ, his son, our Lord . . .

From The Apostles' Creed

In the centuries following the death of Jesus, Christianity developed a promise of permanence which won the hearts of tens of millions of people in the ancient world. This is the message, or "good news," which guaranteed believers an escape from death, or eternal salvation, through the mediation of a figure proclaimed to be coequal with God. To reach this point, the story of Jesus, a charismatic Jewish preacher, was transformed into a full theology.

As reported in Acts, written in approximately 85 B.C.E., Peter states the growing claims of the Jesus movement in arresting terms:

> There was Jesus of Nazareth, a man attested to you by God
> through powers and portents and the miracles God wrought
> through him.... [H]e was not abandoned to Hades, and... his
> flesh knew no corruption. God resurrected this Jesus;...Then let
> every house in Israel know for sure that God made him Lord and
> Christ, this Jesus whom you crucified.[1]

What follows in Acts is the news which made it possible for

Christianity to become a world religion—the presentation of a simple, straight path to permanence:

> When they heard it they were stricken to the heart, and they said to Peter and the rest of the apostles: Men and brothers, what shall we do? Peter said to them: Repent, and let each one of you be baptized in the name of Jesus Christ for the remission of your sins, and you will receive the gift of the Holy Spirit; since for you is the promise, and for your children and for all those far away whom the Lord our God summons to him.[2]

This promise became no less than the promise of salvation, of immortality, the promise of dwelling perpetually with God. Through baptism and belief in Jesus, and through the mediation of the Church, this promise could be fulfilled. The dream of Gilgamesh, which he must renounce at the end of the Epic, was here seemingly realized. In the epistles of Paul and in the Gospel of John, this promise of permanence was reinforced by theological doctrines which left the ground of the historical Jesus and of Judaic thought. The Church fathers subsequently expanded the theology of permanence even further, leading to the full doctrine of the Trinity in the fourth and fifth centuries.

Because the Synoptic Gospels were written at least forty years after Jesus' death, it is difficult to extract an accurate picture of Jesus as an historical figure.[3] As a preacher, Jesus seems to have enjoyed only a small measure of local fame. Indeed, he had gone unnoticed by Roman historians, and achieved prominence in the years after his crucifixion only through the efforts of his disciples and the Gospel writers.

In the Book of Mark, Jesus most clearly comes through as a Galilean preacher proclaiming to the Jews the immanence of the Kingdom of God. This Kingdom, he suggests, will be achieved through the transformation of the human spirit and the world by the imitation of God's mercy and goodness. Jesus' role seems not that of a second David, a conquering prince who will defeat the nations for the redemption of Israel, but rather a Jewish preacher seeking to transform men and women by his message of divine compassion. He is a prophet speaking for God, as did Isaiah or Jeremiah, or a messiah ushering in the new age.

The portents and miracles, which the writers of Matthew, Mark, and

Luke record, represent Jesus' ability as a holy man to concentrate God's power, rather than having power in their own right. Jesus is often reported as saying that he is acting only as an instrument of his Father, a position also taken by Moses. Jesus heals the sick; multiplies loaves and fishes to feed the multitude of his followers;[4] brings back a deceased man, Lazarus, from the dead; and exorcises demons. In these writings, one feels Jesus' compassion for the afflicted, and his willingness to do away with formal differences of class and gender to embrace a common humanity, often symbolized by a democratic sharing of meals.[5]

In the next three centuries, the Jesus movement grew from a despised and persecuted minority to become the dominant religion of the Roman Empire. Where the great mass of people in the Empire were politically powerless, their lives could achieve the redemptive fulfillment and significance they lacked in this world through the promise of individual resurrection and salvation. In order to achieve this, the Jesus movement needed to integrate its developing theology with the bureaucratic power of an earthly institution, the Christian Church. While the delineation of the early development of Christianity has been the subject of libraries of scholarship, it is useful here to highlight some aspects of this development, to show how the process worked consistently to enforce Christianity's guarantee of permanence.[6]

Major steps in this direction can be seen in changes of meaning which marked the transition from Aramaic or Hebrew to Greek and then Latin. The writings which most closely describe the life of Jesus are the Synoptic Gospels of Matthew, Mark, and Luke. These writings in Greek and then Latin contain language which implies a theology for gentile readers in a Hellenized world which differs sharply from the theology that Jesus himself, as a Jew, would have likely embraced in his own language, Aramaic or Hebrew. Consider, for instance, the terms, the "son of God" or "Lord," used to describe him. The Biblical scholar Geza Vermes writes, "In Hebrew or Aramaic 'son of God' is always employed figuratively as a metaphor for a child of God, whereas in Greek addressed to Gentile Christians, grown up in a religious culture filled with gods, sons of gods, and demigods, the New Testament expression tended to be understood literally as 'Son of God,' spelled as it were with a capital letter: that is to say, as someone of the same nature as God." Equally, Vermes makes clear that the term "Lord" carries the idea of "master" or "sir" in the intertestamental period, denoting a person in authority, rather than a deity, as this designation for Jesus came to be interpreted in Christianity.[7]

Vermes makes clear that a similar transformation of meaning can be seen in the depiction of the miraculous birth of Jesus by a virgin through the intermission of the Holy Spirit in fulfillment of the prophesy of Isaiah.[8] Matthew writes, "The birth of Jesus Christ came in this way: Mary his mother was engaged to Joseph, but before they came together she was found to be with child, by the Holy Spirit."[9] The term "virgin" in Isaiah means "young woman," not technically a virgin. In monotheistic Judaism, there could have been no intention of giving a man, like Jesus, divine aspects. What appears in Matthew would make sense only to Hellenized people used to unions between gods and mortals. Matthew also traces the lineage of Jesus back to King David to legitimatize his role as the Messiah.[10] Vermes concludes, "In plain language, Matthew's genealogy and account of the birth reflect an image of Jesus born of a virgin which was exclusively designed for, and meaningful in, the Hellenistic church."[11]

An important break with traditional Judaism, and toward permanence, was in the doctrine of resurrection. The Gospel writers report that Jesus did not die and return to the earth, but was physically resurrected. This belief appears only late in Judaism, and was held chiefly by the Pharisee sect in Jesus' day.[12] The claim to the physical resurrection of Jesus was essential for the emerging Christian Church, as it created the model or exemplar for the physical salvation of its members. The message that believers would be delivered from sin and death by a mystic identification with the crucified Christ is carried in the epistles of Paul, who almost entirely omits mention of the life of Jesus before his resurrection. For Paul and, for the most part, the theologians of the Church, it is through his death, not his life, that Jesus saves the world.[13] Mystic identification with Christ, and so salvation, are achieved by baptism and belief, rather than works. Death, introduced into the world by the first Adam, is thereby defeated.

Another element of permanence was the replacement of Jesus' message of the coming of the Kingdom of God by the idea of personal salvation and the establishment of the Church as the agent of this salvation. The Synoptic Gospels tell us that Jesus believed his role was to usher in the Kingdom of God, an event he seemed to predict would occur in his generation. Thus Jesus is reported as saying, "Truly I tell you that there are some of those who stand here who will not taste of death until they see the son of man coming in his Kingdom."[14] So imminent is this event that Jesus declares, "Let him who is on the housetop not come down to take up what is in his house, and let him who is in the field not turn back to pick up his coat."[15]

However, it was not at all clear that everyone, all the dead, as well as the living, would participate in the Kingdom, when it came. Rather, the Kingdom still generally posed only the *possibility* of collective redemption for the Jewish people, and perhaps the peoples of the world. Individual salvation, with its clear promise of permanence, required no such waiting for a tenuous historical event, no uncertainty, no submersion of individual interests into those of the collective. Its appeal over the traditional Jewish doctrine was incalculable.

By making orthodox belief and ritual practice the conditions for salvation in the *next* world, the Christian Church seemed to diminish the importance of Jesus' ethical message of how to conduct oneself in *this* world. That message had included, for instance, giving one's goods to the poor ("Sell all you have and give it to the poor, and you shall have a treasury in heaven"); dealing with one's enemies with forbearance ("If one strikes you on the right cheek, turn the other one to him also"); and practicing modesty and purity of heart ("Take care not to practice your righteousness publicly before men so as to be seen by them...").[16]

The potential of Jesus' message to effect social change or revolution was, for the most part, not stressed by the early Christian church. The religious historian W.H.C. Frend points out the difference between Jesus and Paul when he writes, "Paul's message was not directed to the outcasts and misfits of society—the inhabitants of the highways and byways—or even primarily to slaves. In this respect the difference between him and his Lord was fundamental."[17] More generally, Frend writes that, in early Christianity, "in contrast to Jesus' teaching, there was no command to 'sell all,' to free the captives; or...to strive to abolish slavery."[18] Such social conservatism reflected, in part, Christianity's preoccupation with the next world, rather than this one. It might also, to some extent, have represented Christianity's debt to the politics of classical thought, which discounted the needs of the common people in favor of the prescriptions of their more enlightened, and more wealthy, rulers. Avoiding social reform also undoubtedly assisted Christianity to survive, although persecution for its first three hundred years, due mostly to its opposition to the official Roman religion, would make the growing Jesus movement difficult and at times problematic.

The message that the Kingdom was at hand, including Jesus' role in ushering it in, and the importance of individual preparation for it by immediate ethical action, was mainly dropped within a century or two. In so doing, the early founders of Christianity jettisoned the potential embarrassment of an historical prediction which did not take place. Far more importantly, they focused exclusively on a seemingly attainable goal of individual salvation or permanence, whose appeal far exceeded that of the unsure coming of the Kingdom of God, as predicted, for example, in Isaiah (see chapter 2).

The Church or Christianity, as a united body of believers, replaced the idea of the Kingdom. Vermes writes, "The concept of a single body of believers, mystically united with the Father through the Son, eased the way for the Church to take the place of the Kingdom of God, that central concept of the Jesus of the Synoptics and of Paul which John to all intents and purposes managed to obliterate."[19]

Another essential factor fostering permanence was the establishment of Jesus' divinity. The claims for divinity would be propounded in the Gospel of John, which has Jesus saying, "You come from things below, I come from things above. You are of this world, I am not of this world."[20] This Gospel abounds with statements proclaiming Jesus' divinity. Thus John writes, "He was in the world, and the world came about through him, and the world did not know him."[21] He also declares, "For God so loved the world that he gave his only son, so that everyone who believes in him may not be destroyed but may have everlasting life."[22]

There is simply nothing in ancient, biblical Judaism that suggests anything like this, that any human being could bridge the immeasurable metaphysical gap between human and God, or be in any way deified. Nor is it plausible that Jesus, as a pious Jew, could have made such a claim of divinity for himself. It is this claim that most clearly separated the growing movement from its Jewish origins, and exclaims why it could not continue as a Jewish sect.

The way in which Christianity portrayed divinity proved particularly appealing. While Judaism, to some extent, combines both awesome power and tender regard in one God, Christianity increasingly relegated God to a more august, distant role. It was Jesus or Christ who took on the duality of God and man. Where God in Christianity seemed to preside over the entire universe, Jesus as God seemed concerned almost exclusively with humankind, particularly with the drama of forgiveness and salvation. In this sense, Jesus provided a tender or accessible bridge into permanence.

As described in the Synoptic Gospels, Jesus was touchingly human. Unlike the lordly Gilgamesh or Homer's aristocratic Achilleus in the *Iliad*, his origins were humble. The son of a lowly carpenter, he was born in a manger; was favored by neither inaccessible wealth nor earthly power; and came from a part of Palestine noted for its rural, unsophisticated populace. Through the text of the Gospels, we see Jesus depicted in various moments of his earthly life. We read of his modest birth, his baptism by John at the river, his ministry to the simple folk of Palestine, his courageous decision to enter Jerusalem, and his painful, heroic death. Yet, particularly in John, Jesus would be declared God, endowed with all divine power, knowledge of all things, eternal life, the power to grant such life to others, and finally, the creation and rulership of the world.

Beyond salvation, the Incarnation of God in Jesus Christ also expressed the deepest desires of human beings to realize the ultimate ideal of human life by a magical identification with divine power. Again and again, Western art would portray this mystical identification of God and a human being in images and sounds of ineffable beauty which captured people's deepest need to realize in themselves qualities attributed to God.

Still another essential element of the Church's guarantee of permanence was in its full endorsement of the idea of the soul. Clearly, the doctrine of resurrection required the doctrine of the soul as its vehicle. Not only did Christianity, through salvation, bodily resurrection, and mystical identification, provide a vehicle for permanence, but in seeing human beings as possessing immortal souls, Christianity directly attributed permanence to people themselves. The doctrine of the immortal soul, prevalent in Platonic thought (see chapter 3), and embraced by Christianity, endowed human beings with immortality in their essential nature.

Far more radically than Judaism, Christianity eventually had to separate the soul from the body in order to facilitate the soul's salvation and eventual eternal life with God. Christianity gave consciousness, the supreme evidence of the soul's existence, a unity, priority, and independence of the body which human experience could hardly sustain. By the time of Saint Augustine (354–430 B.C.E.), this doctrine, deeply influenced by the Platonist philosopher Plotinus, had been firmly embedded in Christian thought.[23] It would continue to haunt Western philosophy into modern times, for example, in the philosophies of René Descartes and Immanuel Kant, as we will see in chapter 5.

Finally, the idea of permanence would find its supreme expression in a doctrine of divinity, the Trinity, which removed God, Christ, and the Holy Spirit, from any historical contingency.[24] The final doctrine of the Trinity would show the full integration of Platonic thought. God would be not an historical figure who created the world, but the eternal continuous source

47

of creation bringing the world into its being and realized (Platonic) forms in each instant. The Son or Christ would be the continuous and eternal manifestation of God's presence in human form, and the Holy Ghost would be God's immanence throughout the world.

While philosophically inclined Church fathers generally endorsed this subtle doctrine, the common people held an idea of God that ran along simpler lines. To them, God *was* an historical creator; Christ was a historical person facilitating salvation and ruling with God in heaven; and the Holy Ghost was the spirit of the true religion.

The Holy Spirit or Holy Ghost initially appears in the Gospels as the spirit of God which promotes the disciples to perform acts of heroism or miracles, and then slowly achieves, in the full doctrine of the Trinity, a co-equal status with God and the Christ. But to the extent this doctrine implied that God was immanent in human beings, it could again be thought to compromise the Judaic distance between human and God, and thereby strict monotheism.

Implicit in Christianity's movement toward a doctrine of permanence was its need to distance itself from Judaism. Hostility to Judaism grew because many Jews, with their emphasis on the letter of the Jewish law and their strict interpretation of monotheism, found Christianity incompatible, and, eventually, a rival religion. When Jews proved resistant to Christian proselytizing, some disciples, initially Paul, turned to the gentile world, offering the same message of salvation. The Gospel writers, particularly Matthew, Luke, and John, did everything they possibly could to distance themselves from the Jews, who, after the Jewish revolt against Rome in 66–73 B.C.E., were considered an obstreperous and hostile minority by the Roman authorities.[25] The hostility to Judaism can be seen most strongly in the Gospel of John, which angrily holds the Jewish leadership responsible for the death of Jesus.[26] Matthew also states this hostility clearly, blaming the whole Jewish people for Jesus' death: "And all the people answered and said: His blood is upon us and on our children."[27]

Despite a continuous threat of persecution as members of an illegal sect, the early Christians saw an immense opportunity to proselytize among the diverse and unhappy subjects of the Roman Empire. This was a world which was falling apart, and in which there was little to hope for. Nationalism ran headlong into Roman authority; economic prosperity seemed more and more elusive; civil service was increasingly corrupt;

power at the top was disorderly and opportunistic; and class oppression and slavery were rampant.

The official Roman religion was sterile, and no competing ideology offered the kind of immediate hope of release from suffering in an increasingly dysfunctional secular world as did Christianity. Roman religion deified natural forces, continuing the pagan tradition exemplified in the Sumerian gods. It also gave divine status to the emperor, and supported the system of class distinction and oppression which was the basis of Roman society. With the promise of salvation potentially open for everyone, Christianity was free to spread its doctrine of permanence throughout the Roman world.

For Christians, taking the Gospel writers as historically accurate, Judaism became predominantly the religion of those who, under the influence of the devil, betrayed Christ, and resisted the "good news." Theologically, however, Judaism was seen as the precursor of Christianity's arrival, so that the meaning of the Old Testament was transformed by Christian theologians into predictions or signs of Christ's life and resurrection.

From that life, in a process which is still the subject of intense scholarly dispute, emerged the West's dominant religion, a religion which promises the ultimate in permanence, immortality, and eternal life with God.

In proclaiming itself the true path to permanence, the Christian Church, in addition to competing with Judaism and Hellenistic paganism, also found itself in competition with a group of believers who, for the most part, considered themselves to be Christian. These were the Gnostics, a cult which was present at virtually the very beginning of Christianity. A number of the Gnostic texts, which were discovered in Egypt at Nag Hammadi in 1945, date from as early as the *Synoptic Gospels*, and perhaps from an even earlier date, and yet were not included in the official canon.[28] Some seem to reflect possibly Buddhist influence, others Zoroastrian, as well as Jewish and Hellenistic sources.

Where the Church preached that only Jesus was from God, and that access to God could only be achieve through him, the Gnostics said that each individual had God within himself or herself. Self-knowledge or enlightenment would then be considered the knowledge of the divine. Where the Catholic Church believed that salvation was outside the individual's power and could only be achieved through its intervention, the Gnostics sought it through individual experience.[29] Where the Church has a clear structure of bishops and priests who possessed knowledge of the true doctrine and administered the sacraments, Gnosticism generally had the loosest of structures, without heiracrchy, officers, or official creeds. Where the orthodox offered the guarantee of salvation through the sacraments of baptism and the Eucharist, under the administration of the Church, the path of Gnosticism was less sure, and could only be achieved by a few.

The official Church claimed its authority from Peter and other apostles to whom Jesus had supposedly appeared after his resurrection. The Gnostics said, instead, that Jesus continued to reveal himself to adept believers as the eternal manifestation of God in human form, and that such knowledge was knowledge of the divine self. The God that was revealed through enlightenment was not the historical, easily graspable figure of either the Hebrew Bible or New Testament, that is, judge, creator, or ruler of the world, but of the same nature as the self. Ultimate authority rested on such knowledge or *gnosis*, rather than on those who had been present at a particular moment with an historical Jesus. Gnostics thus discounted the authority of the Church, resting on apostolic succession. Jesus offered the Gnostics not answers, but an invitation to search. Mere acceptance of doctrine, then, could not result in enlightenment.

It was the Church, not the Gnostics, which prevailed. Essentially, the Church could offer a clearer message of permanence, and to more people, than could the more individualistic and spiritually elitist path of Gnosticism. As Elaine Pagels writes:

> Although major themes of gnostic teaching, such as the discovery of the divine within, appealed to so many that they constituted a major threat to Catholic doctrine, the religious perspectives and methods of gnosticism did not lend themselves to mass religion. In this respect, it was no match for the highly effective system of organization of the Catholic Church, which expressed a unified religious perspective based on the New Testament canon, offered a creed requiring the initiate to confess only the simplest essentials of faith, and celebrated rituals as simple and profound as baptism and communion. The same basic framework of doctrine, ritual, and organization sustains nearly all Christian churches today, whether Roman Catholic, Orthodox, or Protestant.[30]

Once the Church gained the power of the "secular arm," Gnostics were persecuted as heretics.[31] The promise of permanence was promoted not only by doctrine, but also by an authoritarian Church which proclaimed itself as the sole path to salvation, and could enforce its power, and a uniformity of belief, through the "secular arm."

Early Christians had believed that they possessed free choice, and were thus capable of governing themselves. Particularly was this true of the early Christian martyrs, as free will was at the very heart of their opposition. Where once the early Christian communities were a loose federation, with wide-ranging differences of doctrine and practice, and each "church" more or less a reflection of the democracy of believers, the final product was a structure which closely paralleled the hierarchy of the Roman Empire.

A major step toward justifying the authoritarian governance of the Catholic Church was taken by Saint Augustine, whose interpretation of Church doctrine emerged victorious out of the heated battles of his time.[32] As Elaine Pagels writes:

> Instead of freedom of the will and humanity's original royal dignity [as spelled out in Genesis], Augustine emphasizes humanity's enslavement to sin. Humanity is sick, suffering, and helpless, irreparably damaged by the fall, for that "original sin," Augustine insists, involved nothing else than Adam's prideful attempt to establish his own autonomous self-government. Astonishingly, Augustine's radical views prevailed, eclipsing for future generations of western Christians the consensus of more than three centuries of Christian tradition.[33]

Augustine believed not only that the unbaptized had inherited original sin and were incapable of free choice, but that the same was true of those who had accepted the Church's sacraments and theology. All were in need of strict authority, both in religious and secular affairs. Behavior must be coerced, and disagreement or heresy expunged. The potential for permanence offered by salvation was not enough; permanence must also be maintained by authoritarian governance. If human beings were hopelessly corrupted by original sin, a sin genetically inherited from Adam, who died the first death, they needed the authoritarian church to guide or coerce them to salvation.

Augustine's move to affix sinfulness permanently to human nature has had a lasting effect. Pagels writes:

Throughout western history this extreme version of the doctrine
of original sin, when taken as the basis for political structures, has
tended to appeal to those who, for whatever reason, suspect
human motives and the human capacity for self-government. The
counterpoint to the idea of original sin expressed in the hope of
humanity's capacity for moral transformation, whether articulated in utopian or romantic versions or in the sober prose of
Thomas Jefferson, has appealed, conversely, to more optimistic
temperaments.[34]

By the time of Augustine, the Church was no longer in opposition to
Rome, but through the power of its appeal and the energy of its apostles,
now enjoyed the full support of the Empire. As the Empire broke up, the
Church, in association with Christian princes or kings, replaced Rome as
the ruler of Europe until the sixteenth century.

In its early centuries, Christianity transformed its theology by its union
with Platonic thought. In this way, it carried forward the poignancy and directness of its message of salvation, united with a seemingly rock-solid
metaphysics. In the late Middle Ages, it turned to Aristotle. This happened,
in part, because Aristotle became increasingly available with the opening
up of trade with Islam, which had served as a conservator of his works.

At first blush, Aristotle appears less suitable for adoption to Christianity than does Plato, particularly in view of his notion that the soul is tied to
the body, and dies with it. But in the later Middle Ages, his works gained
authority, and he increasingly became the approved Church philosopher,
or "academician," as Saint Thomas Aquinas called him.[35] For one thing,
Aristotle's works were more systematic, more impressive, to the conservative scholastic mind. Plato's iconoclasm, his ability to harbor alternative
notions, and eventually his apparent lack of total assurance in some of his
own doctrines, sat badly in an age of orthodox theology.

In Plato's thought, the soul was of the same nature as God, and therefore could have direct knowledge of him. In Aristotle's thought, God, as interpreted by Thomas, was mostly inaccessible to human reason or
experience. F.C. Copleston sums up Thomas' views:

How, then, can the human mind attain the knowledge even of
the existence of a spiritual being like God? Aquinas's reply is, in
substance, that the human mind, which has as its primary object

of knowledge the essences of corporeal things, can recognize the relation of the object of experience to that on which they are dependent. It is, therefore, justified in affirming the existence of the being on which the things that form the world are dependent. But in regard to the nature of that being the human mind can know it only in so far as it is revealed in finite things. In a famous phrase, we know of God *that* He is rather than *what* He is.[36]

Saint Thomas maintains that the most man can gain is some inkling of God's nature by analogy to man's best qualities, which God possesses in perfection. Not only was God remote for Saint Thomas, as for Aristotle, but Thomas diminished the intermediary role of Christ and the importance of direct spiritual communion with him. This fitted well into a religion which would maintain its power by insisting on the need for a special group of people to mediate between human beings and the ultimate source of their salvation, a group which would control both orthodox ritual and acceptable conduct.

Eventually, the writings of Saint Thomas Aquinas became the official Catholic doctrine. Basing his work on Aristotle, Thomas achieved his goal: to buttress Christian theology and church authority, assuring permanent salvation by the most authoritative philosophy available. It was the need for a more immediate experience of God, and directly of Christ, than was seemingly available in Catholicism, and a theological refusal to mediate God's presence and power through the Church, that led to the Protestant Reformation.

The Christian Commonwealth, uniting an authoritarian Church and secular authority, ruled Europe for over a thousand years. This was a society in which every sector, from the feudal lord to the lowly vassal, played its essential part, combining practical ethics with the ultimate goal of salvation for all its members. This was a society in which virtually everyone supported the idea of a collective means of achieving permanence, a society in which spirituality was generally not an individual quest, as it was for the Gnostics, but one in which believers found full social support only for religious practice enforced by the authorities of both church and state. In this situation, personal failure on earth was redeemed by a collectively guaranteed salvation. Death was a mere passage to a higher goal which all believers could equally enjoy.

In suppressing dissent, the authorities of the Christian Commonwealth removed from society those elements that might point out new possibilities. The elimination of heresy or heterodoxy limited the Church's spiritual resources and virtually assured a static or unprogressive system, which left it vulnerable to the religious and political revolutions of the modern age. Yet even as secularism spread across Europe, and the freedom to question both the classical assumptions behind Christianity and its doctrine increased, major elements of Christian and classical thought endured until the present. Their persistence, despite radically changing social conditions and major advances in science, illustrates how deeply they were ingrained in the psyche of the West.[37]

Chapter Five

In the Grip of Permanence: Descartes through Hegel

When I have seen such interchange of state,
Or state itself confounded to decay;
Ruin hath taught me thus to ruminate,
That Time will come and take my love away.

From Sonnet LXIV by William Shakespeare

In 1517, Martin Luther initiated the Protestant Reformation. In the ensuing two centuries, the Catholic Church lost its hold as the virtually exclusive religion of western Europe, and the Holy Roman Empire dissolved. Although the Church had never achieved full governmental supremacy, for well over a millennium it had fostered a uniform ideology and political order which looked back to the universality of Rome.

The end of the religious wars between Catholics and Protestants, marked by the Treaty of Westphalia in 1648, saw the consolidation of the nation-state in Europe, and the end of the transnational loyalties which had marked the Christian Commonwealth. Where Europe had enjoyed a common culture and, in Latin, a common language, which gave its humanists full mobility, after Westphalia, scholars increasingly focused on their own countries and attached themselves to national institutions.

In the early sixteenth century, a new science began to describe the physical world as no longer centered on the earth, which had been the stage for God's drama, with its cast of human beings lost to sin to be saved by the sending of his only son. This shift occurred partly because of the startling discoveries of Copernicus (1473–1543), Galileo (1564–1642),

Newton (1642–1727), and others, who no longer depicted a stationary earth around which the rest of the universe revolved, but a system in which the earth was just one among many moving around the sun. It was also due to the application of a language—mathematics—which could describe all physical relations without reference to a privileged religious position for the earth. For example, where in Aristotle's physics, the attraction of bodies to a stationary earth is their final cause, in Newtonian physics, gravitational attraction, described in a mathematical formula, is mutual between the body and the earth, and the resulting motion reciprocal. Unified by mathematics, the new science remained international, while the humanities did not.

Where previously technology had been advanced by personal invention and shared use, and so was primarily local in its effect, it now became possible to transmit invention through this universal language. More profoundly, mathematics so facilitated thought that invention became infinitely easier.

Spurred by science, Europe began a huge technological advance which culminated in the Industrial Revolution of the late eighteenth century, and, in fact, is still in progress on a global scale. This advance not only changed the nature of human beings' environment and lifestyle, but also created new, primarily urban, economic classes which demanded a say not only in religious matters, but in secular affairs as well.

From the seventeenth through the nineteenth centuries, most of Europe moved from absolute autocracy, sanctioned theoretically by God, to some form of representative government, although still with gender and severe property limitations on the right to vote. (Universal suffrage would not be granted, for the most part, until well into the twentieth century.) Growing numbers of people in the more advanced sectors of society turned from theology to secular affairs, and from a passive acceptance of the nature of society, as it had existed for over a millennium in the Middle Ages, to a sense of active responsibility.

In philosophy, people increasingly searched for some reflection of their new sense of the physical world, and their new secular and political preoccupations. Yet major philosophers of post-Renaissance western Europe, such as René Descartes, John Locke, Immanuel Kant, and G.W.F. Hegel, while casting their philosophic nets over a world of change, continued to use categories of thought and modes of explanation which looked back to an earlier, timeless world. (Even David Hume, in rejecting these ideas, seems defined by the very categories of thought he was discarding.) Far from being out of step with their age, these philosophers represented the deep ambiguity of human beings caught between their excitement with a new world in the making, and their nostalgia for permanence. They only partially addressed the problems in classical philosophy, which we noted in chapter 3, and left unresolved the contradictions between religion and a philosophy attempting to integrate modern science and social development.

René Descartes

Although a principal founder of modern philosophy, René Descartes (1596–1650) was still a child of the Catholic Church, living in terror that his only mildly unorthodox views might have him burned at the stake, or, at least, censured. In 1633, a papal court condemned Galileo for his writings in astronomy. Galileo, following Copernicus, had maintained that the earth was no longer stationary and so the center of the world, but rather simply part of a far larger physical system which followed scientific laws in which the earth held no privileged position. Furthermore, Galileo argued, the sky could no longer be considered a perfect crystal sphere, and so a reflection of God's mind. With his telescope, Galileo showed that the sky, instead, contained a pitted moon, a planet—Jupiter—with moons of its own, and other planets all circulating around the sun.[1]

Although Galileo recanted and saved his life, Descartes knew full well that Galileo could have been burned at the stake, as had been the Italian philosopher Giordano Bruno in 1600. The French mathematician took no chances; after hearing of Galileo's condemnation, Descartes decided that his own magnum opus, *De Mundo*, an attempt to replace Aristotle's philosophy as a comprehensive guide to the world, should be withdrawn from publication.

Here was a man in the forefront of the scientific revolution, the founder of analytic geometry and a major contributor to optics, who seemed to be breaking new ground in philosophy. Yet despite his modernist views of the sciences and of subjectivity, which are still highly influential, Descartes' philosophic ideas are closer to the thinking of Aristotle and the scholastic philosophy based on it than they initially appear. The same could be said of Descartes' politics, which supported the divinely sanctioned monarchs of his time, who not incidentally were his patrons, and who had little to say in defense of classes of human beings who were unrepresented or oppressed.

Like his religious and philosophic predecessors, Descartes' aim was to secure absolute assurances in an increasingly agitated and insecure world. Although the Church guaranteed salvation, Descartes nevertheless sought to establish "first principles" which would provide complete intellectual security.

Like Plato, Descartes holds that the daily world of experience can provide no such certainties; the chaotic knowledge which comes from the senses is constantly subject to error. To Descartes, one thing seems certain: Whatever the content of his thoughts, he himself is thinking. Therefore, Descartes concludes, he exists. In *Discourse on Method*, he writes perhaps the most famous lines in modern philosophy:

> And finally, considering that all the same thoughts that we have when we are awake can also come to us when we are asleep, without any one of them then being true, I resolved to pretend that nothing which had ever entered my mind was any more true than the illusions of my dreams. But immediately afterwards I became aware that, while I decided thus to think that everything was false, it followed necessarily that I who thought thus must be something; and observing that this truth: *I think, therefore I am,* was so certain and so evident that all the most extravagant suppositions of the sceptics were not capable of shaking it, I judged that I could accept it without scruple as the first principle of the philosophy I was seeking.[2]

From "I think, therefore I am," or "*Cogito ergo sum,*" Descartes makes a huge leap to the conclusion that he is a substance which in *no way* depends on his body. Content with a dualism as radical as anything held by classical or scholastic thought, Descartes never advances any convincing reasons why the subjective reality of thought should not be the product of the body, and not be wholly dependent on it. Equally, he fails to show why the soul should be a separate, independent substance, as he maintains it is, and as it was for Plato. Nor does he explain how the soul, as a metaphysically different entity than the body, can interact with it. His explanation that it does so through the pineal gland is physiologically nonsense, and solves nothing. Nor does he argue convincingly why the soul should be incorruptible or immortal, as he assumes from scholastic philosophy it must be. What is clear is that Descartes still needs to maintain the Platonic soul's independence from the body if it is to experience the Christian drama of salvation and immortality. For Descartes, as for the scholastics, the task of philosophy still remained to justify unquestionable Christian theology.

In this theology, the agent of salvation is, of course, God. But how do we know God exists? Descartes says that he has the *idea* of such a perfect being. But where, he asks, could this idea have come from? Descartes maintains that, as he is an imperfect being himself, he could imagine the other things in the world, such as objects, stars, and men, which are as imperfect as himself, but he could not imagine God. Therefore, his idea must come from outside himself, and can come only from God, who alone is perfect. Therefore, God exists. Another "proof" of God's existence, which Descartes borrows from the scholastic tradition, is called the "ontological proof," which argues that as a perfect being God must exist because his non-existence would be an imperfection. Similarly, Descartes argues that if God did not exist, objects which are known to exist, such as stars and men, would be greater. Therefore God exists, because nothing can be greater than God.

Are such arguments convincing? After all, we can say the word "perfection" without understanding what it means, or without needing a Creator to put this imperfectly understood idea in our mind. And why, we can ask, in considering the "ontological proof," should a definition, even if understood, have any hold on existence? Nevertheless, Descartes professed satisfaction with these arguments, and went on to say, again in conformity with traditional Christian thought, that God, being perfect, is *necessarily* incorporeal and eternal, and that all other things in the universe are dependent on him.

For Descartes, God serves not only as a guarantor of salvation, but also as a guarantor of what we can conceive clearly and distinctly here on earth. Mathematical relations, for example, seem clear and distinct, but, Descartes asks, what if there were a malicious God who was deceiving us? Impossible, Descartes answers, because if God were malicious, he would not be perfect, and the idea we have of God is precisely of perfection. Since for Descartes knowledge of the world is guaranteed by God, who would not deceive us, this knowledge is also, as it is for Plato, perfect and invariant, once it is ascertained.[3]

In this way, Descartes' grounding of knowledge on God exceeds anything that Aristotle might have imagined, or the medieval church demanded. Because, like Plato, Descartes holds the notion of the eternal and incorruptible soul, he also necessarily believes in its permanent or invariant nature. Here, again, Descartes' surety rests on shaky or gratuitous premises and reasoning.

For Descartes, as for Plato, neither human reason, nor the concepts and methods of science, are products of contingent history, but of the timeless qualities of the human soul. Ideas are not enmeshed in the personal and social histories of those who think and articulate them. It would be as if French children could utter *"Je pense, donc je suis"* (I think, therefore I am) without ever having attended a school, just as Plato's slave boy Meno needs only to remember the Pythagorean theorem, because, Plato maintains, it is already a part of his immortal soul.

With God as his guarantor of clear and distinct ideas, Descartes grounds the new physics on the clearest and most distinct notion he believes is available—mathematically expressed interactions. Physics, then, consists for him solely in understanding how matter is agitated by movements according to mathematical laws.

Once God has set the world in motion, matter and momentum are conserved, and the world goes on in endless but ordered movement, and so achieves the intellectual permanence of predictability. Here Descartes outlines the world which soon will be more fully spelled out by Newton's major work in physics, *The Principia*, or, in its full title, *The Mathematical Principles of Natural Philosophy* (1687).

In the moral sphere, Descartes' aim is personal perfection, again in the interest of permanence, or salvation, rather than achieving some beneficial effect in the world by enlisting in a common cause with his fellow human beings. Descartes ends his discussion of morals in the *Discourse* by saying, as might have Aristotle, "I thought I could not do better than to...devote all my life to the cultivation of my reason, and to progress as much as possible in the knowledge of truth, following the method I had prescribed for myself."[4]

In the Aristotelean world, a hierarchy of created beings ascends from inert objects to simpler organisms like fungi or plants, to insects, to mammals, and ultimately to human beings. All the elements of this hierarchy are present in our own organism. But in Descartes' thought, biological organisms are only machines. Between the material world, including plants and animals, and human souls is an unbridgeable metaphysical distance which alienates us from the rest of the natural world. Descartes must make this metaphysical distinction to secure our salvation.

Cartesian philosophy seemed to address two worlds which seemed fairly distinct. The first is the physical world of Isaac Newton, who two generations later explained all phenomena as the result of physical interactions. The second is the world of subjective experience, without direct reference to an objective world at all.

In the first world of mechanics, God leaves matter to be controlled by mathematical natural law—specifically, as Newton would spell out, by the laws of motion and the universal principle of gravitation. For Descartes, this mode of explanation seemed totally adequate to describe all physical interactions.

By considering organisms as physical machines, Cartesian thought could lead to the supposition that one such machine might be man himself. The soul was necessary as a guarantor of the afterlife. But what was it? Unlike Aristotle, Descartes believed that the soul could not be the life-spirit of the body, as it had to survive the body after death. But when Descartes, being a scientist of his age, began to demonstrate how the body seemed to produce sensation, volition, and even elements of what might be called thought, the area left to the soul receded. Cartesian scholar John Cottingham argues that, with the insights of modern science, Descartes might have been forced to admit that even cognition and speech, those elements he holds out as clearly being functions of the soul, could be products of the body. In this way, Descartes seems to be the progenitor of modern neurophysiology (see chapter 9). Cottingham writes:

> [A]pparently Descartes could not envisage the brain or nervous
> system as being capable of... genuine thought or linguistic be-
> havior. Yet this in turn prompts the in one way absurdly hypo-
> thetical but in another way curiously illuminating question:
> would Descartes have maintained his stance on the incorporeality
> of the mind had he been alive today?... Indeed... it is not even
> clear that it [Descartes' position] could survive an appeal to mod-
> ern chess-playing machines...[5]

Even as late as 1890, the American psychologist and philosopher William James remarked in his *Psychology* that there was still insufficient evidence in physiology to establish a physical model for how thought worked, a disclaimer that Sigmund Freud also made in 1895.[6] Nevertheless, Descartes seems to be moving in the direction of making thought a function of the body, rather than a metaphysically different entity. However, had he stated this as a philosophic principle, his theology would have forced him vehemently to deny it.

But Descartes can also be seen as moving in exactly the opposite direction from that of the world as matter and mechanism. Here Descartes can be considered the father of subjectivism, or phenomenology.[7] In this mode of thinking, we can view Descartes as identifying with his own subjectivity, as if he were saying, "I am my experiencing."

Considering everything as individual, subjective experience would prove enormously attractive to the mobile middle class, which was emerging from the collective consciousness of the Christian medieval world and beginning to take on the world as individuals. Such a doctrine can be liberating, as it is in romanticism, which values one's particular perspective above all else. But it can also be seen as limiting, or self-referential, so that there is no direct apprehension of an objective world whose connections or concerns enmesh and transcend the individual. In the case of David Hume, for example we will see that belief in the real world can only occur if the individual *chooses to infer* that the real world exists.

While considered the first modern philosopher, Descartes shows himself increasingly in the grip of earlier ideas:

- While proclaiming an existence based on thought, Descartes concludes that his soul is independent of his body and is a completely different metaphysical substance. The mode in which body and soul interrelate is left unclear.
- Descartes proclaims that God exists, offering a series of proofs based on essentialist or linguistic arguments, and then attributes to God all the powers that the scholastics had attributed to him.
- In particular, he grounds human knowledge, including "clear and distinct ideas," on God's unwillingness to deceive us. With this authority, he attributes to thought considerably more clarity than it has.
- Like Aristotle, he sees the highest human activity not in involvement or commitment, but in contemplation.
- While seeming to endorse both mechanism and subjectivism, Descartes refuses to endorse either, due to his need to maintain a metaphysics necessary for salvation.

In sum, although Descartes desperately wanted to ground the world on God and the soul, such a world was slipping away. Descartes, the inventor of analytic geometry and of the *Cogito*, left thought hopelessly muddled with classical and religious notions, and reduced human beings to observers rather than participants in the world.

John Locke

John Locke (1632–1704) proclaimed a very different philosophy, one which seemed well-adapted to an age of science and of liberal revolution. Nevertheless, it left unsettled major conflicts between science and religion, and failed to resolve key problems already noted in classical thought. Here again, philosophical rigor was sacrificed to retain elements of permanence.

Born some thirty-six years after Descartes in Protestant England, into an age already somewhat more comfortable with the new physics, Locke lived during Europe's first wave of political liberalism. The son of a captain in the Parliamentary army, which had successfully opposed the Crown in the civil wars of the 1640s, Locke inherited his father's distrust of absolute monarchy. Physician to and then political confidant of the Earl of Shaftesbury, one of England's most influential liberal political figures, Locke was directly involved in the events leading up to the Glorious Rebellion of 1689, which overthrew the Catholic and autocratic James II and established a constitutional monarchy in England under William and Mary. By this time, Locke had become a wealthy man, and was deeply committed to maintaining a system that would support private wealth.

In his central *Essay Concerning Human Understanding*, Locke proclaims his purpose as showing "how men, barely by the use of their natural faculties, may attain to all the knowledge they have, without the help of any innate impressions; and may arrive at certainty, without any such original notions or principles."[8] While Locke uses radically different methods than Descartes, his aim is the same—to establish certainty in an increasingly contingent world.

Rather than believing that the mind is stocked with innate ideas, the position of Plato or Descartes, Locke holds that the mind is a blank slate, a *tabula rasa*, which experience writes upon. Once this has happened, the mind can perform its operations on experience, thereby providing a map of the world, and self-knowledge.

Like Plato and Descartes, Locke, for the most part, assumes a fixed set of independent mental capacities. The independence of mind, and its preformed stock of abilities, looks surprisingly like the cognitive souls of Plato, Aristotle, and Descartes, although Locke sometimes hints that these capacities might have been developed by society and embedded in socialized language. Not only is Locke vague about the origins of these mental abilities, he never explains why experience doesn't *already* include components of mind—that is, why it appears initially, as he believes it does, as just pure data upon which the mind can then perform its operations. Later, David Hume, while apparently repudiating classical thought, would hold the same problematic position.

Locke, however, unlike Descartes and Plato, declines to engage in any attempt to argue the antecedent or eternal existence of the soul. He says he simply isn't interested in the question of the soul's origin, or thinks it is impossible to answer. Here it would seem that Locke did not want to confront a still-militant, though now Protestant, church. In Locke's time, dominant Christian notions could sometimes be ignored, but they still could not be contradicted if one wished to exercise political influence.

Nor, despite his medical training, is Locke generally interested in providing any material or physical explanation for mind:

I shall not at present meddle with the physical consideration of the mind; or trouble myself to examine wherein its essence consists; or by what motions of our spirits or alterations of our bodies we come to have any *sensation* by our organs, or any *ideas* in our understandings; and whether those ideas do in their formation, any or all of them, depend on matter or not.[9]

With this huge disclaimer, not only does Locke seem to forgo a physical or organic analysis, but, like Descartes, he also dismisses the notion that ideas can be unconscious, or built into the structure of the mind without the mind being conscious of them. He writes, "To say a notion is imprinted on the mind, and yet at the same time to say, that the mind is ignorant of it, and never yet took notice of it, is to make this impression nothing."[10] Rather, *everything* that the mind knows is based on initially conscious experience, and, directly, on initial perceptions. This emphasis on consciousness, with its evocation of the fully formed soul, would continue in Western thought until the end of the nineteenth century, with the work of Sigmund Freud (see chapter 10).

It should be noted that Locke is not concerned with atomized impressions, such as sensations of yellow, hot, soft, or bitter. Rather, Locke takes as primary more global sensory experiences which, he says, without the mediation of the mind, give us direct knowledge of a particular *object*, such as Mr. Jones at a particular moment. On the other hand, Locke differs from Plato, for whom examples of species exhibit an archetypal idea, or from Aristotle, for whom species are fundamental. Rather, for Locke, words like "man" or "dog" define mere "sorts" or generalizations that the mind pulls from a number of momentary experiences of individual men or dogs.

Despite Locke's seemingly total reliance on sensory experiences and on our processing of them, which might have resulted in pure subjectivism, he still conceives the world as objective because we are not the *cause* of these experiences. This capacity of the world to create sensory experiences or sensory ideas, Locke calls "power."[11]

Locke makes the perception of power a primary experience, something which David Hume would dispute, as would, for different reasons, Immanuel Kant. While Locke describes, for example, how we can observe the sun's power to melt wax, he tends not to focus on our observation of external objects that cause changes in *other* objects. Rather, he focuses on our willing parts of our *own* bodies to move; and on the power of objects to cause ideas in *us*, such as a stone arousing in us the ideas of its hardness and shape. Thus, Locke speaks of "that perception and consciousness we have of the actual entrance of ideas from [external objects]," and again, of the "*actual receiving* of ideas from without that gives us notice of the existence of other things."[12] He writes that anyone who puts his finger in a candle flame "will little doubt that this is something existing without him, which does him harm, and puts him to great pain."[13] But again, Locke confesses to have no idea how such perception works, and appeals to God who has so arranged the world that, in fact, these effects occur.

In describing our conscious experience of the world, Locke posits two basic categories. The "original" or "primary" qualities, such as solidity, extension, figure, motion, rest, and number, are inseparable from bodies, or substances, and are directly communicated to us. These primary qualities are the subject of Newton's physics. Locke also states, however, that bodies have the capacity to produce in us "secondary" qualities, such as colors, sounds, and tastes. The first set of qualities, Locke says, resides in the bodies themselves; the second set exists only in us. This is still another distinction, with its ghostly echo of Platonism, which would haunt philosophy for over two hundred years.

Bodies, or substances, are not directly perceived; rather, Locke says, they are simply notions we have that, because a number of ideas go together, for example, circle, extension, bright and hot, we presuppose a substance, the sun, which produces them. But what the real constitutions of bodies or substances are, Locke confesses he does not know, although he seems to favor the idea that bodies are made up of minute corpuscles.

Locke separates not only primary and secondary qualities, but even more fundamentally, body and spirit. For Locke, the world ends up as dualistic as it is for Descartes:

> The primary ideas we have peculiar to body, as contra-
> distinguished to spirit, are the cohesion of solid, and conse-
> quently separable, parts, and a power of communicating motion
> by impulse.... The ideas we have belonging and peculiar to
> spirit, are thinking, and will, or a power of putting body into mo-
> tion by thought, and, which is consequent to it, liberty.[14]

Locke simply accepts this dualism, and continues with his explanation of the world. As a doctor, he sees an organism's life as the result of the "continued organization" of its parts. The *identity* of the living organism is the transmission of this organization from occasion to occasion of its existence.

In Locke's scheme, "person" or "self" *is* consciousness, or distinctly, self-consciousness; it is the idea we have of ourselves that we are thinking, perceiving, and willing. Although Locke assumes that consciousness is a manifestation of a substance or soul, he does not attempt to prove the soul's existence by this momentary activity, as does Descartes ("I think, therefore I am"). Rather, personal identity is *established* by extending backward into time to remember the similarity of conscious experience.

Locke asks, What determines the actions of the will? The answer is reductive: pleasure and pain. "Free will" is manifested by exercising the will judiciously so that we may secure our true happiness within the possibilities that the world provides. As people differ greatly about what gives happiness (Locke, who lived in the age of exploration, was an avid reader of explorers' accounts of "primitive" or "exotic" peoples), there can be no universal standard of good and evil, although in each society, what causes pleasure and pain creates the local standard. Also, Locke is never clear why "higher" forms of pleasure are better than lower ones. Here, of course,

Locke differs directly with Plato, who holds that the Good is invariant and part of the essential nature of things.

On the other hand, Locke constructs a doctrine of universal natural law based on his surmise of what God intended for all human beings. He writes:

> The Idea of a supreme Being, infinite in power, goodness, and wisdom, whose workmanship we are, and on whom we depend; and the idea of ourselves, as understanding, rational creatures, being such as are clear in us, would, I suppose, if duly considered and pursued, afford such foundations of our duty and rules of action, as might place *morality* amongst the *sciences capable of demonstration*: wherein I doubt not but from self-evident propositions, by necessary consequences, as incontestable as those in mathematics, the measures of right and wrong might be made out...[15]

The confusion here between absolute, permanent standards and the particular ethnocentric standards of different societies is never resolved.

Nevertheless, Locke, unlike the ancients, did not feel, for the most part, that morality comes directly from God, or that morality is innate in an eternal soul. Rather, moral laws can be learned by understanding our nature; for example, that we are social creatures, and wish to be secure and prosperous. Accordingly, we should refrain "from doing hurt to one another," and should be engaged in *"preserving all mankind."*[16] Such moral injunctions should be enforced by devising the necessary laws, with rewards and punishments. Again, Locke's confidence that universal "natural" laws can be so derived contains the echoes of essentialist classical thought.

Like his philosophic predecessor, Thomas Hobbes (d. 1679), Locke believed in a social contract of autonomous individuals who, prior to their entry into civil society, know their individual interests and, to achieve dependable conditions, logically agree to regulation by the state. Hobbes had said that men were so aggressive that they would annihilate themselves unless they were stopped by an all-powerful state. But Hobbes also said that men were rational enough to understand that they needed to agree to its government.

For Locke, the "state of nature" is far more benign. He believed that social institutions, such as private property, and even a money economy, precede the establishment of the state. As men pursue wealth, and, with a money economy, create vast differences between themselves, government, and the social contract which establishes it, becomes absolutely necessary to preserve private property. Ironically, Locke somewhat illogically supported a system in which men without property would be fully bound by the laws, but would be denied the franchise.

As men enter into government to preserve their rights, that is, life, liberty, and private property, government cannot not take them away. Moreover, as Aristotle had said, government must act in the public interest, not in the interest of the governors. It also must not contravene the laws of the people's representatives, which express the people's interests. If it does any of these things, the government forfeits its original legitimacy and the public can justifiably revolt, or individuals can act in their individual interests by killing the sovereign.[17] Unlike Hobbes, who believed that men had forfeited forever their right to revolt when they agreed to form a civil society, Locke maintained revolution as a ready option.

But the "social contract" as a justification for political arrangements has serious problems. Like the doctrine of "original sin," it freezes an act in mythical time, ignoring history and sociology. The fact that people achieve their character by virtue of their socialization, and that their institutions and government are products of a long, previous social history, would eventually make Locke's theory of a "social contract" seem increasingly artificial. In the nineteenth century, Locke's social philosophy began to suffer the same fate as Newtonian physics would in the twentieth.

Locke's theory of revolution proved more enduring. Not only did Locke justify the Glorious Rebellion of 1689, his writings were liberally plundered by Thomas Jefferson in the Declaration of Independence, and were cited well into the nineteenth century as revolts against autocracy spread throughout Europe. Such changes occurred either by violent revolution or by a series of expansions of the franchise. Yet it is sobering to think that Locke's stirring phrases, used by Jefferson, were intended to support the liberties of the major landowners—less than one percent of England's population.

Where Locke seems surefooted and clear about his ideas on human knowledge and politics, he becomes indirect and sometimes vague in his theories of religion. Unlike Plato, religion for Locke in not based on direct experience.[18] Rather, religion comes not as direct knowledge of God's objective reality, but, for the most part, as assent or faith. Such assent or faith is supported by reason, but does not have the same immediate relation to experience as does Locke's understanding of ideas, such as a table, or mental processes, such as remembering. Thus Locke *argues* that God must exist to create the world, as being cannot come from nonbeing. As the Creator is credited with everything in creation, he is powerful and wise. The evidence of his power and wisdom are everywhere. What is more, we could not exist without an intelligent being creating us; hence our existence depends on him. Finally, while God's laws can be discovered by reason, religion, as expressed in the Gospels, and reinforced by the promise of the afterlife, which Locke conventionally credits, complements reason in instilling these laws.

But, for Locke, we have only a *constructed idea* of God. Locke is openly disdainful of "enthusiastic" people who "talk" to God. Our experience of God is different from our experiences of things, such as tables, he says, because things have the directly perceived power to give us an idea of themselves, however unclear or unrelated this idea may be to their true nature. God does not communicate with us in such a direct way.

Locke's notion of God, like Isaac Newton's, is essentially that of a distant Prime Mover, the One who initiated the world and set it in motion, and who established the basis for the moral laws and the grounds for salvation. Compared to the God of the Old Testament, for example, such an entity represents a huge loss. Gone is the fretful but caring father, who can act directly in the present world. Rather, at some point in the unrecoverable past, God had set the world in motion so that it could continue to move forever, like a table of frictionless billiard balls. The Prime Mover had appeared at the first moment, cue in hand, and had made the decisive break.

What Locke and Newton did not resolve in this scenario was the idea of freedom, of which Locke, particularly, was considered the foremost exponent. If God sets the world in motion, is history anything more than a deterministic playing out of motion from the first moment, a tedious bouncing and clacking of the balls into eternity? As a doctor and observer of organisms, Locke suggests otherwise, that in organisms there is a measure of freedom, as there must be in Locke's politics. Again, he leaves the issue unresolved.

As for Christianity, Locke never seriously questions that the "revelations" of the Gospels are true. (Curiously, he says he accepts their claims on credit, due to their depiction of miracles.) The Gospels, in turn, establish divine law, which necessarily includes God's power to reward and punish. Locke says that divine law is obligatory, as obedience to it results in our ultimate happiness or misery in the next life—for which, again, Locke establishes no convincing basis of belief. Nevertheless, Locke's main philosophical position, which is somewhat disassociated from his religious beliefs, is that natural law, implying right conduct, which is God's law, is discoverable through reason, although he lacks conviction that reason can indisputably establish it. Here, in this splitting of religious and philosophic thought, Locke reflects his time.

What Locke was able to do was provide a *modus vivendi*, however qualified, for progressive elements of English and, to some extent, American and continental society, from the Glorious Rebellion to the middle of the nineteenth century:

- The physical sciences could proceed to discover the natural laws with which a rational God had permanently structured the universe.
- Reason, preestablished in the mind, could begin the process of constructing the world and the mind from presumably real sensory experiences, rather than from unassailable, innate ideas of classical philosophy.
- Morals could progress according to an increasingly refined system of ascertaining pleasure and pain, rather than, for the most part, being codes of conducted dictated by God.
- And politics could ground itself in the will of the governed, or, specifically, the propertied class, under the enveloping fabric of natural law humanized by a genial toleration of differences.

Although Locke's philosophy seemed to provide answers for his age, it falters at almost every crucial point in its construction of the world:

- Maintaining a dualistic universe, Locke can tell us nothing about how spirit or mentality is integrated into matter in organisms.
- Nor can he tell us how organisms and their mental functions evolve over time. Although he hints at a sociological explanation for the development of mentality, Locke's reason has the same prefabricated sense that Descartes' has.
- Basing all experience on sensation, Locke ends up with a split system of experiential material (sensations) and processing machinery (mind), which seems inadequate to explain experience. This duality gets us little beyond the problems left to philosophy by Plato and Descartes.
- Locke maintains an artificial distinction between "original" or "primary" qualities, such as solidity, extension, and figure, which

70

are in the bodies, and "secondary" qualities, such as color, sound, and taste, which are in us, and never explains the basis of this distinction.

- Although Locke's doctrine of "power" suggests a direct perception of causality, he does so little to explain it that some of his most perceptive commentators fail even to mention it.

- Locke's view of physics is of a world of matter set into motion by God as Prime Mover, a deterministic world in which laws are divinely determined, which leaves the origin of human freedom unclear.

- Although Locke provides a theory of personality based exclusively on the experience of consciousness, the theory provides no underpinning for his belief in the soul.

- His support for conventional elements of Christianity, particularly the salvation of the soul and its eternal life, has virtually no grounding in his epistemology; and his crediting the Gospels with revelatory truth seems equally without justification in his philosophy.

- The relation between revelatory truth and natural law is hazy at best, and leaves an uncertain support for the laws of civil society. Moreover, it is unclear whether government and civil society are functions of the permanent character of man, natural law, and revelation, or are historically contingent products.

In summary, both Descartes and Locke left philosophy with huge, unresolved problems. While attempting to grasp the immediacy of experience, neither could wean himself away from notions of permanence. While living in an increasingly changing world, both clung to notions which defied change at a number of crucial points. David Hume, who attempted to clean up the mess, would make matters, if anything, even worse.

David Hume

Locke had been, at least to some extent, a man of faith. Scotland's David Hume (1711–1776), the friend of Jean Jacques Rousseau and other members of the French Enlightenment—they called him *"le bon David"*—was an open sceptic.[19] Where Locke had been a doctor, Hume, when he was not philosophizing, was writing history. His *History of England*, however flawed, was, by virtue of its clear style, the standard history for a hundred years.

As a philosopher, Hume genially attacked all traditional authority, religious and philosophic, using what he and his French colleagues deemed the deadliest of weapons—human reason. Although Hume's eighteenth century boasted the most startling advances in science, Hume himself has little to say about science. While he claims to draw upon experimentation, there is little evidence of this in his work. Where Hume prefers using words like "metaphysics" or "occult philosophy" to describe his antagonists' theories, his philosophic target seems to be Plato and the entire system of permanence which he created, much as it is today for postmodernists (see chapter 11). In critiquing Platonic thought, Hume, at the same time, offers what he believes to be a purification of Locke. In so doing, Hume denudes Locke not only of theology, but also appropriates only certain doctrines, and rigidifies these to the point of caricature.

Hume begins by constructing a theory of knowledge on the narrowest of possible foundations: discrete sensations which, he tells us, have no necessary or organic connections with each other. We base our notion of things, then, simply on the conjunction of sensations. In his *A Treatise of Human Nature*, published in 1739, Hume writes:

> [T]he understanding never observes any real connection among objects, and that even the union of cause and effect, when strictly examined, resolves itself into a customary association of ideas. For from thence it evidently follows, that identity is nothing really belonging to these different perceptions, and uniting them together; but is merely a quality, which we attribute to them, because of the union of their ideas in the imagination, when we reflect upon them.[20]

Locke believes experience consists not of sensations, but of things, or what more recent psychologists would call "gestalts." Hume, by contrast, sees as the basis of our experience only atomized sensations, which he never fully defines. The attribution of self-sufficient reality to things, and the idea of their continued existence, are the basis for Newtonian physics. For Hume, these are only constructions and projections, made possible by the "constancy" and "coherence" of perceptions, which we cannot prove.

Hume also maintains that we can never know something's true composition. We can, for example, experience a steady collection of bitter sensations that we call a "lemon," but Hume denies that we can know if a lemon, considered as a thing in itself, is really bitter. Where Locke agrees with this for such "secondary" qualities, he thinks we *can* know the "primary" qualities, those which are dealt with in physics, such as solidity, extension, and motion. Hume denies this as well.

Hume also openly questions the notion that we can experience causation directly. Rather, he says, we infer causation by repeatedly observing the contiguity and succession of events:

> Thus we remember to have seen that species of object we call *flame,* and to have felt that species of sensation we call *heat.* We likewise call to mind their constant conjunction in all past instances. Without any further ceremony, we call the one *cause* and the other *effect,* and infer the existence of the one from that of the other.[21]

But Hume is clear that there is no *direct* experience of causality. Although we can get through life more easily with the notion that flames are hot, this idea is not absolute knowledge but merely a construct from a number of experiences, and a projection from these experiences by which we endow that construct with a constant quality. Hume does not take up the issue of how we make parts of our body move, a fact which provides one of the bases of Locke's notion of causality. He thus denies or neglects both of Locke's justifications for the notion of power, that is, that we experience the world's effects on us and that we have power to affect the world. By denying causality, Hume abstracts human experience from its direct sense of derivation from, and enmeshment in, the causal structure of the world.

In the same vein, Hume sees ideas not as a primary experience, but as notions which are based on immediate sensations, and which normalize such experiences, while never losing some of their initial data. Even a square will merely represent the various squares we have experienced, rather than itself be the archetype or source of such experiences, as Plato would have it.

Similarly, Hume argues against our direct perception of space and time, and attacks the container theory of Descartes, Locke, and Newton, that is, that things or events exist *in* space and time. Rather, Hume maintains, space is a function of objects, of how they are distributed. Time consists of the succession of objects, or the succession of sensations from which our notion of objects arise. Mathematics, as well, becomes for Hume a construct based on transitory sensations, and so lacks the absolute quality ascribed to it by other scientists and other philosophers, starting with Plato.

The same thinking applies to the self or mind, which is, for Hume, simply a collection of perceptions, much like any other object. These perceptions include not only sensations, and the ideas which are based on them, but feelings such as loving and hating, which accompany such perceptions. They accompany them, Hume says, because, for example, we feel love when we receive benefits, and hatred when we receive injuries. The self or mind is not the receptacle of ideas or perceptions, just as time and space do not contain objects, and just as substances do not *have* qualities. Rather, the self or mind is a construct of these qualities or, better, the sensations and feelings which we attribute to one thing—ourselves.

These disclaimers leave Hume no way of explaining reason, which, in his thinking, possesses the same independent character as it does in Plato, Descartes, and Locke. It is as if the mechanism of analysis could be totally abstracted from the world and left unexplained. Even when Hume reflects upon reason, he employs reason, which then escapes his analysis.

To sum up, all these concepts—causality, substances, space, time, and selves or minds—have no basis, for Hume, in direct experience, and are simply constructions based on the assembly of sensations and memories. The world would seem to be nothing but a construct of fragments of experience which then provide us with a tentative *modus operandi* for getting through life, a working hypothesis, which is more or less reliable. This picture of the world, when analyzed carefully, seems so atomized, so implicitly chaotic, that even prior to the development of cognitive psychology or modern neurology, philosophers suspected something was terribly amiss.

The problem is that, while disposing of causality, substances, space, time, and selves or minds, Hume fails to provide any substitute which is not wholly dependent on artificial constructions involving "resemblances," "contiguities," and probabilities, and any idea of where his capacity to analyze might have arisen. As the very existence of the external world is left in doubt, so is the possibility of any dependable scientific laws concerning a physical world. Even the assumption which lies behind modern science—that if certain conditions produce an effect, that effect will always be produced—cannot stand, in Hume's view. Rather, Hume argues, that only continued observation makes such a result likely. As he leaves the origin of reason unexplained, so must he also fail to provide any useful analysis of the relation between thought and the world out of which it arises.

Not only does Hume dispose of causality, substance, time, space, and selves or minds, but he also undercuts any higher justification for morality and politics. Like Locke, Hume seems to base morality on pleasure and pain. He declares, "Reason is, and ought only to be, the slave of the passions, and can never pretend to any other office than to serve and obey them."[22] This is, of course, to turn Plato on his head. For Plato, reason must "tame" the passions, much as a driver tames horses, and it is reason which forms the basis of the ideational world which produces aesthetics and morality. With this doctrine of the subservient role of reason, Hume also denies the existence of free will, the pillar of Plato's and Locke's morality and politics.

For Hume, moral science, then is not normative, not based on "oughts," but descriptive of what is; of what, in fact, causes pleasure and pain. But Hume avoids one reductive implication of this doctrine—that any pleasure is to be sought.[23] Rather he bases his standards, either in morality or taste, including taste in art and literature, on what people of sensitivity and experience opine or do. Morality and taste are, then, simply a function of social cultivation.

What drops out of Hume's system is any standard for action or art which rises above the tastes of society's arbiters, a problem which relativists or ethnocentrists today, such as the philosopher Richard Rorty, are still saddled with (see chapters 11 and 12). Hume's standardbearers, what he called "men of good taste," consisted of a class of men who sought in the genial approbation of their peers the sanction of their morals, the standards of their art, and the justification of their existence. It was, in short, genteel England in the eighteenth century.[24]

Hume thus fails to describe how morality might arise from empathy, that is, from our perception of the needs of others. By reducing moral action to what causes pleasure and pain in the actor, he makes all moral action self-reflexive, to the extent that we are not simply following society's leaders. Nor does he construct any theory of aesthetics that looks to the work of art itself, rather than to the pleasure it causes or to the arbitration of "men of good taste." Both explanations seem simply shallow.

As for Hume's analysis of politics, he relies as heavily on experience as he does for his theories of knowledge and morals. Gone are any notions derived from religion or divine revelation, any discussion of philosopher-kings, or man's essential nature, or any mythology regarding the social contract, a notion he believes only slightly less ridiculous than the divine right of kings. Regarding Locke's social contract, he maintains that, even if at some time in the primordial past, some men entered into some contract, which is doubtful, that act can hardly have any binding validity on the present. Hume writes:

> Were you to preach, in most parts of the world, that political connections are founded altogether on voluntary consent or a mutual promise, the magistrate would soon imprison you as seditious for loosening the ties of obedience; if your friends did not before shut you up as delirious, for advancing such absurdities.[25]

Most governments, Hume maintains, come into being through violence. What creates civic obligation is the judgment that a government's continuance provides more social benefits than its overthrow, with all its possible dangers. In general, he seems content with the British constitutional system as it had evolved in the eighteenth century. "All plans of government," he writes, "which suppose great reformation in the manners of mankind, are plainly imaginary."[26] In this field, for the most part, Hume was an observer, not a participant or a revolutionary.

With this base of thought, Hume attacks religion and the entire structure of permanence which supports it. Plato, we recall, wrote of two worlds. The first is the transitory world of sensation, feeling, and physical experience. The second is the permanent world of ideas, the soul, and God, with the first being an inferior reflection of the second. Hume denies the existence of the permanent world altogether, including God and the soul, and severely restricts what we can be sure of even in the transitory world.[27]

We can think of Hume almost as if he were a legal prosecutor, putting to his defendant, Plato, a series of uncomfortable questions:

"Mr. Plato," he might ask, "what *real* experiences do we have in the world? Are these not merely sensations and feelings? If these experiences are transitory, sir, how can you claim that our ideas, which are based on them, are permanent?

"Do we really experience the *soul*, as you say we do? Or isn't it actually the fact that what we really experience are our own feelings and our impressions? Is not the soul simply a construct of these elements? If these experiences are transitory, sir, how can the soul, which is based on them, be permanent? And if we resemble animals, and seem to form a continuum with them, how can you maintain that our souls are metaphysically different from theirs?

"Sir, do we really *experience* God? If not, what is our warrant for *this* notion?"

Here Hume might bring Descartes to the stand:

"M. Descartes, in your ontological proof of God, you argued that if God is that of which there can be nothing greater, God must exist because his nonexistence would be an imperfection. How, sir, can you argue from a definition? In the absence of experience, isn't it true that whatever we conceive to exist could equally well not exist, and therefore to argue God's existence by definition, before experience, is inconclusive?"

Imagine Locke as Hume's next defendant. Hume might begin:

"Mr. Locke, regarding your argument from the creation to the Creator, if we survey the sorry state of the world, can we argue God's omnipotence, wisdom, or goodness from the nature of creation? How can we, sir, as it exhibits none of these qualities in anything like a pure form? How from such an imperfect world can we derive a God that we would wish to worship? How can you attribute to the Creator more than we find in the creation? There could be many gods or one, or God could have perished after having created the world—how, sir, would we know?"

"On what basis," Hume might ask his three defendants, "can we claim that certain moral principles are permanent or divinely sanctioned, if there are no eternal ideas and there is no warrant for believing in God? If this is so," he might ask Plato, "what warrant have we for believing in the Good?" Or, turning to Descartes and Locke, he might ask, "On what basis can we credit the divinely prescribed morality of the Hebrew Bible or the Gospels?"

Hume might ask all of his defendants, "How can the soul have an eternal life which goes beyond the obvious evidence of our deaths? What is our experience of the afterlife, and on what do you base your belief, other than on your fear of death? If there is no warrant for such a belief, what then can you say of the validity of such notions as heaven and hell, and the incentive of eternal happiness or the fear of damnation? With what justice could we be allowed to suffer forever for what we did, however hideous, in our short life on earth?"

Finally, he might demand of his three defendants: "What is the faculty by which all the above is perceived or understood? If that faculty is what the ancient philosophers called Reason, again, what is your experience of it? If the exercise of your mentality seems as transitory and imperfect as everything else you actually experience, how can you ascribe to it the perfection given to it by the ancients?"

For all of these questions, Hume would believe he would receive no satisfactory answers. He then might make the following closing argument:

"Gentlemen of the jury, we have nothing but our imperfect, transitory experiences as the warrant for our beliefs. You will find that every metaphysical category advanced by the defendants flunks the experiential text. Nothing which our defendants have discussed—that is, nothing in our experience—justifies a flight into metaphysics, perfect knowledge (ideas), the soul, God, the afterlife, or eternal rules of morality. Such notions are mere superstition, gentlemen, and must be discarded. Mankind must see its limitations—such knowledge or notions are simply beyond its experiential capabilities; mankind must content itself with the world it can know. There is no special metaphysical experience; the daily flow of sensation and feelings is all we have."

However powerful a case Hume makes in opposition to such opponents, he fails to make a case himself for a philosophy which deals adequately with life:

- In the end, Hume emerges as a kind of floating, cognitive function, uniting disparate experiences into the constructions we call the real world, human beings, and societies. His detachment is almost total.
- His depiction of direct experience as atomized sensations, upon which he bases everything, seems totally artificial, as would become increasingly clear in modern psychology (see chapters 9 and 10).
- His discounting of causality removes human beings from any direct experience of the world.
- His discrediting of the reality of constructs, again, seems highly artificial, as modern physics underscores (see chapters 7–10).
- His reduction of morality to pleasure and pain, or to the conventions of his time, seems so superficial that it begs for a more profound analysis.

As we have seen, the effect of Hume's scepticism was to cast into doubt the entire scope of classical metaphysics, and its remnants in Descartes and Locke. By demolishing these defenses of permanence, Hume left nothing in its place. By failing to credit causality, bodies, minds, space, and time with any certainty, Hume seemed to deny reality to necessary components of the world, leaving only bits of experience collected and assembled into assumptions and probabilities. This was a world so insubstantial and contingent, and seemingly so alienated from human involvement, that Immanuel

Kant felt called upon by God or the spirit of the age to find what assurances of permanence he could in the very nature of the human mind. His reaction, however, was as extreme and flawed as was the philosophy to which it was reacting.

Immanuel Kant

Where Descartes had found royal patronage, and Locke that of the Earl of Shaftesbury, as well as government service and private wealth, and Hume a collection of patrons, Immanuel Kant (1724–1804) found sustenance as a university professor. His most important work, the *Critique of Pure Reason*[28], was published in 1781, some forty-five years after Hume's *Treatise*. Despite one of the most pedantic and impenetrable writing styles imaginable, Kant made an enormous impact on Western thought. Essentially, Kant proposed the structure of the human mind as an invariant factor in determining key categories, such as space, time, causality, and substance, in seeing the world, not just a gatherer or processor of data, as Locke and Hume would have it. He also offered a very different base for morality and for God than had his philosophic predecessors. In these ways, he reintroduced basic elements of permanence.

Kant begins by attacking Locke's and Hume's view of the mind. For Kant, the mind is not a *tabula rasa* which experience writes upon, but is itself a highly structured mechanism which transfigures reality. Innate ideas, which Locke and Hume dismiss, are reestablished in the very structure of the mind as fixed conditions of experience. Kant writes in his preface to the *Critique of Pure Reason*:

> Hitherto it has been supposed that all our knowledge must conform to the objects:...The experiment therefore ought to be made, whether we should not succeed better with the problems of metaphysic, by assuming that the objects must conform to our mode of cognition...[29]

Kant then defines, point by point, how our cognitive mechanisms structure our experiential world. The first element is space. He concludes, "Space is nothing but the form of all phenomena [experience] of the external senses; it is the subjective condition of our sensibility, without which no external intuition is possible for us."[30] According to Kant, the space which the mind gives us as an absolute condition of our perception is the space described by Isaac Newton. But Kant fails to deal with the fact that the mind may only achieve this category of space through a process of maturation, and that this category may not be unique; that alternative concepts of space may be equally viable. Later, developmental psychologists, following the twentieth-century Swiss psychologist Jean Piaget, would indeed show how infants and small children construct a sense of space which, particularly in the early stages, has few of the elements which Kant thought were fully present in the mind from the beginning. Then, too, the development of non-Euclidean geometries in the nineteenth century, and their use in modern physics, would establish alternative concepts of space (see chapter 7).

Kant treats time in the same way as space. Just as the subjective condition of space structures our external perceptions, so does our mind impose time as the formal condition structuring *all* our experience, both internal and external.

As for causality, Kant, unlike Hume, looks for its basis not in inference and probability, but again in the mind's very structure. While holding that the concept of a 'cause,' and the idea that any fact of experience has a cause, is found in the mind's structure, Kant leaves the determination of any *particular* cause to empirical science.

Finally, the concept of a substance is also given in the invariant structure of the mind as a *condition* of our experience of objects. In all these instances, Kant's explanation, while problematic in many respects, does suggest the role of mind or the brain in creating experience, and thus helps lay the basis for the cognitive psychology and neurophysiology of a later day (see, particularly, chapter 9).

All these categories—space, time, causality, and substance—are, according to Kant, the mind's innate, absolute properties. Their effects as they operate in experience—and so for the world they represent—are unified in a process called "synthesis." This is the mind's most essential activity. Synthesis is the ground for the assertion, "I think," although Kant is, I believe, hopelessly vague about how the process of unification works, or what its result looks like. Unlike Descartes, Kant denies that we can derive a theory of a unified soul as substance from the assertion, "I think," or that we can prove a list of the soul's supposed qualities, such as immateriality, incorruptibility, and spirituality.

What Kant shares, however, with Descartes, Locke, and Hume, and therefore Plato, is the idea of reason as an absolute given, rather than simply a function of a material organism which develops in time and operates in time. A primary example of how reason works is mathematics. For Plato and for Kant, unlike for Hume, mathematical concepts are derived by the mind *a priori*, that is, without external experience. These concepts, and their interrelationships, form the structure of natural law.

Basing his physical ideas of the world on Newton, Kant holds that mathematical formulations of process, as opposed to physical explanations, *are* science. Greek thinkers before Plato and Aristotle had used the supposed properties of earth, air, fire, and water—heaviness, lightness, dryness, and moisture—to explain why matter behaves as it does. The medieval scholars added elements like sympathy, which accounted for magnetic attraction. Descartes reduced all physical reactions to the direct action of matter on matter.

It was Newton who proclaimed the full mathematization of science. Newton's law of gravitation is purely mathematical, as gravitation itself cannot be explained as a result of the physical nature of matter; it is simply a mathematical expression of what can be observed. Likewise, for example, in Newton's second law of motion ($F = ma$, force equals mass times acceleration), force is anything that gives acceleration to a mass, but need not be physically known at all. Although Newton's contemporaries strongly criticized his avoidance of physical explanations, the triumph of Newtonian science carried the field. Kant totally endorses Newton, to the point that he cannot imagine alternative systems of mathematics being used to explain physical phenomena.

Newton's mathematics is not only the basis for all physical explanations, but it underlies all reality as a universal structure.[31] For Kant, as for some physicists, this underlying structure of reality is the mind of God.

To be sure, Kant would hold that empirical investigation is necessary for science, but science, in the apt words of Kantian scholar Michael Friedman, is "framed" or "nested" within Kant's transcendental principles.[32] Because these principles are eternal or invariant, nature, which these laws describe, is as permanent and unchanging as it is for Aristotle. Furthermore, according to Kant, how experimentation is conducted, what it is looking for, and how hypotheses are to be tested, are regulated by rational principles of the mind, which are also *a priori*.

What we actually experience, the *phenomenon*, while related to the real world or world-in-itself, the *noumenon*, is not, for Kant, the same thing. Agreeing with Locke and Hume, Kant says that the *noumenon* can never actually be known, but his reason for this position differs from theirs. For Kant, the *noumenon* is the world without its structuring by the human mind.

But, we can ask, if we cannot know the real world, how can we achieve the kinds of assurances about the nature of existence that were the aim and product of scholastic philosophy? How can Kant make the leap between the *noumenon* and the human mind?

The answer to these and other questions in philosophy, Kant finds in the nature of God. Alternatively, Kant finds answers to these questions in the unconditioned, nonempirical structure of the mind.

Within the timeless world of reason, Kant posits a fully Platonic God as the Being of beings who contains the potentiality of all that can be thought. God is the cause of all things—negatively, because God alone is able to define each thing according to every possibility that the thing itself does not realize; and positively, because God, as the synthesis of all possibilities, holds in his nature the possibility of each individual thing. Finally, the interrelation of all things exists in the mind of God, who thus defines the natural laws and the mathematics behind them, and so opens nature up to the human mind or reason, which partakes of God's nature.

While reason requires these functions of God, Kant is clear that the *reasonableness* of God's existence does not constitute a *proof* that God exists. In seeking a proof of God or of God's nature, Kant finds it unsatisfying to argue from the nature of creation to a divine Creator; nor is it possible for him to go from conditioned experience to an unconditioned Creator. He writes, "That unconditioned necessity, which we require as the last support of all things, is the true abyss of human reason."[33]

Having said this, however, Kant, like Descartes, then posits the existence of God from the very grandeur of his conception of him. He writes:

> For how could there ever be an experience that should be adequate
> to an idea? It is in the very nature of an idea that no experience can
> ever be adequate to it. The transcendental idea of a necessary and
> all-sufficient original Being is so overwhelming, so high above
> everything empirical, which is always conditioned, that we can
> never find in experience enough material to fill such a concept...[34]

It is almost as if Kant were saying that any idea, such as that of God, which is so impressive or overwhelming, must be true, a position similar to that of Descartes.

It is, then, this God who structures and defines the universe, and it is God's nature in which human reason participates. This ultimately mystical identification with the Creator is what underlies our quest for truth because God's truth is embedded in ourselves. This identification is what unites us with the ultimate nature of things and provides us our sense of participation in the world.

When Kant deals with morality, his methods are strikingly similar to the ways he handles the theory of knowledge. Rather than a pragmatic exercise of reason which helps us identify what makes us happy, which Locke and Hume propose, morality, for Kant, is an ideal or transcendental activity of reason which guides us to do what we need to do to *deserve* to be happy. By referring to the *ought*, Kant lifts morality out of any enmeshment in the pragmatic, empirical world, which, he tells us, we know only as representation, and, so, not as reality. Morality then enters into the pure possibility or *freedom* of influencing or causing effects in the empirical world.

Such an ethical system cannot prescribe specific outcomes, just as Kant's rational structure of science cannot foresee specific findings. Rather, Kant says simply: a) that, when developing general maxims of conduct, if we will the end, we should also will the means; and b) that we should act as if the maxims, through our will, were to become a general law of conduct (the "Kantian imperative"). Only morality which follows this rational form is worthy of respect; love, loyalty, and other passions are not involved. Nor does Kant deal with the sociology or history of morals, their enmeshment in their culture. Although Kant does have a practical streak,[35] and his ethics are not as formalistic or purely intellectual as they might seem, one wonders why Kant's moral law would create adequate motivation. One might ask why respect for moral conduct should be limited to that ordained by pure reason—what is the role of sympathy or compassion? Even within Kant's own reasoning, it is also not clear how human beings, who live in a Newtonian, deterministic universe, can be as morally free as Kant believes they are.

How does Kant justify his view of morality? Cannily, he argues that morality gives rise to beliefs which provide its supporting structure. As one's progress toward moral perfection takes time, Kant believes there must be an afterlife where this progress can continue. Morality also causes him to believe in a certain kind of God. Kant states that there must be a God who would actually *cause* happiness to be the result of moral conduct, although the necessity of his nature, though reasonable, cannot be proven. Kant writes:

> That will must be omnipotent, in order that the whole of nature and its relation to morality and the world may be subject to it; omniscient, that it may know the most secret springs of our sentiments and their moral worth; omnipresent, that it may be near for supplying immediately all that is required by the highest interests of the world; eternal that this harmony of nature and freedom may never fail, and so on.[36]

Thus Kant gives to God all the qualities ascribed to the gods by the Sumerians, because it is reasonable that God should have them.

Kant's arguments for the existence of God, because such a Being is necessary to ground morality, are as close as he comes to a proof of God's existence. For Kantian scholar Allen W. Wood, these arguments "do not provide reasons that directly produce belief in God or immortality. What they show is that morally disposed people are involved in a kind of practical irrationality unless they believe in a future life and a providential and gracious Deity."[37]

Such a God will also be the moral ruler of the universe, and his laws, accordingly, will be followed by a voluntary community seeking the highest good. For Kant, the true nature of the church is to be such an intentional community, rather than to be a stage for ecclesiastical ceremonies, and an authority, which he believed many churches were, that infantilize human thought through their interpretations of divine revelation.

A similar sense for the transcendental, as opposed to the practical, structures Kant's view of politics. Here he argues that the political state is a product not of an historic, voluntary contract which people make in their own interests, as it is for Locke, but a product of the timeless dictates of reason without direct reference to need. It is an arrangement that allows for the mutual freedom of all its members. Such an arrangement has nothing directly to do with social justice or social welfare, but rather with the self-protection of its members' freedom to act. Ironically, in exercising this function, the government acquires the right of "domination," that is, the power to coerce behavior or compliance if the passions of citizens override their reason.

One of the freedoms to act is the freedom to acquire property. As this freedom necessarily involves conflict with others and the danger of theft, the state must logically exist to establish rules so that such property may be safely held. Kant states illogically, however, that only people with property are self-sufficient, and therefore only such people can be full citizens and exercise the franchise.

Here, Kant grounds his politics on what he believes to be the transcendental nature of reason. Each ruler must so rule that his or her laws are those that would arise from the united and presumably enlightened will of all. This idea is the counterpart of Kant's moral imperative, which says that an act is right if it could become a universal law of behavior. This kind of legislation can arise either through the democratic process or through the thought experiments of nondemocratic leaders *imagining* what would arise from the united will of all.[38] Thus social insurance, which would later be enacted by Otto von Bismarck, chancellor of a united Germany in the late nineteenth century, is possible, although by no means required, with this line of thought.

However, if the ruler does not act according to the united will, or the ruler is oppressive, Kant, unlike Locke, denies citizens the right to revolution, as this sends society back to the unreasonable state of nature. Rather, unless the government has reverted to anarchy or mass murder, Kant prescribes gradual reform leading to republican rule, the form of government which can best realize the united will. Here Kant, in his later writings, is clearly reacting to the extremes of the French Revolution, which began in 1789, and in a few years degenerated into the Terror. Ironically, the French Revolution, in the name of reason, reached extremes which men of Kant's temperament found intolerable.

Finally, Kant does not stop, as does Locke, at national borders, but envisions an international order based on reason or right, and composed of enlightened states which guarantees perpetual international peace.[39] The right of individuals to a perfect constitution thus embraces the whole globe. Such an order rests on reason, on the power of an unseen world to control the phenomenal world of history and experience. It is an ideal order, not one which is immediately realizable.

Though Kant believed he had accomplished his purpose of implicating mind in the nature of science, morality, and politics, and had provided at least a rationale for a belief in God and a moral order, he left philosophy in considerable distress.

- Kant makes the split between the permanent structure of the mind and the body an unbridgeable gulf, with mind and reason as detached from the physical world as they are in Plato.
- He lifts consciousness to a supreme position, without defining its actual nature.
- He separates appearance *(phenomenon)* and reality *(noumenon)* from each other, without providing a clear sense of how they can be unified.
- He defines physical laws in a Newtonian manner, which looks to an external Creator, rather than to the world itself, as their author. However, Kant's sense that God is the underlying structure of the world *can* be seen as making the world itself responsible for its own laws.
- Kant leaves freedom unexplained.
- He allies reason to God, and states that it is fixed and invariant, and totally detached from any process of development, either within an individual or in the history of a society, and makes it resistant to any cross-cultural analysis.
- He finds science, dictated by human reason, equally absolute, and resistant to change.
- He bases morality on what is reasonable, and argues that God should exist because it is reasonable that such a Being should support a moral order.
- He grounds politics on reason free from historical contingency or human need.

Permanence or invariance prevails throughout. By basing his deepest views on what a reasonable world, including human beings, God, and the laws of nature, *should* be, Kant lifts philosophy into the normative rather than the real.

As generations of philosophy professors pored over Kant's dense texts, the conflicting schools of interpretation multiplied to the point of dissonance, making it difficult even for committed Kantians to continue with anything more than tendencies or lines of thought derived from the structure which Kant had tried so hard to make rock-solid. One dubious accomplishment of Kant was to make a seemingly definitive break between philosophy and common understanding, reserving philosophy for the experts. Concrete examples seemed to have dropped out of philosophic discourse, to be replaced by artificially constructed words, or neologisms, and often hopelessly unclear terminology.[40] Philosophy, always a contentious science, assumed a level of controversy and preoccupation with intramural conflicts which rivaled the worse days of the scholastics.

Yet, behind the perhaps pretentious structure of Kant's language was a person filled with awe at the majesty of the universe, and with a sense of responsibility for helping us fulfill our role in it. How hard he worked, how strongly he believed in the sanctity of his mission.

That something lies beyond the phenomenal world, a deeper reality which is of the very nature of the mind and of God, and which unites rationality, morality, politics, and religion, Kant had no doubt, although he could not prove its existence. This surpassing vision, which has its origins in Plato, leaves the ground of experience and builds into a region of supposition which, in the words of William James, requires a "will to believe."

George Wilhelm Friedrich Hegel

Perhaps the most influential philosopher of the last 150 years, George Wilhelm Friedrich Hegel (1770–1831) can initially best be seen as a reaction to Kant.[41] Like Kant, Hegel was a totally dedicated philosophy professor, with little else in his life but his encompassing visions, his lectures, notes, and books.

Once Kant had established his philosophy and his particular style of exposition, philosophy in Germany, and, to a large extent, in the rest of Europe, could *only* be a reaction to him. In Hegel's case, the result is an alternative structure of permanence built on Kantian foundations. These are, briefly:

- A permanent or fixed Reason;
- A permanent logical structure of ideas;
- A permanent or fixed nature defined by Newtonian laws; and
- A permanent God, who is ultimately Reason, and who establishes the nature of minds, reality, and morality.

The deciding political event in Hegel's life, which took place when he was just nineteen, was the fall of the Bastille in 1789. The French Revolution, and the subsequent career of Napoleon, meant for Hegel that history could no longer be considered as the static maintenance of tradition, or the playing out of man's essential nature, or the repeated enactment of man's salvation. As Hegel developed his ideas in reaction to Kant, he saw his task as integrating Kant into a theory embracing fundamental change.

For Hegel, history is the progress of Reason, otherwise translated as mind, realizing itself. Hegel writes:

> Thus Reason is the *substance* [of our historic world] in the sense that it is that whereby and wherein all reality has its being and subsistence.... It lives on itself, and it is itself the material upon which it works. Just as Reason is its own presupposition and absolute goal, so it is the activation of that goal in world history—bringing it forth from the inner source to external manifestation, not only in the natural universe but also in the spiritual.[42]

History is, then, a rational process leading to an end. That process takes place, for Hegel, in the development of Reason, or Spirit, as it manifests itself in the world. The end of history results from Spirit knowing itself and creating a conformity between the freedom it needs to know itself, and the social conditions or the "state" which promotes that freedom. Perhaps Hegel's most famous line is, "World history is the progress in the consciousness of freedom..."[43]

Like Plato and Kant, Hegel sees the soul as an agent which acts on, but, with some qualifications, is still ultimately independent of, the material world. Hegel also attributes full independence to the World Spirit, which has the complete autonomy which the Hebrews attributed to God. Like Plato and Kant, Hegel sees no ultimate distinction between the human soul and the World Spirit, or God. Rather, one's soul is of the very substance of God, and in its purity participates in all of God's qualities and actions. (This notion, suggested by Kant, is also very close to the Gnosticism of people like Meister Eckhart.)

It is God who wills history, or the "progress in the consciousness of freedom" which underlies all the surface contingencies of historical process. History is admittedly a horror story of human suffering; Hegel calls it a "slaughter-bench."[44] Its justification or redemption is its inevitable progress toward freedom in conformity with God's will. God's will, Hegel writes, "we are here calling the Idea of freedom."[45]

Unlike Plato and Kant, Hegel attempts an accommodation between reason and the passions. Rather than reason simply disciplining the passions, as Plato and Kant say it should, the passions should eventually become reasonable by virtue of the civilizing progress of the social order through time.

Citizens, then, will be virtuous and compassionate, not because they are *compelled* to be, but because they are so conditioned by their social up-bringing that they *wish* to be. Thus, the goal of history is to create a state or society that allies the private interests or passions of citizens acting in free-dom, with the state's rational goals. The ideal state is, then, that social order which reflects the World Spirit, even as it fulfills all the now-rational per-sonal desires of its citizens to work for the common good.

With this idealistic scenario, Hegel spins out a modal history. Greek culture, Hegel believes, seemed to have been created by free, self-conscious individuals, but when one looks closely, one sees that its morality was cus-tomary, rather than individually chosen. Because Socrates questioned this morality, according to Hegel, he was put to death. By contrast, the Roman world denied outward freedom to individuals, causing them to retreat into private philosophies of individual consciousness.

Christianity, Hegel believes, assumed the helplessness of individuals in the social order and emphasized their private spirituality. (Jesus said, "Ren-der unto Caesar what is Caesar's, and unto God what is God's.") The trans-formation of the outer world to conform to the developing freedom of the inner Christian spirit remained unrealized. During the Middle Ages, the Catholic Church denied individual consciousness and seriously compro-mised the spiritual nature of religion by selling material indulgences. Thus, Martin Luther, in questioning indulgences and insisting that there be no in-termediary between God and man, affirmed the primacy of individual con-sciousness. The Reformation was a triumph of the "Germanic people," who, in their simplicity of heart, did away with the pomp and worldliness of the Catholic Church.

From then on, Hegel maintains, the history of the Germanic (essen-tially European) world was an attempt to make social institutions support rational, individual consciousness. The rationality of the French Revolu-tion, with its Declaration of the Rights of Man and Citizen, was perverted by the Terror, because it had been imposed on the French people, rather than having been achieved organically. But the lessons of that revolution were absorbed in Germany, which created constitutional monarchies with rational laws and guarantees of individual rights, acceptable to its rational and free citizens. The rhythm of thesis (for example, Greek morality), an-tithesis (Socratic questioning), and synthesis (Christian consciousness) is played out in history, round after round, until this final resolution. Al-though Hegel would have us believe that history had reached its apex in the Prussian state, he, in fact, wrote during a period of reaction in which the Prussian government lacked an effective parliament, imposed strict censorship, and generally denied citizens virtually any say in the governing process.

While Hegel was somewhat more liberal than the then-current Prussian administration—he believed in trial by jury, freedom of expression, and at least a weak legislature—he was, by our current standards, a political conservative. At the end of his life, for example, he argued against the proposed British Reform Act, which expanded the franchise in 1832. Although the idea, harbored by modern philosophers like Karl Popper, that Hegel was a proto-fascist seems unfair,[46] Hegel's often-exaggerated style permits such a reading.[47]

The important issue, however, is not Hegel's lack of clarity about the history of his time, but his reasoning about how freedom of consciousness can be enhanced through the social order. This freedom, Hegel believes, is not simply "negative freedom," that is, the ability to do what one likes without constraint. One's likes are derived from the particular society in which one lives, and if that society is in an early stage of social development, one's likes will be underdeveloped. However, in an advanced organic community, one's desires will be those which advance the true interests of the citizenry, and thus will maximize freedom.[48] By an organic community, Hegel means one in which social change comes from within and builds on what the community has already achieved, rather than such change being arbitrarily imposed, as it was in the French Revolution.[49]

Parallel to such development of society is the mind's or Spirit's increasing knowledge of itself, that is, its knowledge of the *phenomena* of its own operation. Hence the title of Hegel's masterwork, *The Phenomenology of Mind*,[50] which traces the development of this knowledge. Similar to his construction of social history, Hegel spins out a history of knowledge where the inadequacies of each stage serve as the prod to humankind to move on to a more advanced stage. Thus, to summarize briefly, Hegel passes from "sense-certainty," which lacks the ability to describe itself, to perception, which classifies knowledge according to universal symbols, but lacks the ability to make itself more coherent or predictable. He then moves on to understanding, which establishes laws, such as Newton's law of gravity, but fails to grasp these as its own mental constructs. The final stage is self-consciousness, which sees the phenomenal world as its own creation, and can understand its own operations.

For Hegel, still another path, in addition to social and intellectual history, to his understanding of the working of reason, is his analysis of logic. Logic, he finds, reveals the nature of God before the creation of the world or of individual minds.[51] The World Spirit, or God's mind, underlies the natural laws of the universe and the operations of individual minds; that is why the world is intelligible. The content of the World Spirit conceptually is the "absolute idea," which is very similar to Plato's set of interrelated ideas, or, more recently, to Alfred North Whitehead's God in his role of advancing the world toward complexity (see chapter 7). It is the basis of the forms of all specific instances in the world, from triangles to birds to poems, which are held in a unity in the divine mind. In this sense, the world, as it is for Whitehead, is the completion of God's nature, which, as mere idea, is deficiently real.

History, cognition, and logic all illustrate God's work in developing the world. This towering structure of thought proclaims permanence at virtually every level:

- We have already mentioned Hegel's endorsement of Kant's structure of permanence, which includes a permanent Reason; an invariant, logical structure of ideas; an invariant or permanent nature, and an autonomous, permanent God.
- Hegel, however, goes beyond perhaps even Kant in magnifying the nature of God so that God embraces all mind, and instigates all significant social process, thus ensuring history's outcome and its permanent worth in the achievement of freedom.
- Hegel structures an invariant rhythm of social process, the opposition of thesis and antithesis, which ends in a new stage of development. He also prescribes a parallel structure of development in human consciousness, and in logic.

Hegel's notion that human desires arise from communities; that humans achieve their full potential in an organic community in which they participate; and that the highest form of freedom is community responsibility, would be a major source for the philosophy of John Dewey, as we will see in chapter 10. The notion that human history is teleological, or purposive, and that it progresses through stages of thesis, antithesis, and synthesis, would be interpreted by Karl Marx, in its final act, as the capitalist class or bourgeoisie exploiting the proletariat, leading to the *inevitable* Communist Revolution (see chapters 11 and 12). (Ironically, the revolution would still require active revolutionaries, Lenin's Bolsheviks, to

make it happen.) While Dewey would divest himself of virtually every feature of Hegelian permanence, Marx would retain Hegel's teleological view
of history.

With Hegel, the Western world's long rumination on permanence achieved
its final major statement. Even though, in the twentieth century, as the
American philosopher Joseph Margolis has pointed out, thinkers as disparate as Karl Popper, Hilary Putnam, Jurgen Habermas, Hans-Georg
Gadamer, and W.V. Quine would all evoke notions of permanence, the concept would never again achieve the status of the total explanation of reality
it enjoyed in the history of Western thought through Hegel.[52] The world
would move on, leaving endorsement of the idea of permanence more as an
exercise in nostalgia than as a scheme which its proponents themselves
found convincing and fully adequate. These developments would take place
not only in the theory of knowledge, in the sciences, and in social thought,
but also in people's grasp of their own history and social structures.

Before we take up those changes which have brought permanence
under attack, let us summarize how notions of permanence have fit together
during this four-thousand-year history; how, in fact, Western thought and
religion have reflected what might be called a "permanence complex."

Chapter Six

The Permanence Complex

But thy eternal summer shall not fade,
Nor lose possession of that fair thou owest;
Nor shall Death brag thou wander'st in his shade,
When in eternal lines to time thou grow'st.

From Sonnet XVIII by William Shakespeare

It is time to take stock. In part I, we have traced elements of a developing story—
the history of the belief in permanence in the West. This story has unfolded
over a four-thousand-year period, from the world of ancient Sumer to the
nineteenth-century Prussian state. Its authors have included the unknown
scribes who recorded *The Epic of Gilgamesh;* the writers of the Old and
New Testaments; and philosophers as varied as Plato and Aristotle, the
French mathematician René Descartes, the English physician and political
activist John Locke, and the German metaphysicians Immanuel Kant and
George Wilhelm Friedrich Hegel.

The chief elements of belief in permanence have been notions of the
soul, of God, and of eternal ideas. A derivative notion from eternal ideas, as
we have seen, has been a split between appearance and reality. Most of our
authors have also included the concept of determinism, in the form of fixed
natural laws and guidance or inevitability in the process of human history.

Now it is time to see how all these various elements fit together; how
they form a complex of ideas. What I mean by a "complex" is any scheme
of ideas whose joining together is determined by a psychological motive. In
this case, in what I call the "permanence complex," the motive is the
human need to feel secure in a threatening world.

93

In analyzing such a complex, we can start with almost any element to construct the whole, as each element implies and reinforces the others. We can then see how the complex maintains itself as a scheme of mutual implication, and how the whole thereby gains in power. Simultaneously, as we will also see, it thereby becomes more vulnerable.

The Soul

A key element of the "permanence complex" is a belief in an entity that is our essential nature and that survives the death of the body—the soul. Descartes, for instance, as a modern man, attempted to show how perception and even thinking can be considered bodily functions. At a certain point, however, he was forced to stop, as it was necessary for him to maintain the soul's autonomy. Only if the soul is free of the body can it be saved and live eternally with God. As an anxious and devout Christian, Descartes needed to preserve this idea if the soul was to fulfill its traditional promise of permanence.

Here, it might appear that the soul owes its very existence to the idea of God. More plausibly, however, the soul can trace its origins to direct human experience rather than to theology. Let us return to the mythical Garden of Eden, or to its equivalent, the natural world. There, in what the seventeenth-century philosophers called the "state of nature," animals pursue their animal existence in real time. If they encounter some noxious substance, which they are genetically programmed to evade, they evade it. When they experience hunger and spot prey, which their elders have taught them to pursue, or which they are genetically programmed to pursue, they pursue it. The higher animals even obtain, by active memory, a sense of stable entities existing in the garden, such as trees and tigers.

But when the primordial man, Adam, can feel the contrast between his immediate reality (the tiger now), and a past reality (the tiger last week), a new element has been introduced. And when Adam is aware of his ability to see today's tiger, or even more significantly, his ability to remember or imagine a tiger that is not in front of him, he has taken an important step toward self-consciousness. The primordial state of Adam's "innocence" isn't broken by his awareness of good and evil, but rather by a far more basic awareness, his self-conscious awareness of being in the garden.[1] Adam thereby achieves an independence from the external world, and becomes an "I" in contrast to the external world, which is an "it."

94

This "I," or self, is also nurtured as we grow up and are defined by other people, or as we define ourselves. Adam and Eve may say, in the presence of their son, "Isn't Abel cute?" Abel may then say of himself, "I am more lovable than my brother, Cain."[2] This developing self-consciousness, it seems to me, is the psychological basis of what is called the soul.

From this self-consciousness, philosophy, exemplified by Plato, makes a huge leap by defining the soul as a substance requiring nothing but itself in order to exist. Since this notion has affected all subsequent Western thought, we need to look at it closely.

Platonic philosophy radically transfigured awareness of our growing psychic capacities into a self-sufficient metaphysical entity or substance. It also detached the "soul" from the body. By contrast, Aristotle, we remember, spoke of the soul as the life of the body, which dies when the body itself dies. Platonic philosophy, and later keepers of the belief in the soul, see it as separate and eternal. In doing so, they consider useless any attempt to create a somatic base for psychic activity, or see the soul ultimately as a manifestation of the body. The soul has literally been lifted out of the natural order in which it develops.

Why did this happen? One clear motive is that, by becoming a metaphysical substance, the soul achieves independence from contingencies, those events which occur immediately, such as tigers, and those which will occur in the future, such as our death and the death of those we love.

The idea of the soul can be seen operating here as a defense mechanism. In psychoanalysis, we learn that, as children, we invent defense mechanisms to adapt to disturbing family situations; we then continue to use such defenses in situations in adult life in which they are inappropriate. An abused child, for example, in periods of stress, may go numb as a way of emotionally escaping a beating. The same individual, in later life, may continue to feel numb during a period of stress, and so be unable to handle a present stressful situation constructively, even though there may be no physical threat, as there was in childhood.

In turn, a belief in the "soul" defends itself against all attacks. For example, the defense against admitting unconscious impulses to consciousness, a topic dear to Freud's heart, is not based just on their social unacceptability, such as sexual attraction to a parent, but on fear of the loss of the adequacy and autonomy of consciousness. To admit such weakness is to accept the power of contingent events over our mentality, and so admit implicitly weaknesses of the soul before other contingencies of life.

In the *Phaedo* of Plato, Simmias, one of the figures in the dialogue, makes an analogy between the soul's relation to the body, and harmony's relation to the strings of the harp. Just as harmony would be lost if the strings broke, so would the soul be vulnerable to the body's decay at death.[3] The analogy is plausible, but Socrates dismisses it out of hand. Rather, he continues to foster his view of the soul as an independent, eternal, and invulnerable substance. Here, not only is the soul resistant to contingency in life, but it endures forever after death.

In order to secure such resistance, it is necessary that the soul be entirely different from the world of process, which is subject to decay and death. Permanence has its price, however, and a very high one. Nothing we know of the physical world, or of our own bodies, is useful in any way in understanding this now metaphysically different entity called the "soul." The idea of the soul makes it virtually impossible for us to see how mentality arises from the world, and most immediately, from our bodies, and particularly from our brain. It cuts off consciousness from its source in the physical world and radically overemphasizes its independence and centrality.

The notion of the soul as a metaphysically different entity has still another drawback. How does something which is metaphysically different from the body interact with the body? This is an issue which troubled Descartes, who located the point of interaction in the unlikely pineal gland. The problem has its counterpart, which we saw in Judaism, in the difficulty that mortal human beings have in establishing any reliable interaction with a metaphysically different God.

Not surprisingly, however, the soul seems very similar to God. The soul, like God, is detached from the natural world altogether, being made of an entirely different substance; it has no definable origin, except perhaps in God Himself. Yet it is capable of intervening in events through its apparent capacity to move the material world. The soul is extended into eternity, that is, beyond physical death. Again, a similar existence is attributed to God.

God

The notion of the divine is initially plural, as it is in *The Epic of Gilgamesh*, and represents the varied forces of the world. Originally, all these forces are considered magical and powerful, and the notion of the divine is in no way separate from the causal ebb and flow of momentary experience.[4] In time, however, stable identities are formed of entities such as the sun, winds, and animals, which are then abstracted from the flow of existence and endowed with personalities and worshiped. Like the natural forces which they personify, and unlike themselves, the worshipers see the gods as all-powerful and in control of what occurs in the world. As personalities or egos, the gods not only protect them from life's contingencies, but are omniscient, omnipotent, and immortal, all the qualities which the worshipers would like for themselves. It is the gods who create the world, who order its events, and who dictate the fate of the worshipers. They, in turn, offer the gods prayer and sacrifice.

Jewish monotheism represents the parallel growth of the idea of a single God and the ego. One is never too far in front of the other; the worshipers unify the active forces of the world in one personage at the same time they create their own egos. In commenting on his biblical cycle of novels, *Joseph and His Brothers*, Thomas Mann writes:

> I dwelled on the birth of the Ego out of the mythical collective, the Abrahamatic Ego which is pretentious enough to assume that man should serve only the Highest, from which assumption the discovery of God followed. The claim of the human ego to central importance is the premise for the discovery of God...[5]

God might represent not only human pretentiousness, but also a further projection of the ego's need for permanence. God, unlike the earlier "pagan" gods, is taken out of nature and made totally free of any contingency. Like the pagan gods, however, the Hebrew God is omniscient, omnipotent, and immortal, but far greater in stature than any single god—wiser, more powerful, unifying all the elements of permanence into one entity. In Judaism, Yahweh is also the great companion, the tender parent, the beloved, providing association with the eternal and the well-being of the believers, *if* he is obeyed.

God's very strength, however, creates a problem. Not only is God metaphysically different from human beings, but God's absolute power makes him difficult to approach. Human beings may solicit but there is no way to compel God's attention, or to move him.

Christianity attempts to remedy this problem by ensuring eternal salvation through the mediation of Jesus, or Christ. It is Jesus, or Christ, who serves as a bridge between God's august power and human beings, and who ensures salvation through human faith and/or by Christ's election. Maximum assurance is provided by the concept of predestination, by which a person's soul is selected for salvation from the beginning of time, and so is not subject to any of life's contingencies, such as the need for moral conduct or conversion to faith, which might affect its eligibility.[6] It is also Christ who represents a more accessible projection than does the Jewish God of the human wish to have all the powers of a god or God.

In incorporating, particularly, Platonic ideas into its theology, Christianity further enhanced its endorsement of permanence. By moving away from the life of Jesus, portrayed in the Synoptic Gospels, we find that John and the Church fathers reconstructed Jesus as an eternal manifestation of God, rather than as a contingent, historical figure. God also ceased to be even similar to an historical personage, as He is portrayed in Hebrew Bible, but in the Trinity became a metaphysical entity, existing for all time, constantly creating the world. The Holy Ghost further emphasized permanence by making God's eternal nature immanent throughout the universe, a notion found in Greek thought, Gnosticism, and the works of Kant and Hegel.

Eternal Ideas

As we saw, ideas as motive forces probably have their origins in the specific deities of the pagan world. The deities of the sun, winds, animals, and ax, for instance, are believed to impart form to matter, to prescribe their customary actions, and, in some cases, to animate them, precisely the later role of ideas or essences in Greek thought. As the number of gods diminishes to one, God's sphere of action increases from the limited powers of, say, the moon, to the full autonomy of a single ego operating throughout the entire world. This development, as Thomas Mann suggests, parallels the development of the human ego.

Fairly early in human history, ideas become wedded to words, forming an internal language and an important basis for the formation of self-consciousness. This self-consciousness, in turn, plays a vital role in the formation of the idea of God. Ideas, like the "soul" and "God," then become abstracted from physical process.

When ideas become independent of perception, and from their origin in experience, they become independent of the real world altogether. They are then fully formed, eternal, and incorruptible, as they are for Plato, and closely associated with the soul and God, having gone through the same transformation. We may die, our real-time experiences may perish, but the major components of our mentality will endure. Here, ideas, representing the mind's functioning, have secured the same permanence as have the soul and God.

Ideas then operate *on* matter, endowing it with form and purpose. For Plato, ideas "participate" in matter, lending it forms and persuading it to excellence. They, like God and the soul, are not part of the natural world, or of the same stuff as physical existence, but exist in an eternal realm.

By God's immanence, as in the Holy Ghost, or by the participation of eternal ideas, experience is rescued from its contingency. Although experience and the world of process perish, the ideal realization of forms lives forever. This, in turn, secures the eternal existence not only of ideas and souls, but also of our acts, and of art—the "eternal lines to time" of which Shakespeare sings.

Here, again, we pay a huge price for considering ideas in this way. It becomes impossible to trace how ideas arise from physical processes; how they are enmeshed in physical fields, social reality, and history; and how they perish with physical destruction and social and historical change.[7] The notion of an independent idea exactly mirrors the notion of God and the soul, that is, the notion of a self-sufficient substance requiring nothing but itself in order to exist. It should also be pointed out that, if we cannot seek the origin of ideas and logic in our own culture, we are blocked from understanding this process in other cultures, indeed, of understanding other cultures at all.

Nor, with the Platonic view of ideas, can we believe that ideas or schemes develop as a child matures. Plato's Meno simply "remembers" the fully elaborate proof of the Pythagorean theorem. It would be well into the twentieth century before psychologists like Jean Piaget would trace the origin of most of our common conceptions of the world to a combination of genetics and childhood development guided by culture. This is a problem which vitiates many of Kant's categories, such as his uniform and preformed notions of time, space, causality, and substance.

For Plato, Kant, and Hegel, ideas, like the gods, become unified in one abstract entity. The model for such unification is mathematics, but Plato and Kant imply that such unification carries through for the entire ideational world. Mathematics, with its property of eternity or invariance, develops side by side with science, providing it ever-more intricate explanations of the physical world, or models yielding predictable or deterministic results. We then see the ephemeral physical world as having a more basic substructure with all the qualities of the ideal world—eternity, rationality, and unity.

AT WAR WITH TIME

In Plato, Kant, and Hegel, this unification of ideas exists in the nature of God, who creates the world, endowing it with forms, intelligibility, and invariant and rational laws. In the case of Hegel, God also endows history with a final end, the ideal state in which human beings, unified with God through reason, achieve self-conscious freedom resulting in moral action. Attributing the historic creation of the world to God carries the enormous liability of arguing against any theory which gives the world itself responsibility for the creation of its own forms or laws. Attributing the motive force in history to God argues against the contingency of history, or the contingent role that human beings play in making that history. Any alternative teleological theory, such as Marx's, has the same effect.[8]

The soul, God, and eternal ideas are all codependent instances of what I am calling the "permanence complex." Each borrows from the others to create seemingly independent concepts. Categories may shift, but there is always a single motive—permanence or security.

Appearance and Reality

In Western religion and thought, we can see the permanence complex in operation in still other ways, in the split between appearance and reality. Plato effects a dramatic reversal in the reality quotient of the physical world versus the world of ideas, the soul, and God. We should think that the physical world, being more tangible and immediate, would be more real than the intangible world, but Plato says no, the physical world is deficiently real. Ideas, the soul, and God form the *true* reality; our physical world is only an appearance.

It is not hard to look for Plato's motive. Separating the ideal world from the world of experience, which is subject to decay, is necessary to secure its permanence. The same motive operates in attributing a different metaphysical nature, that of true reality, to the ideal world. The permanence of Aristotelean essences have the same effect.

The suspicion of perceptual experience hangs on into modern thought. From Descartes through Hegel, philosophers have been troubled by the seeming inadequacy of perceptual experience to represent the "true" nature of things. Even Locke, echoing the Greek philosopher Democritus two thousand years earlier, believed that those elements which can be expressed mathematically, such as geometric shape, are "primary" qualities *of* the object, where "blue" or "sweet," for example, are "secondary" qualities *from* the object.

Kant espouses what seems to be the ultimate split between appearance—what he calls the *phenomenon*—and reality, the things-in-themselves—the *noumenon*. At times, for Kant, the *noumenon* is the physical world of Newton, a world of hard, lifeless bodies obeying the laws of motion and the law of universal gravitation. In this interpretation, the *phenomenon* seems like a scientist in a spaceship circulating through the *noumenal* world, speaking a different language from the beings he cannot see and conditioning all he does see with the convolutions of his mind. At other times, Kant speaks of the *noumenon* as an ideational reality, in the manner of Plato. Here Kant represents an extreme endpoint of the logic of permanence, in which permanence is a function of the invariant, divine mind. Like Plato, Kant suggests that human beings partake of this mind, and therefore can discern the world's ultimate meaning or natural structure.

For Hegel, the physical world sometimes seems to disappear altogether, and become simply phenomena or experience. True knowledge, then, becomes the mind knowing its own thinking about this phenomenal world, and thus knowing itself.

The Laws of Nature and History

Creation stories in both Sumerian religion and Judaism—indeed, throughout the ancient world, including Greece—assume the prior existence of chaotic, inert matter. It is the gods, or God, who give matter form and animate it, and set it in motion according to fixed laws.

In the *Opticks*, published in 1704, Newton wrote: "All things being considered, it seems probable to me, that God in the beginning formed matter in solid, massy, hard, impenetrable, moveable particles, of such sizes and figures, and with such other properties, and in such proportion to space, as most conduced to the end for which he formed them..."[9] But Newton's view of matter as impenetrable and passive is the result not of any investigation into its nature, but, for the most part, of a predisposition stemming from the religious and intellectual tradition to which Newton was heir. That matter might itself be capable of the spontaneous generation of order would arise in the biology and quantum field theory of the twentieth century (see chapter 8).

We can thus see the nature of the Newtonian world as a function of monotheism and of Greek thought.[10] In the seventeenth, eighteenth, and early nineteenth centuries, the laws of nature, as well as the forms which matter takes, could only be given by that agent which possesses full power and independence from the physical world, that is, God.

A high price is paid for this alliance of religion and science in the cause of permanence. If matter is brutish and passive, it is incapable of organizing itself—that is, it can have no responsibility for nature's laws or for the construction of organisms. If that is so, there is no point in inquiring how the laws or organisms originate. Laws can be "discovered," that is, we can read the mind of God, the Prime Mover, through his traces in the physical world, as we can with the origin of organisms, but there is no agency we can directly discern, that is, none residing in the world itself, except perhaps the nature of our own minds.

Moreover, the laws established by this eternal Being will themselves presumably be unchangeable, as like will create like (although we might have had an eternal Creator addicted to change, or a God, as Hegel says, who promotes the growth of freedom through history). In Aristotle, transience is relegated to a lower order of causality called accident, as opposed to the permanent order controlled by God-given essences. History, for Aristotle, can accomplish little beyond exhibiting essential forms—that "little" being variations attributed to accident. Again, there will be a bias against observing change, or understanding its origin. Instead of evolutionary change or historical process, the world will seem permanent.

Not only this: If the soul is permanent and invariant, so must be its products, including science. Kant's and Hegel's invariant reason (or Descartes' soul) fits in easily with the absolute invariance of Newtonian science, as it does with the set of ideas whose eternal relations are fixed forever. These are exemplified by a unified, eternal mathematics which unifies all physical processes.

The same problem besets human history. If the soul, God, or God's laws are eternal or invariant, so must be the substructure of history. Historical events then will be a mere gloss on history's real text, as they are ultimately for Aristotle. The only alternative, within the permanence complex, to explain real change is to see change as God's unfolding self-knowledge as manifested in history—the alternative of Hegel.

Either way, such thinking results in the idea that there is only one inner track and endpoint of history for all humankind, with one eventual set of ideal human or political institutions. In this scenario, Hegel sees one culture—the Prussian state, or northern Europe—as superior to all the rest, implying that its "burden" or "historical obligation" is to take over all the others. A similar sense of ideal absolutism affects Plato's republic, the Christian Commonwealth of the Middle Ages, and Kant's rational state. Another variant of seeing history as a manifestation of God or of some ultimately derivative teleological principle is that all human history becomes preparation for the inevitable establishment of God's Kingdom, or the full self-realization of the World Spirit, the enlightenment, or the "dictatorship of the proletariat."

So firmly entrenched is the permanence complex in Western thought that it is difficult to see it, just as the most common phenomena in physics, such as gravity, are often the last to be observed. But ideas of permanence are very much with us. Take expressions like "In God we trust," which underpins the United States' monetary system; or "One nation, under God," our political or historical course; or most recently, similar uses of religious phrases by political leaders and religious fundamentalists. Or think of how many of us really do believe in the survival of our souls after death, or in the timeless survival of good deeds or works of art.

The permanence complex has persisted so long because it meets the deepest human need, the need for security in a world in which we are vulnerable and mortal. And so we have dreamed our wishes and thought them real, and now we find them deeply embedded in the very structure of our lives.

The permanence complex, of course, ultimately looks to a static world. It says that, beneath the flux of existence, the deeper realities are eternal. Although many of us still believe in many of its key concepts, it is hard to ignore the fact that the permanence complex, as a unifying system of Western thought, no longer looks as solid as it once did. What has undermined it has been our grudging acceptance of the universe's capacity for self-generated change. This acceptance has resulted from advances in scientific and social thought, as well as movements in history and social structures, and our perceptions of them in social and political theory. Basic notions which stood our ancestors well for millennia are under sharp attack. The permanence complex, in which these notions were embedded, is coming unstuck. Its very strength, its logical interrelationship, the co-dependence of its ideas, has become its weakness.

PART
II

Convergence

INTRODUCTION

Origin of man now proved.—Metaphysic must
flourish.—He who understands baboon would
do more toward metaphysics than Locke.

From *Charles Darwin's Notebooks*[1]

In the middle of the nineteenth century, a major doctrine of change emerged:
Darwin's theory of evolution. Here was the beginning, at least, of an explanation of how species evolved. Charles Darwin, a British biologist, directly challenged some of the basic underpinnings of Western thought: the Judeo-Christian doctrine of a single, divine, creative act; Aristotle's notion of stable species; and, implicitly, the idea of a fixed natural order held by all the Western philosophers we have cited, from Plato to Hegel.

After Darwin, changes in science and thought, as well as disturbing historical events, came thick and fast. The entire structure of permanence and certainty which had been erected for four thousand years came under attack. In part II, we will look at those changes, and suggest a new way of thinking about the universe and our role in it.

The Fragmentation of Knowledge

Most educated people at the beginning of the twenty-first century consider themselves to be specialists. One person might be a biochemist, another a tax lawyer, another a computer programmer. Yet what is needed for the task of understanding our culture's evolution, and of framing a new cultural paradigm, is the generalist's capacity to look at our culture's many dimensions and to put together ideas from disparate sources.

The fragmentation of humanistic learning, which makes this task difficult, began with the compartmentalization of the medieval university into separate faculties. After the Renaissance, it was furthered by an increasing differentiation of the workforce in an industrializing economy.

Even as late as the second half of the eighteenth century, Thomas Jefferson, Benjamin Franklin, and some of their colleagues could still have reasonably claimed to have mastered the known fields of human thought. This knowledge was not just passive. Such persons could ideally hold public office; design a building; conduct a scientific experiment; read the Greek, Latin, and possibly Hebrew classics in their original languages; correspond in several modern languages with friends on the European continent; and write tracts or books for that small subset of society called "men of good taste."

By the beginning of the nineteenth century, it generally was no longer possible for university-educated people to speak for the civilization as a whole, or professionally to do more than one thing well. From Johann Wolfgang von Goethe (d. 1832) to William James (d. 1910), a few exceptional individuals struggled to unify the world in their own minds. In our time, virtually no one even tries, and the educated general public, for the most part, has given up the task.

Today, even more than the humanistic disciplines or the social sciences, the physical sciences have staked out areas restricted by credentials and increasingly recondite languages to their own professionals, completing the fragmentation of knowledge. One result has been to make it difficult for anyone to speak for the culture as a whole. University professors look now almost exclusively to their respective fields. Particularly in the United States, they have abandoned their earlier role as secular ministers and speak less and less to the general public, or even to their own colleagues.

The British physicist, statesman, and novelist C.P. Snow, in his often-quoted 1959 Rede Lecture on *The Two Cultures and the Scientific Revolution*,[2] lamented the existence of separate scientific and literary cultures, but the fragmentation of thought seems beyond repair. Even philosophy, the supposedly most general discipline, has lost contact with the educated public and has itself become a specialized science, which has, in turn, fragmented itself into separate areas. Most Americans today would be hard-pressed to name one living American philosopher.

University education, not to speak of the public schools, has failed to offer a corrective. Particularly in the last fifty years, most colleges and universities have sacrificed the notion of general education in favor of superficial area requirements, or worse, no requirements at all.[3] Compared to Europe, most American secondary schools, with the exception of a few private academies, fail to provide an adequate background of general education. The Renaissance dream of the liberal arts and sciences providing a genuine enlightenment of the mind has given way to specialization and an anxious vocationalism.

Grasping a major paradigm shift in the culture is, then, particularly difficult.[4] But difficult as the task seems to be, we cannot acquiesce in views of the world which may no longer make sense, and which represent the unchallenged legacies of earlier periods. We live in an age of extraordinary transition, a transition perhaps more important than the change in scientific thought represented by Copernicus, Galileo, and Newton. In short, we are on the edge of a new world. Why should we miss the significance of the moment in which we live, and fail to respond to it adequately? If the fragments of a new world lie all around us, waiting for us to put together a new system of meaning, we should make the attempt, and draw what implications we can to shape our own lives and create a better society for the future.

Contemporary Philosophy and the Permanence Complex

One reason for constructing a new paradigm is that philosophy since Hegel has not fully responded to the challenge. Surveying twentieth-century philosophy, the American philosopher Joseph Margolis declares that "the entire tail-end of the century is obsessed with the threatened loss of invariance."[5] He sees permanence, or invariance, still asserting itself in several key areas. The first is the philosophy of science, where Margolis finds that a number of philosophers, who are quite willing to see science as a product of history, nevertheless insist that the laws of physical nature themselves do not change. He writes:

> Increasingly, since the French Revolution, the Western world has pursued a curious line of thought. It has persuaded itself that, in human affairs, there is genuine historical novelty.... Nevertheless, this new sense of history is characteristically not permitted to challenge the prevailing assumption that, through it all, purely physical events remain subject to the invariant, exceptionless laws of nature.[6]

A second vestige of permanence can be found in the notion that human nature or reason is eternal or invariant. This is an idea closely tied into the invariance of science, and is supported by a number of recent or contemporary philosophers.[7] As we saw in chapter 5, Kant and Hegel argued that the structure of science is given by human reason, which interprets and rationalizes the physical world. For them, reason is also the language of a rational God, who created the physical world and infuses it with the rationality of his mind. As reason is invariant, so must be nature's laws. Similar dependence on permanence, Margolis notes, can be found in twentieth-century philosophers specializing in other areas, such as history and morality.[8]

Our task in part II is not to take up the complex web of philosophic thought in the last three quarters of the twentieth century; others such as Joseph Margolis and John Passmore have made this the subject of full and rewarding studies.[9] Our task is, rather, to hew to the theme of this book by attempting to put together out of a variety of sources, the basis for a new way of thinking and acting which can supplant a now-questionable belief in permanence as the dominant paradigm of Western thought.

Sources for a New Paradigm

Accordingly, in part II, we will review as succinctly and as accurately as we can developments in the last 150 years, and particularly in the last seventy-five, across major scientific disciplines, and in history and human experience, which can be seen as converging on a new way of thinking. Particularly in the physical and biological sciences, we will rely heavily on a relative handful of representative scientists who have seen, in the advances in their fields, implications for a new view of the world. In some cases their work is controversial, and its final worth not settled. Many other scientists could have been chosen. The work represented here illustrates not only the excitement of modern science but the fact that its basic findings are still in flux, and that any conclusions we reach must, accordingly, be tentative.

Wherever possible, our scientists and other thinkers speak in their own voices. Here and there, their language is somewhat technical, but I think it makes more sense to struggle with it, and gain some of its spirit, than reduce it to some least common denominator.

As in part I, the choice of sources made here is quite personal. Anyone's effort to comprehend the whole of our current situation cannot be based on encyclopedic knowledge, but must pick and choose its directional points.[10]

Our point of departure in attempting to construct a new paradigm is to review, briefly, key developments in biology, mathematics, psychology, and neurology which occurred roughly from Darwin's *Origin of Species* in 1859, to the foundation of quantum mechanics, seventy years later. We then turn to the work of Alfred North Whitehead, who framed a general philosophy in response to these new developments in science, particularly in physics. Whitehead, who had already established his reputation as a mathematician and theoretical physicist, outlines a theory of how the world advances into complexity. That theory still provides a highly useful physical model for conceiving of a world based on process rather than on permanence. Whitehead's unwillingness to fully credit his own thinking, and his resort to notions of permanence, mirror the ambiguity of much of modern philosophy.

Following the discussion of Whitehead, we will take up more recent developments in physics, cosmology, and biology; and then in neuroscience, artificial intelligence, and cognitive psychology. These developments strongly suggest a universe based on self-organization, contingency, and relationship, and demolish virtually every trace of permanence in scientific thought. This new view of the universe achieves a surprisingly adequate human or social dimension in the thinking of the social psychologist George Herbert Mead, the psychiatrist Harry Stack Sullivan, and the ego psychologist Jane Loevinger.

The philosopher John Dewey can be seen at the center of this group. His grounding of philosophy in the engaged or purposeful situation, which includes both the physical field and the social setting, is fundamental for a new epistemology. From this perspective, he reevaluates the Western tradition, and provides a general mode of thought which is not only an antidote to a sterile permanence, but also a call to an engaged activism.

We then turn to the contemporary situation, to which any new view of the world must respond. Today, not only do we lack any assurance of our physical continuity in the universe, or the surety of scientific knowledge, but the state of the twenty-first century, which includes annihilating wars, genocide, overpopulation, massive poverty, environmental pollution, and, most recently, terrorism, makes clear that humanity's position in history is contingent and precarious. No longer can we assume either the essential goodness of human beings, or a final, beneficial outcome.

While failing to respond to a number of serious world problems, such as increasing poverty in the global South and in our own country, or continuing racial and gender oppression, today's globalized economy can be seen as eroding political democracy and weakening our will to work for change. The intellectual edge for reform, once supplied in part by the academy, has been blunted by the partial withdrawal of academics from political involvement.[11] Political participation, so vital in a democracy, has receded, with the voting record of the young and the poor at the very bottom of the scale. In addition, a post–World War II cultural philosophy of deconstructionism, while attacking notions of permanence, has failed to provide an alternative basis for committed action.

With the world indeed in flux, and with traditional modes of certainty under severe attack, we find, however, that we do have a philosophic convergence of ideas which can provide us with an emotional and intellectual basis for action. Our thesis is that philosophy without activism is deficiently real. Our conclusion, accordingly, outlines an activist approach. I believe this activism offers a role for people today which is both fulfilling and life-enhancing, and also provides the basis for developing or strengthening social institutions which affirm human life without the dubious prop of permanence. If this new view lacks the kind of assurance provided by older notions, it may be the best we can devise in a universe in which total security and intellectual truthfulness are incompatible.

Chapter Seven

Alfred North Whitehead: Toward a Physical Model

*The great point to be kept in mind is that
normally an advance in science will show that
statements of various religious beliefs require
some sort of modification . . . . If the religion is a
sound expression of truth, this modification will
only exhibit more adequately the exact point
which is of importance.*

Alfred North Whitehead[1]

One of the last full attempts at a general philosophy in the West was made by the British mathematician and philosopher Alfred North Whitehead (1861–1947). The son of a vicar, Whitehead became one of the leading theoretical mathematicians of his age. In 1910, he and Bertrand Russell published *Principia Mathematica*,[2] which attempted to express all mathematics in symbolic logic. Several years later, Whitehead produced a number of works in the philosophy of science, including an alternative to Einstein's theory of relativity, and then moved into general philosophy.

These later works can be seen as a response to the first phase of a scientific revolution that began in the mid-nineteenth century, scarcely a generation after the death of Hegel, and continued unabated through the appearance of Whitehead's principal philosophic work, *Process and Reality*, in 1929.[3] In responding to the new developments in science, Whitehead made a major break with Western philosophy, although, like Virginia Woolf in literature, he considered himself in the philosophic mainstream. The model he proposed of organic process throughout the universe, while needing adjustment, would be confirmed in many ways by subsequent developments in science (see chapters 8 and 9).

In this chapter, we will first attempt to outline the new developments in science before 1929. We will then look at Whitehead's response, and his creation of a philosophic explanation of how the world generates its own order and advances toward complexity.

The Scientific Revolution

BIOLOGY

In 1859, with *On the Origin of Species*,[4] Charles Darwin politely but directly attacked the Judeo-Christian tradition which held that, at a stroke, God created all the living species which we presently find on the earth. Darwin's theory of evolution was thus also an attack on the Aristotelean notion that these species were eternal and had been present from the beginning.

Darwin's theory, as elaborated by subsequent genetic research, states that the complex, multicellular organisms present on the earth today have evolved from simple, unicellular organisms, which, in turn, had developed from far simpler proto-organic compounds over almost four billion years. The central driving mechanism of evolution, Darwinism maintains, is chance variation in genetic material, which can render the organisms more viable or reproducible in their particular environments.[5] The result of evolution is increasing complexity measurable by the proliferation of the organisms' different kinds of cells, and by the increasing elaborateness of the organisms' functions.

Such complexity is also measurable by the organisms' growing intelligence, which generally has the same effect of making them more viable. Darwinism is clear that this mental activity depends on an increasingly elaborate bodily substructure of neurons. By making mentality dependent on the physical world, and by demonstrating the continuity between man and lower organisms, *The Descent of Man*, which appeared in 1871, strongly attacked the notion of a self-sufficient and eternal soul.

In some ways, Darwin's revolution resembled the revolution initiated by Copernicus, Kepler, and Galileo. By showing that the earth no longer has a privileged position in the cosmos, these sixteenth- and seventeenth-century astronomers had put into question the unique status of human beings as the center of a metaphysical drama requiring God's special attention, including the dispatch of his son, to effect the salvation of humankind. Darwin, by showing the continuity between animals and human beings, equally puts our special status into question. Implicitly, his revolution questions the notion that human beings uniquely have souls, or that a soul can be a separate metaphysical substance, by showing that human intelligence is a continuous development from the animal world.

Darwin's theory does not dispel the notion of God as the Prime Mover, but does question God's role as the poetic creator of the contemporary world's biological forms. As evolution seems to describe an autonomous process conducted by living organisms themselves, it tends to remove biology from the kind of deterministic thinking which, in Darwin's day, still dominated physics. Despite the prominent social status of Darwin's family, he was viciously attacked, not only in scientific circles, but particularly in churches across the entire spectrum of English society. His theory of evolution is no esoteric matter, but clearly one that was perceived as vitally affecting the security of common people. The attacks would continue for another hundred and fifty years, to the present day.

Other developments in biology were to follow, with important implications for human thought. For example, Darwin assumes that changes of species will be gradual, based on incremental mutation. For the most part, he failed to deal with the multiple effects of slight alterations of genes, known as "pleiotropy." With organisms opting for unified coherence or composition, relatively minor genetic alterations prompt significant reconfigurations. An organism's phenotype, or observable characteristics, will then be substantially changed, achieving a new unified form, although the initial *gene* changes may be negligible. Observation of this phenomenon has resulted in a substantial amount of rethinking about biological change since Darwin's time, and has led to a shifting of models from the linear causality of physics to integrated mathematical-logical systems, and to models analogous to the world of art and aesthetics. (See Whitehead's discussion of this issue below, and chapter 8).

Darwin also does not deal adequately with how organisms interact with all the other species around them. What he fails to take into consideration is how a small change in one species might trigger a complex mutual adjustment in a number of codependent organisms, and so might affect their continuing viability. For example, if one species which eats another were to increase, the second species might all but disappear. If, in turn, that species lives off a third, the third species might increase, and so on. Darwin's original theory also generally fails to account for how living things influence or even basically restructure their physical environment—the sea, land, or atmosphere—by such actions as trapping energy, emitting gases, and forming rocks or soil made of organic material. Here again, biology would opt increasingly for models stressing a complex system of interrelationships, called the biosphere.

PHYSICS

The mechanics of Galileo and Newton, which formed the physical model and hence the substructure of Western thought from Descartes to Hegel, changed substantially with the development of field theory and relativity physics. The fact that physics could so fundamentally change created a revolution in expectations, suggesting that physical theory was vulnerable in a way that Newtonian mechanists, for two hundred years, had thought impossible.[6]

Newtonian physics had assumed that bodies require nothing but themselves in order to exist, and operate in a single, comprehensive containing grid of independent spatial and temporal coordinates (three for space and one for time for each point-event). In their relation to each other, material substances or objects then will follow exactly Newton's laws of motion, as well as the universal law of gravitation, which work invariantly, regardless of time or place.

As matter and energy are conserved, this means that the system, once set in motion, presumably by God as Prime Mover, will continue forever, and that every effect is predetermined. Thus, it was thought at least theoretically possible that mathematics and physics can account for every motion and combination of matter, and so the presentation of the world at any moment, past, present, or future.

As a matter of practice, however, the difficulties of calculating the interaction of even a limited number of bodies, such as the planets in the solar system—what came to be known as the "n-body problem"—became clear, as did the impossibility of knowing at some starting point the position and momentum of every body. Absolute determinism was simply impossible in practice, if not in theory—that is, the idea that for every effect there is a cause, and for that cause, a still more remote cause or set of causes, back to the beginning of the world.

As the interaction of bodies result in friction or heat, Newtonian physics interprets this as meaning that order, particularly that found in tightly packed bodies, such as complex molecules and organisms, or in astronomical systems, such as the solar system, must eventually disappear. All forms of order, it was thought, will wind down into a state of chaotic equilibrium, known as the "heat death," or "entropy," unless God occasionally intervenes to reestablish forms of order, as Newton believed he would.

As the new physics developed in opposition to Newtonian mechanics, objects were no longer considered self-sufficient substances requiring nothing but themselves in order to exist. Rather, as the Scotch physicist James Clerk Maxwell (d. 1879) proposed, they became focal regions of their electromagnetic and gravitational fields, just as, reciprocally, they generated these fields. Whitehead explains:

> The physical things which we term stars, planets, lumps of matter, molecules, electrons, protons, quanta of energy, are each to be conceived as modifications of conditions within space-time, extending throughout its whole range. There is a focal region, which in common speech is where the thing is. But its influence streams away from it with finite velocity throughout the utmost recesses of space and time ... [A]t every instantaneous point-event, within or without the focal region, the modification to be ascribed to this thing is antecedent to, or successive to, the corresponding modification introduced by that thing at another point-event. Thus if we endeavor to conceive a complete instance of the existence of the physical thing in question, we cannot confine ourselves to one part of space or to one moment of time.[7]

Time and space, which Galileo, Descartes, and Newton thought to be a single system of coordinates, had to be reconceived as properties of fields and their interrelations, and lost their independent character.

By the end of the nineteenth century, physicists had determined that the speed of light is not affected by relative motion. In 1905, Albert Einstein's special theory of relativity accounts for the constancy of the speed of light by making time and space variable. For example, the speed of light will be the same between two stationary observers, and between an observer and an approaching spaceship emitting light. In the latter case, the length of an object on the approaching spaceship, as measured by the stationary observer (that is, the observer who sees himself as stationary relative to the coordinate frame in which the spaceship is moving), will appear shorter than when the spaceship is standing still relative to the observer, or when the object is measured by an observer on the spaceship itself. Equally, a moving clock on the approaching spaceship will appear to the stationary observer to run slower.[8]

The special theory describes the relation of bodies at rest with regard to each other or in uniform motion, but gravitational fields establish different conditions. One of the predictions of Einstein's general relativity theory (1916) is that rays of light will curve in a gravitational field as seen by someone not in the field. From the point of view of general relativity theory, gravity can be seen as an effect of the curvature of space-time that is *caused* by matter. With such a distortion, a Euclidean system of space, that is, a space in which light moves in straight lines from point to point, will no longer hold. It also follows that if a body's gravitational mass becomes too great, it will be impossible for any light to escape from it; that is, it will establish a "black hole."

Relativity physics made clear that the geometry of space and time is determined by the presence of objects, and that a single "objective" view of the universe is no longer fully possible. Euclidean geometry was no longer adequate to describe physical relations, as it had been in the old physics, when space and time had formed an independent grid. The idea that objects *create* the geometry of space and time subtly began to suggest that objects create their own laws as well, as opposed to "obeying" invariant laws imposed upon them, presumably by God. Nevertheless, relativity theory did nothing by itself to attack the notion of determinism, although it greatly complicated how determinism can be mathematically expressed.

Finally, relativity physics implicitly attacked the Kantian theory of space and time. If the geometry of space and time is controlled by objects, space and time can hardly be categories or conditions of the human mind.

MATHEMATICS[9]

For well over two thousand years, mathematics occupied an unassailable place in human thought. Plato had described mathematics as the epitome of the world of ideas. In Plato's daily world of process and experience, mathematical ideas persuade matter to achieve its forms, and the regularities of its interactions. For Plato, as for Kant and Hegel, mathematics is also in the very nature of the divine mind and the human soul.

That Aristotle saw mathematics as an abstraction from nature, and its development as an activity of the essential and therefore invariant human mind, did not change this fundamental view of mathematics' perfection and invariability. Well into the eighteenth century, mathematics was deemed a perfect structure, discoverable by man, which would reveal the truths of the physical world. Here physical relationships are considered as subsets of mathematics, whether it be Greek conic sections or Newton's calculus. Mathematical theories underlay the discovery of laws in every field—astronomy, mechanics, optics, and hydrodynamics.

These laws were considered invariant, eternal, and universal. For example, Newton's mathematical expression of the law of gravitation was thought to be the true description of how all bodies interact at all times and at all places in the universe. Such laws, therefore, represent the structure of a universe for which every event is predetermined by its derivation from the eternal laws. Although mathematics eventually became influential in establishing laws in the biological and human sciences as well, these laws were generally considered more modest, that is, mere expressions of contingent phenomena or researchers' attempts at expressing regularities of behavior, rather than representing nature's absolute truths. These so-called "soft sciences" involving human beings or biological organisms usually left more room for indeterminacy or freedom, and, for that reason, were somewhat disparaged.

By the beginning of the nineteenth century, both the divine authorship of the world and absolutism in politics, thought, and science were being challenged. Even in the eighteenth century, Hume had questioned the absolutism of mathematics, as its axioms, he claimed, are derived from sensations. Kant met this challenge by saying that mathematics is not inherent in the physical world or derived from sensory experience, but directly reflects the invariant nature of the human mind, and *therefore* is still single, unified, and absolute. He also suggested that these attributes are reinforced by the participation of human reason in the divine mind.

In the following decades, with the appearance of non-Euclidian geometries, such as those of Nikolai Lobachevsky (1793–1856) and Georg Riemann (1826–66), and alternative mathematics by William R. Hamilton (1805–65), Arthur Cayley (1821–95), and others, mathematics began to lose these attributes. Why should one system be used, as opposed to another? Could any one system lay claim to absolute truth? As mathematical historian Morris Kline puts it:

> Evidently in the early 19th century no branch of mathematics was
> logically secure. The real number system, algebra, and Euclidean

and the newer non-Euclidean and projective geometries had either inadequate or no foundations at all.... One could justifiably say that nothing in mathematics had been soundly established.[10]

Nor was the applicability of mathematics automatic, as it had been in the past. Kline writes:

Thus the sad conclusion which mathematicians were obliged to draw is that there is no truth in mathematics, that is, truth in the sense of laws about the real world. The axioms of the basic structures of arithmetic and geometry are suggested by experience, and the structures as a consequence have a limited applicability. Just where they are applicable can be determined only by experience.[11]

In the early twentieth century, attempts by mathematicians to reestablish a unified foundation split mathematics into a number of hostile camps. These camps included those who thought mathematics could be derived from logic, such as Alfred North Whitehead and Bertrand Russell; the intuitionists, like Jules Henri Poincaré; a formalist school, led by David Hilbert; and a set-theoretic school, initiated by Ernst Zermelo. The fall from grace of mathematics as a "science whose conclusions are not only infallible but truths about our universe and, as some would maintain, truths in any possible universe"[12] would accelerate in the period after 1929.

PSYCHOLOGY AND NEUROLOGY[13]

Descartes, Locke, Kant, Hegel, and even Hume, had been preoccupied with autonomous and self-conscious mental functioning, which all but Hume thought to be the product of a self-sufficient, substantive soul. In the late nineteenth and early twentieth centuries, a series of advances in psychology and physiology began to open up radically different ways of interpreting mental activity.

Western thinkers, such as John Locke, had indicated that *how* thoughts produce motions in the body, or *how* the external world produces experience in us, is largely beyond understanding. By the end of the nineteenth century, scientists began to believe that eventually they could find correlations between physiological and mental states—a process which, ironically, Descartes had initiated—although they realized that this task would not be easy.

Intensive work on animals began to break down the exclusive human claim to mentality implicit in the notion of the soul, particularly the Christian notion that human beings alone are the soul's possessors, and so uniquely can be candidates for salvation. This work complemented Darwinism in attacking the exclusiveness of human mentality. Successful work on conditioned responses around 1900, for example, was conducted on both animals and human beings. This work suggested that human intention could no longer be considered the exclusive product of self-consciousness, as it was subject to the kind of physical manipulation that was effective with animals.

Debate between the first neurologists who localized functions in specific areas of the brain, and those who saw the brain operating holistically, dominated neurology in the nineteenth and early twentieth centuries. Resolution of this debate through definitive findings was hampered enormously by the lack of experimental methods and adequate equipment which could yield specific information about neural firing and synaptic communication, and thus could map which neurons or sets of neurons were involved in any given experience or action. For example, it was well into the twentieth century before equipment was sensitive enough to pick up the firing of a single neuron. As the necessary technology became available, the workings of the brain began to be subject to scientific research which treated it as just another, if more complex, biological mechanism (see chapter 9).

This research was complemented by the mainstream of psychology, which, just before the outbreak of World War I, became dominated by behaviorism, founded by John B. Watson. Behaviorism, which continued into the 1960s, rejects consideration of internal representations altogether.[14] Rather, it tends simply to measure incoming stimuli and outgoing responses or behavior, and views the brain as essentially a switching or connecting device. In so doing, it reduces the mind to a mechanism, and thus implicitly attacks the idea of the soul as a spiritual, metaphysically different entity than the body.

Holistic thinking, which was supported by early research in cognitive and particularly Gestalt psychology, attacked both the notions of sensations as a basic unit of mentality, and ideas as independent objects in the mind. Such psychologists talked instead of gestalts, schemes, and fields of mental organization. For the most part, the technology to ground this kind of research in physiology, however, did not become available until the end of World War II.

The claims for the soul as a unitary substance had always rested on the pervasiveness of human consciousness. In this respect, it is fascinating to go back to the writings of Descartes, Locke, Hume, Kant, and Hegel, as well as William James, and see how fixated they seem on consciousness. However, research and clinical experience with dreams and neurosis, initiated by Sigmund Freud (1856–1939) and others, suggested that consciousness was only a small part of mental functioning, and that a great deal of such activity occurs below the level of consciousness (see chapter 10). In addition, work by sociologists and anthropologists, such as Émile Durkheim, Franz Boas, and Bronislaw Malinowski, suggested that much of what can be called a person's worldview or implicit philosophy, is collectively and unconsciously held.[15]

Finally, work in biology would continue to show the evolution of intelligence from animal forms. Work in child development would show the development of categories of thought, and so question the idea of consciousness as an invariant substance, or Kant's view that the mind has invariant categories.

Thus, by 1929, the sciences were questioning the traditional description of mind given by religion and philosophy, and particularly the independence of conscious reason from the animal body, the physical world, and the prevailing culture. This, in turn, would change the conception of science. If reason is not fixed, but is a product of development, both biological and historical, this means that science itself, whose structure was thought to be the product of eternal and invariant reason, must now be considered to be a developmental process. Gradually, the aura of permanence and divinity which had surrounded the human mind was beginning to give way to a developmental process.

Whitehead's Response

Alfred North Whitehead made a major attempt to incorporate the new developments into his philosophy, particularly those in physics. What impresses one in Whitehead's work is his vision of an active universe structuring itself, rather than being determined. The result is a philosophy which makes a major break with four-thousand-year-old notions of permanence. Although, as we will see, the break is not clean, Whitehead nevertheless helped point philosophy in a new direction.

Whitehead creates a sense of an active universe by using organisms, rather than things, or inert matter, as his basic unit, a notion suggested both by Aristotle and Locke. Whitehead attempts to build the physical and mental worlds out of his understanding that each such element of the world experiences itself. This is as true for the simplest element, such as an electron, as for the most complex, a human being. By ascribing experience to all being, Whitehead breaks down the metaphysical wall between the physical and biological worlds.

For Whitehead, the Platonic description of experience, with its ideas like red, round, or what the philosophers call *qualia*, is inadequate because they are the conceptual form which feelings take. The description is also inadequate because it ignores the integration of the sensations or objects into larger wholes, a notion based not only on field physics but on William James' depiction of the conscious field.[16] In this mode of thinking, a threatening bear which we perceive in the woods is at the center of our conscious field which includes the bear's surroundings, particularly highlighting our routes of escape, a construction opposed to Locke's isolated objects or Hume's separate sensations.

For Whitehead, the same thinking applies to propositions. A proposition is embedded in an "environment" out of which it comes, and to which it initially relates. "All men are created equal" had an *original* environment, the experience of Thomas Jefferson in the eighteenth century, to which it initially referred, however later its reference might be extended, say, to social relations in the twentieth or twenty-first centuries.

Another reason that Whitehead considers Platonic description inadequate is that perception is not just a mental activity, but a physical one, what Whitehead calls a "prehension." For Whitehead, perception ultimately rests on our absorbing energy, for example, photons, from another source. Expressed in field theory, that source is part of our physical field. In this sense, a stone which we see or prehend is both part of our field and part of us. The percept is then not *just* a "representation" of the object, as Descartes maintained. The mind is not, for Whitehead, as it was for Descartes, a substance which requires nothing but itself in order to exist, and which can then simply entertain itself with its own Platonic ideas, such as round and red. Rather, the mind consists of its physical constituencies, including neurons, blood, and, at the physical level, its field's electromagnetic and gravitational forces, which sometimes includes the prehended stone. In this way, Whitehead attacks the discontinuity between mind and body, and between the mental and physical worlds.

But perception, for Whitehead, is not direct, as it is for Locke and Hume. We do not directly perceive ideas like round or red. Rather, the perceiver's body will transform the original energetic stimuli into the high-level perceptions, which Locke and Hume called "simple ideas." For Whitehead, such ideas are, then, abstractions and cannot adequately describe our full experience. Whitehead also asserts plainly, as did Locke, that we *feel* influence, or, technically, a vectorial, or directional, reference to an outside cause, for example, a blow on the head, which sends us reeling, or a candle flame, which burns our hand.

We should note that such direct evidence of causation contradicts Hume, and also questions Kant's need to designate causation as a category of the mind. However, Whitehead would also say that due to the complexity of the human brain, the neurons probably mimic causality, rather than directly experience it, as lower organisms may do.

Whitehead sees the same processes involved in creating purpose as in perception. He believes that what produces the body's purpose or subjective aim, to the extent it is centrally controlled, is a qualitative adjustment of the Platonic ideas of the impulses contributed by the cells, as mediated and reenacted by the nerves and the brain, and of the Platonic ideas of the impulses generated by the brain without direct relation to the rest of the body. This creation of purpose is the spontaneous result of the conjunction of these ideas. The mixture of perception and purpose, as these are centralized, is the organism's "presiding personality." This transformation of energy into mentality and purpose is the core notion in Whitehead's thought.

Whitehead holds that what distinguishes living things from the inert world, which operates according to physical laws, is this working of purpose or direction. Whitehead writes, "In the case of an animal, the mental states enter into the plan of the total organism and thus modify the plans of the successive subordinate organisms until the smallest organisms, such as electrons, are reached."[17]

An example is thirst. There is a physical feeling, and there is a conceptual form which the physical feeling takes. This form is an urge toward the future realization of a fact, the drinking of water, a change which, in this case, will stimulate the complex of cells, called the organism, to seek water, and will eventually involve the absorption of new elements into the organism's constitution.[18]

Whitehead is also concerned with how organisms respond to external stimuli with a certain originality. He explains this by saying that as the external stimuli or data come in, they are objective; when they are integrated into the organism, they are private and subjective. They can then prompt the organism to some new response. The capacity for novelty is a function of the organism's complexity.

For simple, inert matter, absorbed data are passively registered. This would be the absorption, say, of an electron into an atom. A living organism may also passively perceive data, for example, the organism's realization of a "green tree out there." Whitehead would call such a realization a "positive prehension." But negative prehensions, that is, experiences which are *instigated by* but not *realized in* the data, are ways he believes the world advances into novelty.

For Whitehead, human consciousness generally involves negative prehensions which can be translated as propositions. Consciousness always includes some realization that looks beyond the body's immediate delivery. Even a statement like "This ball is red," carries the idea that the ball might be some other color, a notion, incidentally, which Freud also advances. Other propositions, such as "This ball is not red," or "This ball might be blue," or "I'd like to be a doctor," more clearly show the relation between consciousness as mere awareness and consciousness as the vehicle of purpose, or what Whitehead calls the "subjective aim."

Whitehead's explanation of the creation of novelty applies not only to appetites, intentions, and behavior, but also to the formation and evolution of organisms. Whitehead explains that a new subjective form arises to guide the composition of the organism's felt Platonic ideas as they readjust to new inputs from the environment. Such inputs might be a high-speed particle altering a genetic molecule, or a new element in the organism's chemical environment. This would be Whitehead's explanation of how pleiotropic adjustment occurs, in which the total organism reconfigures itself in response to small genetic changes.

Today, scientists are increasingly using complex computer models to represent mental or organic processes. The models show how adjustments at the informational or symbolic level predict and direct adjustments or reconfigurations at the material or energetic level. If one substitutes the more modern idea of "information" for Whitehead's Platonic ideas, and then attempts to determine how information adjusts in the organism to organize organic processes, as in the quenching of thirst, or to configure the organism, as in pleiotropy, Whitehead's thought has a quite contemporary ring (see chapters 8 and 9).

Whitehead also suggests that the adjustments in the organism which organize organic process are essentially aesthetic. (This aesthetic valuation of symbolic adjustment is what mathematicians, he tells us, frequently refer to as "beautiful" proofs.)[19] He explains the world's advance into novel complexity as aesthetic, writing that "the teleology of the world is directed to the production of Beauty."[20] Whitehead here suggests that there is some genuine analogy between the integration of a mathematical system; the readjustment of a biochemical balance as in the quenching of thirst; the way an organism creates a new composition as a result of slight alterations of the genes (pleiotropy); and the way an artist alters an entire painting to adjust to changes of color or shape in a small section, or creates the artwork itself from paint and canvas.

Art, which is "deficiently real," projects the full realization of concrete fact in the physical world, just as a diagram or blueprint of a building anticipates its construction. Whitehead says, "It requires Art to evoke into consciousness the finite perfections which lie ready for human achievement."[21] This advances not only the organic roots of art, but also its prophetic role in the world's historic progress. Whitehead suggests that standards of beauty may not be merely cultural, but also reflect their relation to organic integration and complexity, an idea which lifts artistic standards out of total cultural relativism (see chapter 12).

Finally, Whitehead holds that organisms create not only their own internal organization and consequent forms, but also their regular modes of interaction, which are called the "natural laws." In both these ways, the world advances into novelty. That this is done spontaneously throughout the universe, what Whitehead calls the "creative advance," is his supreme insight. The origin of creativity and order is implicit in the very nature of the world. Whitehead takes this idea partly from biology and partly from his own work in physics, in which objects create their own ordered fields, which reflect their constituents' interaction. Objects thus do not follow God's laws, as Newton said they did; rather, Whitehead believes, they create them. In physics, this notion seems an enormously useful corrective to Newtonian determinism. In biology, by emphasizing the way in which an organism achieves integration in itself and with its larger environment, Whitehead points to what may be the weakness of present-day Darwinian theory (see chapter 8).[22]

When Whitehead surveys the world, he finds evidence everywhere for the creative advance, that is, the growth of complexity or "intensity of experience." This is, he believes, the world's indisputable progress as it transforms chaotic nature into all its complex forms and laws. The progress toward complexity is apparent at every level, from quantum particles, through molecular structures, to biological organisms and human beings. There is no doubt that complexity is growing on this planet, if not throughout the reaches of the universe. Four billion years ago there was no life here at all; today there are highly complex organic forms. Whitehead attempts to explain this phenomenon through a philosophy based not on permanence but on self-generated process.

However, this explanation of the creation of organic forms or systems does not suffice. Whitehead must go beyond the data and their interrelations to find an ultimate source for the world's novelty. In this "second explanation," he says that purpose, or the subjective aim, instead of emerging from an integration of feeling, guides the organism from the outset. For Whitehead, this guidance comes from the "primordial nature of God," which contains all possible combination of ideas. God's "judgment" is his supplying the emerging subjective aim which is particularly relevant to that organism.[23]

In raising this second mode of explanation, Whitehead reverts to notions of permanence which lie at the base of Western thought from Plato to Hegel, and to the religion of his youth. Whitehead, like many modern philosophers, as Joseph Margolis points out, is simply unwilling to carry through on the primary thrust of his ideas.

In many ways, Whitehead's "primordial nature of God" looks very much like Plato's God or Hegel's World Spirit. It also resembles the single, unified, and absolute mathematics which, as we have seen, began to dissolve in the nineteenth century, and which Whitehead and Bertrand Russell attempted to save through their *Principia Mathematica*. If the unification of ideas is highly questionable in mathematics, the unification of all ideas in the world is even more so. What is the relation between $2 + 2 = 4$ and Jefferson's idea that all men are created equal, although both are ideas? Coexistence or mere membership in the class of God's mind does not imply a necessary relation. Our idea of integration is based on structure and limit, precisely what seems missing here. As the notion of God expands to include any possible relation, or the inclusion of any entity, it loses any semblance to this ideal.[24]

For Whitehead, as for Kant and Hegel, God's nature forms the basis for all potentiality in the world. Whitehead asks: How can novelty enter the world if it is not already somewhere? As Whitehead seems to be denying the possibility of novelty altogether, he must find its source in the mind of God.

It is God who supplies the plan or set of eternal ideas which persuades each organism to achieve what complexity or organic beauty it is capable of, and which guides the organism toward novelty. Each result is relevant particularly to that organism and represents a particular selection from the infinite interrelation of ideas which constitutes God's nature.[25]

At first blush, this is not how evolution proceeds, at least as Darwin explains it. Rather than a purposeful operation involving the total organism, the evolution of individuals and eventually of species proceeds by random variation of genetic material, which then produces a phenotype that is supported by the environment—that is, when the organism survives and multiplies. Purposefulness seems curiously absent, and would seem closer to what Aristotle would call accident, or randomness.

But the rearrangement of the total organism following relatively minor genetic changes, or pleiotropy, suggests a drive for order which is not accidental, but which may not be inconsistent with Darwinian evolution. Equally, the organism's choice of organic development following regular mathematical forms suggests that more than accident is involved (see chapter 8).

What does not seem evident, however, is any central direction for the universe as a whole. The sheer proliferation of forms belies any such central vision. How many different tries there have been in the biological world, how many false starts; as the biologist Stephen Jay Gould points out, whole genera have perished irrevocably in the Paleozoic past.[26] Even in Whitehead's time, one could walk through a biological museum, with its glass cases of fossils and preserved species, from mollusks to mammals, and sense the energy and fecundity of the biological world, but also its seeming lack of unified direction. Is it meaningful, as Whitehead suggests, to think that this variety achieves unification in the mind of God?

By invoking God as the initiator of organic compositions, and the world's aesthetic unifier, Whitehead thereby reestablishes determinism, a problem faced by philosophers from Plato to Hegel. In Whitehead's thought, God is immanent in the world, guiding each organism. Although Whitehead says there is freedom, this mechanism for limiting it seems enormously powerful.

As God is necessarily ubiquitous, God would also be responsible for results which are clearly destructive, or Whitehead would be forced to parcel out good results to God and bad results to other agencies. The first position would sully Whitehead's notion of God; the second would make attributing results to God dependent on Whitehead's moral or aesthetic judgments.

Whitehead must here deal with the problem raised by Hume, of arguing from an imperfect creation to a perfect Creator.

How does Whitehead deal with the related problem of evil? It is not reassuring. He writes: "The revolts of destructive evil, purely self-regarding, are dismissed into their triviality of merely individual facts; and yet the good they did achieve in individual joy, in individual sorrow, in the introduction of needed contrasts, is yet saved by its relation to the completed whole."[27] If one thinks of evils such as the Holocaust, this becomes patently wishful thinking, although Whitehead is right, for example, that stealing may be satisfying for the thief, however destructive it is for the victim. Yet to say, as Whitehead seems to be doing here, that premature death, suffering, or genocide are somehow "saved" by being absorbed into God's nature, is to argue them away (see chapter 12).

Such salvation occurs, Whitehead says, because the world, as a completed fact, is God's "consequent nature," a concept close to Hegel's. In this sense, God is the entire world, which constitutes an ultimate theory of immanence. Not only is God *in* everything, but everything *is* God. In this sense, the world is a holy place. Every effort is part of a divine effort, and nothing is lost or wasted. Here the distinction between God and the world dissolves, as do Whitehead's arguments for God's separate role. It then does not matter whether one sees the world's complexity as the work of God, or of the world itself. For if the world is God, or is infused with God through and through, if it is holy and charged with divine energy, the problems for thought created by the Hebraic God who is metaphysically separate from the universe, or the distant God of Isaac Newton, do not arise.

Whitehead's ultimate argument for God's persuasive work in the world, like Plato's, is the intuition which artists know as art, and moralists know as right, and workmen know as effective, and statesmen know as just, and organisms know, or feel, as healthy. All men seek the Good, Plato tells us, and all men choose it, if they know what it is, for when they find it, it is supposedly persuasive. But not all effects in the world are benign; this persuasion does not always work. Nor, if one considers the *particular* conditioning power of one's culture or upbringing, is there any *universal* element which has such persuasive power. However, the world's general growth toward complexity, and the role of ideas and art in history and culture, would argue that a drive toward complexity is perhaps in the nature of things. Whether this drive comes from God or from the universe remains open (see chapter 12).

While denying a sectarian religious purpose, Whitehead's "second explanation" seems to be particularly concerned with reformulating the Judeo-Christian tradition in the light of the modern world so it can continue to deliver its principal object—an abiding sense of permanence. While concerned with process, Whitehead here posits an eternal, unified set of ideas; a God who unifies these ideas and guides each occasion; a God who sanctions every aesthetic and moral act in God's nature; and the permanent deposit of all effort in God as well. Plato or Hegel could hardly have asked for anything more.

Despite these problems, Whitehead, particularly in his "first explanation," provides a wealth of suggestion as to how the universe moves toward complexity and beauty, and thereby provides a physical model that looks surprisingly contemporary and useful in reconfiguring thought. While his "second explanation" reinstalls God as the final cause of the process, it is also possible to see in Whitehead's philosophy how the universe itself takes responsibility for its own advance. Whether or not the universe is holy; whether it is useful to speak of the universe as divine, or its drive toward complexity and beauty as God's, seems less important than Whitehead's overall vision in which intelligence, embedded in all beings, drives the universe forward to whatever perfections it is capable of achieving.

His awe before the universe is like Plato's or Kant's. Lucien Price recorded Whitehead saying, "Here we are with our finite being and physical senses in the presence of a universe whose possibilities are infinite, and even though we may not apprehend them, those infinite possibilities are actualities."[28]

It is this sense of wonder which filled the scientists of the twentieth century, and as permanence fell away, provided for many of them, and for those who read their work, the spiritual equivalent of an earlier religion. Elements of the Whiteheadian view of the world, whether consciously adopted or reached independently, seem to infuse the thinking of the other writers we will consider, who together offer an alternative to permanence.

Chapter Eight

The Creative Advance: The New Physics and Biology

> *We are, quite literally, in a new world, a much more*
> *peculiar place than it seemed a few centuries back,*
> *harder to make sense of, riskier to speculate about,*
> *and alive with information which is becoming more*
> *accessible and bewildering at the same time. It*
> *sometimes seems that there is not just more to be*
> *learned, there is* everything *to be learned.*

Lewis Thomas[1]

The physical model we have of the world subtly underpins our conceptions of every other aspect of life. For example, the self-sufficient souls or individuals of Descartes and Locke fitted in well with the self-sufficiency of Newtonian particles in space and time. When the physical model changed, it began to exert a subtle influence on our ideas about psychology and society. Our task in the next four chapters is to show how this realignment has occurred; for example, how psychology has reflected field theory in physics, or a sense of contingency in human history has paralleled indeterminacy in the biological and physical sciences. The result has been a concerted attack on permanence, not only in the sciences, but across the whole range of human thought.

By 1929, the notion of the self-sufficiency of objects in absolute time and space had died with Newtonian physics. In relativity physics, established by Albert Einstein in his special (1905) and general (1916) theories, scientists began to maintain that time and space are not absolute, but the functions of objects in relation. For some quantum physicists, even such qualities of particles as their charges and masses are now definable only by their interaction with each other.

Modern biology is advancing a similarly relational view of the world. Biologists now maintain that organisms can only be viewed in relation to each other and to their immediate environment, and ultimately to the entire biosphere.

Modern cosmologists take the same tack, arguing that each level of the cosmos—organism, ecosystem, earth, solar system, galaxy—is dependent on the next larger scale for both its creation and state of energetic disequilibrium, which allows it to maintain itself or to evolve. Again, interaction and interdependence are deemed essential.

This relational view of the world, which is still largely in development, is similar in many ways to that of preliterate peoples, who see themselves enmeshed in a field of relationships full of powerful forces, which lend each individual its shape, energy, and motion. If modern science has returned to this ancient view of the world, it has done so at a level of sophistication which preliterate human beings could not have even imagined.

Another major feature of the new science has been the abandonment of determinism. The absolute regularities of cause and effect, in this mode of thought, constitute the physical laws; reciprocally, each sequence of cause and effect illustrates these laws' operation. This is the world which Newton, and even Einstein, envisaged.

By contrast, modern quantum mechanics has found it simply impossible to maintain the idea of determinism, that is, of strictly identifiable effects from strictly identifiable causes. Rather, it works with what it calls "probability amplitudes," and often with information instead of physical models.

Indeterminacy has always been a factor in biology and the human sciences because of the complexity of the data. What is different in modern biology is that the twentieth century provided researchers with the tools to see indeterminacy in action at the molecular level, and to chart how, at this level, organisms put their constituents together and react to their environments. These actions, which are predictable in general, are still indeterminable in detail.

Still another feature, particularly of the new physics, has been the importance of the observer, as opposed to his or her anonymity or dismissal in classical physics. In relativity physics, the position of the observer is crucial; and in quantum physics, any explanation of the action of particles must include the act of observation. Not unexpectedly, the new physics has ended up more as a description of experimental processes, possible viewpoints, or models, than as a description of an "objective" or physical world.

Finally, a new cosmology has questioned the universe's very endurance. Once thought timeless and essentially static, the universe is now seen as an historical process, which could possibly have a beginning or an end. Some physicists also believe it is possible that this universe may not be the only one, and that other outcomes, including different laws of nature, are possible. Such theories, while still highly speculative, undermine the assurance we might have of eternal regularities in nature to which all process must conform.

The major casualty in this new view of the physical world has been permanence:

- If objects are no longer self-sufficient in time and space, and if their properties are dependent on relationship, they can no longer be considered permanent in any traditional sense.
- If the laws of nature are indeterminate, and the product of relations among the elements of the universe themselves, rather than imposed by an external God, they will lack the permanent character previously ascribed to them.
- If the act of observation and the experimental process are inextricable components of our picture of reality, still another element of indeterminacy, and hence, impermanence, has been introduced.
- If species are in evolution, and are co-dependent with each other and with their environment, they will be seen as enmeshed in time. Any feature which they demonstrate, such as intelligence or mind, will be a product of this historical process.
- Finally, if the universe itself is an historical product, it, too, may be regarded as less than eternal.

The world of Plato, Kant, and Hegel becomes, then, only a first approximation of a world which, when seen more closely, refuses to stay still. This physical model suggests a world in which we are implicated, no longer as passive worshipers, but as active observers and creators.

The New Physics: Quantum Mechanics and Cosmology

Even before Einstein's initial publications in relativity theory,[2] quantum mechanics was taking its first steps toward a more fully realized explanation of the subatomic world. That history began in 1900, when the German physicist Max Planck (1858–1947) introduced the quantum. Essentially, Planck said, the energy contained in radiation is found in discrete units, or quanta, rather than over a continuous range, as Newton had assumed.

Eventually, by 1911, the British physicist Ernest Rutherford formed an incomplete picture of an atom which corresponded to experimental observations of the discontinuous way atoms absorb or emit energy. The Danish physicist Niels Bohr then proposed that the atom is not a large mass, like a "plum pudding," as had been imagined, but rather has a small nucleus (10^{12} centimeters) surrounded by electrons in a limited set of prescribed "orbits" at different distances from the nucleus, representing different levels of energy. If the electrons change their orbits, the atoms need to absorb or emit energy in the kind of units Planck had discovered. Bohr, however, had no idea how an electron jumps from orbit to orbit, or why it doesn't radiate light when it stays in orbit, or why the electron doesn't collapse into the nucleus.

In 1926, physicists cleared up some of these difficulties by adopting a notion, developed by Louis de Broglie, a French physicist, who showed how electrons are really "standing waves," with distinct patterns and energy levels. Terms describing waves, like "wavelength" and "frequency," became commensurate with terms describing particles, such as "momentum" and "energy." But problems continued to plague the theory, as it now presented no possibility of consistent physical or visual models.

These problems were dealt with by considering the wave a statement of *probability*, that is, the probability of finding an electron at a particular point. The path of the electron could be plotted, but not its exact location at any given moment, thus allowing it to have the character of both a particle and a wave.

According to German physicist Werner Heisenberg, the electron's position was unknowable because the *way* it could be known fatally disrupted the information that was being sought. In classical physics, it had always been possible to compensate for observational methods. For example, light reflected from a falling body, which enables the observer to record its fall, does not appreciably alter the body's path. A change of temperature contributed by a thermometer to a liquid being measured can be calculated and compensated for. But quantum mechanics offered a dilemma which came to be known as the "uncertainty principle." If the experimenter uses a long wavelength photon, or "blunt instrument," to observe an electron, its low momentum or energy will not significantly disrupt the electron's momentum, but the electron's position will be less accurately known. An analogy would be to have a blindfolded person try to locate a thimble by touching it with a chair. Using a short wavelength photon, or "fine instrument," will more accurately measure the electron's position, but because of the photon's high energy, this instrument will seriously disrupt the electron's path.[3] Here the analogy might be to have the blindfolded person use a small but powerful magnet to locate the thimble, but then not know to what extent the magnet had caused the thimble to move.

Because of these difficulties, strict causality or determinism in the classical Newtonian form was no longer achievable, although in principle one could measure the particles' probable distribution in the future. The cause of the problem posed by Heisenberg's uncertainty principle, which still has not been solved, is the interference of human beings in the phenomena being studied. This occurs not in the way suggested by Kant, with forms of understanding such as time, space, and causality being properties of the human mind, but by humans imposing the direct physical relationship of measurement.

While most of the scientific community accepted this uncertainty, and the abandonment of classical causality, Einstein pointedly did not, and strove throughout the rest of his life to find some way around the problem.[4] Most of the next generation of physicists embraced probabilities without guilt, rather than insisting on exactly observable relations between causes and effects. For example, Richard P. Feynman, a Nobel Prize–winning contributor to quantum mechanics, describes physical calculations entirely in terms of probabilities, without indicating the slightest need to present a physical model or to allude to certainties of cause and effect underneath them. Almost gleefully, he declares that "the way we have to describe nature is generally incomprehensible to us." Quantum electrodynamics (QED), the study of light and matter, he claims, is based entirely on calculating probabilities.

> So this framework of amplitudes has *no experimental doubt* about it: you can have all the philosophical worries you want as to what the amplitudes mean (if, indeed, they mean anything at all), but because physics is an experimental science and the framework agrees with experiment, it's good enough for us so far.[5]

The new physics reached its triumph in the 1970s in constructing what has come to be known as "the standard model." But this model, despite its explanatory power, has continued to pose serious problems. The four identified physical forces—strong molecular forces, electromagnetism, weak forces, and gravity—have not been integrated into one system which explains physical phenomena. The model includes more than sixty kinds of interacting elementary particles which it generally does not explain, and more than a dozen arbitrary constants describing their interactions. Attempts to incorporate gravitation into its explanations have thus far led to meaningless calculations, and have been abandoned.[6]

A unified theory is the great prize, but, as the American physicist Robert K. Adair points out, the necessary measurements will need to be made at very small distances and will involve very high energies, and are thus beyond present technical capacity. If physical models need to be experimentally verified, as in the past, Adair questions whether more progress can presently be made.[7]

In the 1980s, attempts to construct a single, unified scheme, in which the properties of particles are a result of their interactions, failed. Some of these difficulties were alleviated by the "superstring theory," which allows particles to be conceived as small multi-dimensional strings or lines, rather than as points. However, according to Adair, superstring theory, for all its promise of a unified theory, still poses the kind of arbitrariness which has plagued physics for decades. A unified theory, or theory of everything (TOE), still has not been found.[8] Again, the kind of certainty which Newtonian physics promised has now proven illusive or unobtainable.

When we turn to cosmology, the same kind of uncertainty seems to prevail. The writing of modern cosmological history began in 1929, when the American astronomer Edwin Hubble observed that galaxies (now thought to number a humbling 100 billion) were all moving away from each other. Hubble set himself the imposing task of explaining the birth of all physical matter, space, and time—the universe. Hubble posited that the universe began 10 or 20 billion years ago, when everything was condensed to an infinitely small space and an infinitely dense mass, which then exploded—the "big bang."

This explanation, however, leaves the future existence of the universe uncertain.[9] In current parlance, the decision rests with the "omega factor," the ratio of the density of matter in the universe to the theoretical "critical density" of matter sufficient to generate enough gravitational force to counteract the expansion. If the omega factor is less than one, the universe expands forever. If it is one, the universe expands at an ever slower rate to the limit of stasis; if it is larger than one, the universe eventually contracts toward the "big crunch."[10]

In 1970, British physicists Roger Penrose and Stephen Hawking attempted to create a theoretical structure for Hubble's history. Essentially, they sought to demonstrate theoretically that massive collapsing stars might achieve the "singularity" of the infinitely small space and infinitely dense mass that Hubble had suggested as the conditions at the beginning of the universe.[11] Such singularities are associated with the mathematical solutions for black holes, thought to be prevalent throughout the universe, from which light cannot escape because of the gravitational pull of their masses.[12]

Lee Smolin, an American gravitational physicist, proposes a different, highly speculative, and currently untestable thesis for the history of the cosmos. Smolin maintains that, even if a unified theory in physics explaining all particle interactions were successful, it still would not answer the question of how the parameters for these interactions were chosen. These are the sizes, the masses, and charges of the particles, and the strength of the four main forces. Smolin finds it highly improbable that the universe should demonstrate this particular set of numbers; he estimates the chances of this happening as one in 10^{229}. The only way such improbability can be explained, according to Smolin, is by the universe's history.[13]

To give a homey illustration, if I observe a crowd in a street at a certain moment, I will find the probability of this particular crowd appearing at that moment as almost infinitely remote if I multiply the probabilities of its various elements, for example, the distribution of people, their height, weight, dress, physiognomy, and movement. To explain such a phenomenon, we automatically resort to history by, say, citing the publication of the latest election news, which might have brought the crowd into the street; by the social history of the country; and minutely, by the personal biographies and physical histories of each member of the crowd, and their evolutionary history as organisms.

The answer, then, must lie, Smolin believes, not in particle physics but in the history of the cosmos.[14] Smolin hypothesizes that our universe is just one of a huge number of universes which have appeared or will appear in the future. The uniformity we observe in the laws of nature in our universe, and the highly unlikely occurrence of the particular set of the parameters of its basic particles and forces undergirding those laws, need not rest just in the nature of things, he believes, but also in the historical circumstances of our particular universe's birth.

As opposed to Roger Penrose and Stephen Hawking, Smolin hypothesizes that "singularities," with the infinite numbers describing their contraction or density, don't occur. Rather, new universes result from black holes contracting to an extreme, but not infinite, density (that is, 10^{79}, the density of an atomic nucleus), and then exploding, in the way we see our universe exploding in the "big bang." There is thus a condensation and a "bounce"—not, strictly speaking, a total end or beginning. Smolin writes:

> This expanding region may then develop much like our own universe. It may first of all go through a period of inflation and become very big. If conditions develop suitably, galaxies and stars may form, so that in time this new "universe" may become a copy of our world. Long after this, intelligent beings may evolve who, looking back, might be tempted to believe that they lived in a universe that was born in an infinitely dense singularity, before which there was no time. But in reality they would be living in a new region of space and time created by an explosion following the collapse of a star to a black hole in our part of the universe.[15]

Such speculations on the origin of the cosmos illustrate a science still very much in flux, a radically different state than the Newtonian certainties of an earlier period.[16] While anything like consensus about the origin and future of our universe has not been reached,[17] modern cosmologists have been more in agreement about the relational character of cosmology *within* the galaxies of our universe. The conventional wisdom is that, far from being mere collections of matter, galaxies are self-regulating systems which produce stars of various sizes, including the more massive ones, which may become black holes. A feedback system delicately regulates the rate of star formation produced from molecular clouds in the interstellar medium. When the clouds are cool, they condense through gravity to produce the stars, but then heat up with energy from the stars' nuclear reactions and explosions which prevent further condensation of the clouds, and the consequent production of more stars. Finally, pressure waves created by supernova explosions of massive stars may well initiate the process of star formation in nearby molecular clouds.

According to Smolin, one cannot talk about any part of this system in isolation; rather, it is an integrated ecosystem. This is a radically different view of the universe than our previous images of an inert, inactive, random spattering of eternal, solitary stars; or of a Newtonian clock created and set in motion by God, presumably hovering outside his creation; or, more recently, a homogenous volume of maximally entropic, or chaotic, gas.

In the nineteenth century, scientists concluded that all organized forms of matter would inevitably break down into what they called the "heat death," that is, the random, disorganized motion of their parts. Smolin and most physicists today believe, however, that this is true only for isolated systems. By contrast, they see the universe as a non-equilibrium system sustaining each subsidiary system, that is, the galactic cluster sustaining the galaxy, the galaxy sustaining the solar system, the solar system sustaining the earth, and so on.

Without such support, each subsidiary system in the universe would indeed inevitably achieve equilibrium. For the earth, for example, this would represent the end of its capacity to sustain life.[18] As a highly organized system, life would quickly disintegrate into entropic disorganization, but for the fact that the earth is part of a larger system which supplies it with a steady flow of energy and a ready means of returning energy into space.

As we saw in part I, the models of the universe from Sumer through Newton envisaged a primal state of chaos ordered by the gods or God. Smolin describes a highly different model:

> [T]he possibility of conceiving the universe, as a whole, as a self-organized system, in which a variety of improbable structures—and indeed life itself—exist permanently, without need of pilot or other external agent, offers us the possibility of constructing a scientific cosmology that is finally liberated from the crippling duality that lies behind Plato's myth. It is clear that if the natural state of matter is chaos, an external intelligence is needed to explain the order and beauty of the world. But if life, order, and structure are the natural state of the cosmos itself, then our existence, indeed our spirit, might finally be comprehended as created naturally, by the world, rather than unnaturally and in opposition to it.[19]

The major elements of the new physics—the breakdown of classical causality, the reliance on information and alternative mathematical models, the involvement of the observer in the observed, the relational codependence of phenomena as opposed to their self-sufficiency, the emphasis on self-generated rather than imposed order, and on historical development rather than a single, instantaneous creation—would find their counterparts in biology as well.

The New Biology

Rather than biology being considered a separate and specious field, as it was by physicists in the nineteenth century, it has now become part of an integrated system of thought which includes relativity and quantum physics and cosmology. Similar to these fields, the explanations of the new biology are relational and non-deterministic, its subjects self-organizing, and the field increasingly reliant on the informational sciences and computers. Examples of this work are provided here principally by biologists Lynn Margulis and Dorian Sagan, microbiologist Stuart A. Kauffman, and environmentalist James Lovelock.[20]

In *Microcosmos*, Margulis and Sagan write out a history of life on this planet. Their choice in writing a history, rather than an ahistorical textbook, carries the message that the explanation of the origins of biological forms can be found in historical processes. Margulis and Sagan begin by showing, in a mode similar to Smolin's, how the chemical compounds of the earth's atmosphere and surface resulted from their celestial birth, and by their interaction with a higher sustaining structure, the sun and star system.[21]

This was an occasion of what Margulis and Sagan, and Kauffman, call a state of "disequilibrium." Just as Smolin speaks of the need for disequilibrium for the creation of stars, Margulis and Sagan, and Kauffman, see disequilibrium necessary for the creation, maintenance, and evolution of living things. This state has maximum potential, as it hovers between normative or repetitive order and chaos. From the point of view of information theory, such a state requires the maximal amount of information to describe it. Both extreme order and chaos require less information. For example, a highly structured crystal requires as little information to describe as does the chaotic or random motion of gas molecules.

Disequilibrium is being studied by a number of researchers, such as Nobel Prize–winning chemist Ilya Prigogine and Per Bak, a colleague of Kauffman at the Santa Fe Institute. The subjects of these studies range from oscillations, resonance, and turbulence effects, to biochemical reactions. Prigogine calls this "physics of nonequilibrium processes" a new science, which defines how matter under various conditions of disequilibrium or-ganizes itself into definable forms.[22] The particularities of these forms—for example, the placement or momentum of individual molecules—and even the timing of these forms' histories, are not predictable, but their ultimate general characteristics are. Sometimes popularly called "chaos theory," the new science is applicable to a wide range of phenomena, including the kinds of cosmological effects described by Hawking and Smolin, the chem-ical and biological phenomena discussed by Margulis and Sagan, and Kauffman, and the ecological effects depicted by Lovelock.[23]

A maximally complex state of disequilibrium, such as is studied by chaos theory, was present at the earth's beginning, and, according to Mar-gulis and Sagan, made the origin of life entirely plausible. The most com-mon amino acids of present-day organisms, they point out, can be produced in the laboratory by bombarding replications of earth's early at-mosphere with various energy sources. Certain groups of molecules "self-catalyze a series of surprisingly intricate and orderly or cyclical reactions," which mimic those of living cells.[24]

Similar assumptions about the plausibility of life's generation are held by Kauffman, who disputes the idea that the spontaneous generation of life is a highly improbable event. Rather, he says, the creation of "a self-reproducing system of complex organic molecules, capable of a metabo-lism coordinating the flow of small molecules and energy needed for reproduction and capable of further evolution" is easy to imagine. The ori-gin of life, he believes, was "law-like and governed by new principles of self-organization in complex webs of catalysts."[25] In such a self-sustaining system, which Kauffman has been able to model on computers, he sees the origin of life.[26]

Kauffman's position is thus not to look for the origins of life in some improbable "frozen accident" which gave us the genetic code and the structure of organic metabolism, much less the action of a supreme deity, but in the predictable behavior of readily available chemical compounds. His position is that spontaneous order is a ready option throughout the world.[27] Not only does he demonstrate that such order is replicable in mathematical and computerized modeling, but also, negatively, that if such spontaneous self-organization was not an option, the statistical possibility of life originating by chance would be too improbable.[28]

Darwinism destroyed the naïve Platonic notion of the creation of fully formed species from the mind of God. But *Platonism* is not so easy to dispose of. Kauffman's task is to show how the forms of organization achieved by organisms lie within the contingent, historical provenance of the self-organizing materials, rather than being preestablished Platonic forms waiting for realization. He must show why organisms opt for certain forms, and how these forms result from an organism's relations to its environment and from the interaction of its own molecular constituents. In attempting to show the origin of the physical world from quantum mechanical particles, modern cosmologists are undertaking a similar task. Kauffman generally attempts such explanations, while sometimes seeming to slide into Platonism. In doing so, he provides an exciting microbiological base for thinking about the origin of life, its organization of processes and forms, and its evolution.[29]

Just as Smolin describes the self-organization of galaxies, Kauffman describes the self-organization of proto-living processes in what he calls "random-grammar models":

> The catalytic and other chemical rules governing the ways enzymes catalyze ligation and cleavage among proteins can be thought of as a kind of *grammar*. In this grammar, strings of symbols act on strings of symbols to yield strings of symbols.... Given this basic idea, we may generalize to *random grammars*. Each such grammar is a kind of hypothetical set of chemical laws. Each will yield a world of symbol strings and their joint transformations.... [T]he kinds of compositional sets of symbol strings that emerge in systems in which strings act on strings to produce strings become models of functional integration, transformation, and coevolution.[30]

Kauffman's use of "grammars" raises the possible notion that the grammars are indeed predetermined or eternal Platonic forms, that they exist in some timeless realm. But, first of all, their efficacy rests on the particular, historically achieved parameters of this universe, and the corresponding way its elements necessarily relate to each other. The grammars also are achieved in time, through organic processes.

Whitehead would say their Platonic forms would be "deficiently real" until those processes have occurred. But here, as in quantum physics, cosmology, and chaos theory, physical facts are being considered as information. One way to avoid Platonism is to say that researchers deal with physical facts *as* information, rather than that physical facts *are* information. By this distinction, I mean the difference between a self-sufficient, ideal composition and the focus of a real, that is, physical prehensive field. The question then becomes, what is the appropriate informational model?

In microbiology, for example, an analogy is usually made between a computer program and a system of genes. In this sense, the gene system is a program which guides the organism's development.[31] Here, both Kauffman and the more orthodox Darwinist John Tyler Bonner raise the problem that the genetic code does not have adequate information to directly control all the many steps necessary to produce the final product, the phenotype.[32]

Kauffman speculates on how Platonism and historicism can coexist, or, in other words, how the history of organisms functions so that the organisms are not mere shadows of Platonic forms. "Biology," he writes, "is a deeply historical science which may yet be the locus of law. An old debate wonders what it might be, in a historical science, to exhibit laws. Grammar models promise answers for such issues.... This may be just the conceptual scheme we need: a locus of law, accident, design, selection, ever unfolding and transforming in novel functionally integrated forms."[33]

Kauffman asks, is there a family of natural forms, and what is its relation to natural selection? For example, like Margulis and Sagan, he sees spherical cell membranes as examples of spontaneous order, and sees that "many aspects of organismic form must reflect the natural properties of the building blocks from which organisms construct themselves."[34]

This line of thinking produces exciting results. Physicist Donald E. Ingber has researched the design of organic structures. Here he finds mathematically describable structures, which distribute and balance mechanical stresses—what Ingber calls "tensegrity." He writes:

> That nature applies common assembly rules is implied by the recurrence—at scales from the molecular to the macroscopic—of certain patterns, such as spirals, pentagons and triangulated forms. These patterns appear in structures ranging from highly regular crystals to relatively irregular proteins and in organisms as diverse as viruses, plankton and humans. After all, both organic and inorganic matter are made of the same building blocks: atoms of carbon, hydrogen, oxygen, nitrogen and phosphorous. The only difference is how the atoms are arranged in three-dimensional space.

This phenomenon, in which components join together to form larger, stable structures having new properties that could not have been predicted from the characteristics of their individual parts, is known as self-assembly.[35]

Like the other scientists we have discussed, Ingber sees the same principles possibly operating at every scale in the universe: the atomic nucleus, molecules, sub-cellular structures, and unicellular and multicellular organisms, as well as the solar system and galaxies. The work of Kauffman and Ingber suggests that showing how self-generation and informational forms or laws can work together, in relation to natural selection, is the major task for biology in the twenty-first century.[36]

Another important aspect of modern biology is its intense concern with the interrelationship of organisms. Margulis and Sagan, and Kauffman, maintain that individual organisms cannot be seen as self-sufficient units, the way Plato or Descartes conceived of the individual soul or Newton conceived of the individual object in space and time. Margulis and Sagan point out that "the view of evolution as chronic bloody competition among individuals and species, a popular distortion of Darwin's notion of 'survival of the fittest,' dissolves before a new view of continual cooperation, strong interaction, and mutual dependence among life forms."[37]

For example, Margulis and Sagan show how, in the first two billion years of life, the non-nucleated bacteria which inhabited the earth shared their genetic material by passing it off and taking it in from other organisms in the environment. This new genetic material enabled these bacteria to perform functions which their own DNA did not permit and to pass on these new functions to further generations.[38] According to these authors, organisms like ours only trade genetic material through sexual reproduction with our own species which creates the new generation—our children—but that such trading does not genetically affect *us*. They point out with some whimsy that these *limits* of human sexuality are compensated for, to some extent, by the ability of humans, and other complex organisms, to share information and ideas.

Margulis and Sagan also tell us that, in addition to sharing genetic material, early microorganisms combined symbiotically. For example, human cell mitochondria, which are vital to our use of oxygen, were originally independent organisms which combined and lived with early microorganisms. The nuclei of our cells are the result of mergers with bacteria, as are the chloroplasts in plants, which make edible food from water and sunlight. There is also accumulating evidence of the early ancestry of the rods and cones in our eyes, and of our brain neurons from early ciliated spirochetes. If spirochetes are truly the ancestors of our brain cells and neurons, Margulis and Sagan speculate, then our concepts and thought processes are based on chemical and physical abilities latent in bacteria.[39]

If this is so, the structure of thought becomes at least partially historical, embedded in the developmental history of life on this planet, to which we are recent heirs—although, as Kauffman would maintain, still with ahistorical features. This is a radical departure from the universality of Reason posited by philosophers from Plato to Hegel.

In 1956, one of the principal architects of artificial intelligence, John von Neumann, observed that logic and mathematics, which are built on organic capacity, owe their features to the history of organisms. He argued that if languages around the world take various forms, if they are historical facts and not logical necessities, it is only reasonable to assume the same for mathematics and logic. These, according to von Neumann, may well be *secondary* languages, "built on the primary language truly used by the central nervous system."[40]

The models presented by Margulis and Sagan, and by Kauffman, demolish the notion that ideas and the world, or minds and bodies, can be metaphysically separated in the way portrayed in Judeo-Christianity, classical philosophy, or the modern thought of Descartes and Kant. Von Neumann posits that even mathematics, the supreme example of Platonic idealism, is embedded in organisms and is a product of their history, rather than, as Plato would say, independent and eternal. Mentality, the biologists tell us, is a function of the body and has a four-billion-year history. In this scenario, intelligence is wrapped into the history of the organism, and into its complex adjustments to its environment. What elements of Platonic structure still endure in the forms of an historically conditioned intelligence remain to be determined.

Margulis and Sagan sum up:

Like cities, individual organisms are not Platonic forms with definite borders. They are cumulative beings with self-sufficient subsections and amorphous tendencies. And just as they are composites of species, they are also the working parts of larger superorganisms, the largest of which is the planetary patina. An organelle inside an amoeba within the intestinal tract of a mammal in the forest on this planet lives in a world within many worlds. Each provides its own frame of reference and its own reality.[41]

Shaping the Environment

The pioneering work of James Lovelock adds an environmental perspective to this view of biology, which carries an impetus for action. His Gaia hypothesis, named after the Greek goddess of the earth, represents still another qualification to Darwinist theory. Where Darwin had taken the earth's material environment as a given, Lovelock proposes that the "origin of species" is dependent on the evolution of a supporting *material* environment, which living things have played and continue to play a major role in shaping. Lovelock writes:

> Now we are at the limits of Darwin's vision. We begin to see that organisms do not just adapt to a world certified by geologists in the building on the other side of the campus. We no longer see the word *adapt* as a passive verb but one that is active also. Organisms can, and nearly always do, change their environment as well as adapt to it.[42]

Lovelock shows how living things, through their four-billion-year history, have regulated such factors as the temperature, oxidation, and acidity levels in the earth's atmosphere, oceans, and crust, making these states comfortable for evolving life forms. As species have evolved, so have their ecosystems, each tuned finely to the other.

Lovelock's work parallels Margulis and Sagan's as he relates the history of the earth as an evolving ecosystem. Here again is a full-scale attack on the notion of an isolated individual or species and on invariant laws disengaged from history, which seems fully commensurate with developments in physics and cosmology. By emphasizing how living things have shaped their past environments, these scientists call for a responsible role for human beings, presently the dominant species, in influencing our environment.

As life has evolved toward complexity, it has presented the possibility of greater control over all aspects of life, including the environment, our genetic system, and projections of our own intelligence, as represented by computers. If in some respects, we sum up the physical world in our being, as philosophers as early as Aristotle said we do, we also now hold its future evolution, at least on earth, in our hands.

An Evolutionary Epistemology

In our discussion of Whitehead, we saw that the relations of organisms to their environment, and the interrelation of their own constituents, which prompt not only the creation of mental phenomena, such as perception and intention, but also evolution, might be conceived as the processing or configuring of information. In quantum mechanics, informational models essentially have become what scientists deal with. A similar development seems indicated in microbiology, as we have seen in the work of Stuart A. Kauffman. (We will turn to information theory in chapter 9.)

Such considerations have given rise to the development of an evolutionary theory of knowledge and mind in the writings of contemporary American philosophers J.T. Fraser and Alexander J. Argyros.[43] They start with the idea of a universe evolving in time and increasing in complexity, as do the scientists we have reviewed. While higher forms of order are "nested" in lower forms of order, Fraser and Argyros maintain, they are not reducible to lower forms. For example, while biological organisms obey the laws of both quantum mechanics and chemistry, they also add forms of order of their own, such as cell formation or the means to react to stimuli, operations which are found in neither quantum mechanics nor chemistry. Equally, human beings obey the laws of organisms, but add distinctly human forms of order based on their more complex neurological organization and culture. Human beings develop languages, libraries, and computers. Fraser and Argyros rank all entities in an evolutionary hierarchy according to the kinds of progressively more complex messages or information they can register, process, manipulate, and transmit.

Because Fraser and Argyros believe we are, simultaneously, quantum mechanical entities, chemical entities, organisms, and human beings, we process information or perceive in all the ways our simpler constituents do. For example, like a rock, we fall in response to gravity, because both we and rocks know or, in Argyros' special use of the term, "represent," our environment in this mode of information processing.[44] Argyros points out, "A poem does not exist for a raccoon, except as a series of auditory or visual stimuli that are not perceived as poetry but as environmental noise."[45] The raccoon cannot hear the poem, schematize its meaning, or talk about it.

The way in which an organism handles information determines the kind of world it inhabits. Consider the notion of time. Lower biological organisms have a present but no past or future experience, because of the way they process information. Higher biological organisms, with an orienting self, experience an increasing spread of past, present, and future. Through history, telescopes, and computers, human beings have expanded our sense of time and space, and thus have extended our world.

The processing of information at the quantum mechanical, chemical, and lower organic levels in the brain challenges the exclusive focus on consciousness in Western thought from Plato to William James, and opens up the notion of the unconscious in a way which radically exceeds that of Freud (see chapter 10). A key question is the extent to which such knowledge is available to our conscious mind. Fraser and Argyros suggest that it is available "intuitively." We certainly "know" that we are gravitational objects at some level which does not include self-conscious knowledge of Newton's universal law. We can also react to stimuli in ways which more closely resemble the responses of animals than human beings—say, when we jump at a loud shout, rather than reacting to its linguistic content.[46] Fraser also suggests that stages of mental maturation, as charted by Jean Piaget,[47] recapitulate earlier phases of evolution.[48] Finally, Fraser and Argyros maintain that in our *conscious experience*, although we do not perceive in the ways of quantum mechanical particles or chemicals, we can reconstruct these modes of perception or information processing through scientific methodology.

Seeing information handling as the substructure of evolution has other uses as well. Here we can translate Whitehead's somewhat vague "intensity of experience," which he held up as the standard for evolutionary progress, into complexity of information processing.[49] The notion also makes more credible Whitehead's idea of aligning beauty with the complexity of organic development, as it makes beauty a successful way of organizing information. In this sense, holding a number of disparate elements in balance is the aesthetic analogue of holding a number of disparate elements in the environment for processing.

Complexity, which is the basis of beauty, is, then, not an entirely culturally relative factor, although the complex artistic object must also be seen in relation to its cultural environment. In this sense, Argyros maintains that he and Fraser offer a concrete rebuttal to cultural relativism and to the anti-foundationalism of current deconstructionist theory.[50]

With this evolutionary epistemology, Argyros sees cultural evolution as an extension of the universe's evolution. While Fraser considers culture as the last stage of information processing, and treats culture somewhat like an organism, Argyros believes—rightly, I think—that, because a culture itself does not experience something, it is best evaluated by its effects on individuals. By expanding the basis of individual identity through socialization, and by expanding the individual's information base and the sophistication of information processing, culture creates a continuously expanding world for individual experience.[51]

In sum, the position of Fraser and Argyros reinforces major points made by Whitehead and by theorists of the new physics and biology:

- We can define evolution as advancing complexity created by interrelationship and self-organization.
- Complexity can be measured by an increasing capacity to integrate and respond to higher orders of information.
- Higher orders of capacity subsume lower orders.
- Beauty is an analogue of complexity, and may have an evolutionary role in fostering it.
- Advancing complexity provides some independent or nonrelative basis for judging progress in evolution, history, and aesthetics.

This developing position is also reflected in those sciences directly concerned with mind to which we will next turn, that is, neurophysiology, artificial intelligence, and cognition.

Chapter Nine

The Mind in Nature

CLOWN:. . . *But tell me true, are you not mad indeed?*
Or do you but counterfeit?
MALVOLIO: *Believe me, I am not; I tell thee true.*
CLOWN: *Nay, I'll ne'er believe a madman till I see*
his brains.

From Shakespeare's *Twelfth Night*, Act IV, Scene 2

In the last two chapters, we have seen how modern physics has attacked the notion of a self-sufficient particle with predetermined characteristics, and the notion of the natural world as the product of a single, historical act. We have also seen how modern biology has questioned the notion of self-sufficient species, in favor of species existing in intimate codependence with other species and the physical environment. In this chapter, we will examine how the mind is embedded in nature, and how intelligence is expressible as information. As we will see, no longer can we think of our minds or souls as metaphysically different from the natural world, but as perhaps its supreme product.

In analyzing the neural system, the French neurophysiologist Jean-Pierre Changeux, and the American neurophysiologist and Nobel laureate Gerald M. Edelman, use the same kind of analysis we saw with physics and cosmology. In the world of neurophysiology, as in physics and biology, these scientists find that organisms create their own complexity and laws, in codependence with their environment. The mind becomes the result of a traceable scientific process. This analysis invokes none of the major tenets of permanence: a single, divinely produced event creating the world out of chaos; a set of disembodied Platonic ideas participating in matter and deciding its forms and relations; an eternal, immaterial, individual soul; or the invariant, imposed laws of nature or history, determining process.

After reviewing the work of Changeux and Edelman, we will turn to the closely allied and supportive fields of artificial intelligence and cognition. Today, researchers are continuing the work of connecting mind and body begun but dropped by René Descartes, as they are no longer inhibited by the need to uphold his concept of the self-sufficient soul. Rather, provided with an immensely useful tool for modeling, the computer, they are, bit by bit, recreating the mind as an informational system, and with even the possibility of a different physical base than the brain. Far from being the static, permanent structure which thinkers from Plato through Kant and, to some extent, even Hegel, believed it was, we now can see reason or intelligence, embodied in computers, as evolving at a rate orders of magnitude faster than in the biological world.

Neurophysiology: The Relation of Mind and Body

For thousands of years, human beings have speculated about the relation between the mind and brain.[1] In the nineteenth century, this speculation began to be replaced by hard research, including gross anatomical charting of the brain, microscopic observation of neural tissue, and the recording of how surgery and trauma to specific areas of the brain affect perception and behavior.

However, prior to the twentieth century, hard evidence relating neural activity and behavior was virtually nonexistent. The firings of even the largest, individual animal neurons could not be adequately recorded with microelectrodes until the late 1920s, when it became possible to distinguish their sounds from the noise in the amplifier. Only fairly gross cellular features could be seen with a light microscope until the 1950s, when the electron microscope arrived, radically enhancing magnification. Visualizing energy expenditure in the brain, used in identifying areas involved in particular neural processes, required the development of positron-emission tomography, or PET scanning, which only became available in the late 1970s. Equally, or perhaps more, important, neurology had to await the full development of microbiology after World War II, as well as computer modeling and cybernetics, a science analyzing control and communication systems in organisms and machines.[2]

Finally, modern neurophysiology had to move away decisively from the *reflex arc explanation*, which said that every response is triggered by a specific stimulus operating through a single pathway in the brain. This was the neural counterpart of behavioristic psychology which, from its founding in 1913 until the 1960s, as we saw in chapter 7, had treated the brain as a telephone exchange connecting inputs with behavior, but otherwise a black box with no discernible functions. With the demise of behavioristic psychology, neurophysiology could undertake in earnest to understand how neurons are associated in the brain, and how they cooperatively interact with one another to provide motor responses, perception, thought, memory, and intention.

The result has been an extraordinary burst of research which has had major implications for contemporary philosophic notions of human mentality. Many philosophers have yet to address these implications, much less the even more radical implications posed by artificial intelligence.

A more forthcoming attitude toward scientific progress would also affect how philosophy addresses its own history. If past pronouncements are disproved, these can no longer be considered, in William James' phrase, "live options." Philosophical speculations can no longer be entertained based on taste, predilection, or religious commitment, except as landmarks in the history of thought, but must be subject to the test of available evidence:

- When Plato says ideas appear in the mind in a preformed, self-sufficient state, he ignores the fact that information is processed neurologically to create such ideas. At the same time, he obviates any need for understanding evolution, embryological development, postnatal physical and social experience, and the history of society, which form the generative and conditioning forces for these ideas. Plato implicitly dismisses the entire notion of the embodiment of the mind in the brain, the brain in the larger organism, the organism in its environment, and even, to some extent, the individual in society.
- Aristotle is simply wrong when he attributes absolute stability to the "essential" nature of species, and, particularly, to human beings, including their aims or final causes.
- So, too, is Descartes in error in locating the connection between an immaterial soul and the material body in the pineal gland. Not only is such a connective function in this gland a fiction, but, more

basically, the Cartesian dualism of mind and body becomes increasingly implausible in the light of overwhelming evidence for the embodiment of mind.

- Locke's notion that the mind is a *tabula rasa* awaiting the imprint of perception is unsustainable in the light of what we know of the genetically guided organization of the brain.
- The same is true of Hume's view of perception as atomistic sensations, since it fails to account for how the human brain actually organizes the perceptual world.
- Kant's a priori categories of time, space, and causation ignore the developmental history of these notions in children and the human species, although his explanation strongly suggests the important conditioning role of neural organization in creating experience.
- The same considerations apply to Hegel's timeless Reason.

These positions no longer make sense in the light of contemporary scientific research. Consider, as an example of such research, how neurophysiologist Jean-Pierre Changeux physicalizes thirst:

> We drink when we have lost water...This water loss causes a reduction in the blood volume and a change in its salt concentration. These variations in physico-chemical properties provoke a desire to drink, through the intermediary of the nervous system. Only a few neurons are involved. They are localized in a precise region of the brain—the hypothalamus...When [Angiotensin II] is injected into the blood or applied directly to the specialized neurons of the hypothalamus, bursts of impulses are released. Oscillating neurons, similar to those of the cricket or sea slug... become active. Angiotensin II starts the "impulse clocks" of the hypothalamus and when its concentration passes a threshold, the animal will soon begin to drink.[3]

In this example, thirst is a biochemical and neural set of reactions accounting for a mental state and for behavior. In Changeux's description of thirst, the neural oscillations occur in an energetic system open to the outside world, which, as we have seen, happens with life systems in relation to their environment, the earth's biosphere in relation to the sun, and star systems in relation to their galaxies. In this case, the cells draw energy from the outside world by consuming nutritive substances, such as glucose.

Also, as in these cases, a state of disequilibrium is required. Here, disequilibrium is induced by an unequal distribution of ions across the cell membranes. When the electric potential passes a certain point, the neural transmissions occur.[4]

Identifying this set of reactions is made possible by developments in science, including microbiology and cybernetics, as well as by the "physics of nonequilibrium processes." Advances in scientific equipment and research techniques, which have only occurred in the last few decades, have also been crucial. Changeux's example also makes clear that the relational mode of thought, employed in this book, bridging different scales from galaxies to atomic nuclei, and different levels of organization, from the quantum mechanical to organisms, is demonstrated in the study of the brain, the "seat of the soul."

Cooperation by physicists, microbiologists, computer scientists, and psychologists thus mirrors the way the world is organized. The enmeshment of fields of thought in each other reflects the deeper enmeshment of physical realities.

In dealing with perception, research in neurophysiology has advanced to the point that it makes sense to think of it as a complex experience of the body, with concentrations of activity located specifically in various cooperating parts of the brain. Such a description strongly contrasts with earlier views, from Plato through Locke, which saw perception as a function of the soul, analogous to its looking through a window onto the world.

Using cross-disciplinary research, Changeux gives us an explanation which physicalizes what was once thought a metaphysically distinct mental function. Perception, he says, takes place when the "sense organs project to distinct cortical areas after relay in the thalamus.... A first level of representation of the world in the cortex thus consists of territories distributed like continents, each corresponding to a major category of physical signal, reaching the organism through impulses in the sensory nerves."[5] In this explanation, which involves specific sets of neurons and which depends on electrical and chemical activity, we have a distinctly physical explanation of perception which tradition had long assigned to the metaphysically different world of the mind.[6]

Equally with consciousness, neurophysiologists have wrestled with the supremely difficult task of providing its physiological basis.[7] Not only have the technical difficulties been formidable, and the neurology itself blindingly complicated, but the brain has shown extraordinary plasticity, so that various mental functions are capable of being performed by different parts of the brain, and with different arrangements. Here is Changeux's tentative stab at describing the relation between neurophysiology and consciousness:

> Operations on mental objects, and above all their results, will be "perceived" by a *surveillance system*, composed of very divergent neurons (such as those in the brainstem) and their reentries. The existence of regulatory loops with reentries at several organizational levels of the brain could lead to high-amplitude oscillations…. These linkages and relationships, these "spider's webs," this regulatory system would function *as a whole*. Can one say that consciousness emerges from all this? Yes, if one takes the word "emerge" literally, as an iceberg emerges from the water. But it is sufficient to say that consciousness *is* the functioning of this regulatory system. Man no longer has a need for the "Spirit"; it is enough for him to be Neuronal Man.[8]

Neurophysiologists particularly, because their domain is the physical base of mental activity, have been in the forefront of attacking every vestige of the notion of the soul, its independence from the body, and its insulation from the physical contingencies of time and space. Appetites, emotions, thinking, and consciousness are all potentially describable in neurological terms. In order to conduct these functions, the human brain needs to have arrived at a state of sufficient complexity. After the acceptance of Darwinian evolution, the story of human creation in one moment of divine inspiration is no longer an option. The creation of human beings, including our minds, must be explained as a result of our development in time.

To tell the story of human neurological development, we will use the version of neurophysiologist Gerald M. Edelman.[9] Like Changeux, Edelman tells his story without recourse to a soul or a self-contained consciousness, and, as we will see, without assuming that the brain "processes" information with a fixed program, as does a simple or early generation computer. As does Changeux, Edelman also attacks the notion that the brain's development is fully determined by its genetic programming; what creates this indeterminacy is its complex, partially random history.

Edelman writes about the brain's evolutionary history, its development in the embryo, and in the life of the individual, in a manner recalling Lee

154

Smolin, Lynn Margulis and Dorian Sagan, Stuart Kauffman, Alexander Argyros, and others we have discussed. It is the brain's emergence from a multi-layered and open-ended history, and the contingent character of its operation, which deliver mental life from determinism, thus allowing human beings their measure of freedom. We should note that Edelman's reliance on Darwinist random selection distinguishes his explanation of evolution and development from particularly that of Stuart Kauffman, who emphasizes self-generated organization as a complementary track to random selection.

For Edelman, the brain's development through natural selection, its growth in the embryo, and its maturation in the life of a socially developing human being, all show similarities, suggesting a unified mode of explanation, which Edelman calls "neural Darwinism." Change results through the random creation of variation; recognition of the variation's "fit," or selection, in its environment; and its consequent replication. In this scenario, there is no determining teleology, that is, a prescription of where the process must go. Its unpredictability then becomes its measure of freedom.[10]

The model, Edelman writes, is Darwin's explanation of the evolution of species. This is a process in which, we will recall, the environment "selects" those variants which allow the species to survive. No prior specific information about what the organism faces in the environment is provided. Nor is there a supreme intelligence guiding the process.[11]

A superb example Edelman uses is the immune system. (His research on the immune system won him the Nobel Prize in 1972.) Here he finds the organism genetically guided to produce a random display of antibodies. When foreign molecules threaten the organism, some of the antibodies can lock onto and neutralize them. Those antibodies are then stimulated to divide and reproduce. This increases the density of those particular antibodies which can lock onto and neutralize *more* of the threatening molecules of the same type. This increases the organism's immunity or capacity to defend itself against those molecules in the present as well as in the future, and thus to survive. In this crucial operation, only indirectly regulated by genes, and activated through unpredictable environmental inputs, there is no fully determined prior program. Rather, a selective process operates with a fair measure of contingency.[12]

Edelman also shows in detail how brain development during embryology often operates according to selective principles, again without following a strict program. While genes guide such a complex development, they cannot completely control it. Specifically, Edelman shows how brain cells may vary because of genetic mutation, and how they unpredictably migrate. He also shows how these cells can adhere to each other or lose adhesion, and how the brain areas map onto each other. All this occurs under the general guidance of specific molecules and genes, while allowing a significant area of variation.[13] He also demonstrates how synapses and mappings are reinforced or diminished because of usage prompted by behavior or experience. Here is still another contingency—a changing and demanding outside world, including other people.[14]

We have already seen Changeux's description of how the perceptual maps work. In Edelman's explanation, incoming data are mapped selectively in various areas of the brain. The neural maps then signal each other back and forth to create a composite perception, which is called "global mapping."[15] This composite perception may, in turn, signal other parts of the brain which control motor responses.

These behavioral responses are directed by "values" housed in other areas (the hedonic and limbic centers) of the brain. Such value-directed responses enhance the organism's chances to survive, for example, by enabling a man to follow a tiger, thereby allowing him to track it or avoid it. Neural responses which "work," for example, by keeping "important" objects, such as tigers, in the visual field will be enhanced. Those that don't will be diminished, as a result of Darwinist selection.[16]

Memory continuously enhances the effectiveness of this system. Memory is not "dead storage" of invariant bits of information; rather, it is a continuous process of recategorizing as new inputs are received. This means, for example, that we will continually refine our image of a particular tiger as we acquire more perceptual experience of it, and of the category of tigers as we see more of them. Edelman shows the rich variety of ways human beings categorize data, which sharply contrasts with the strict logic and invariant languages of earlier generations of computers and computational systems. What range of felines tigers belong to, for example, may also vary widely from culture to culture.

The continuous interchange between the real-time perceptual system and the areas of the brain concerned with survival, informed by memory, creates what Edelman calls "primary consciousness." This form of consciousness is created by connecting memories important for survival—a dangerous tiger, for example—with a perception in the present—

this tiger now. Primary consciousness is thus, in Edelman's phrase, a "remembered present."[17]

The scene is "coherent" because the mind arranges it according to survival priorities, an explanation similar to that of William James, who maintained that "interest" coordinates the conscious field. Thus, the tiger will be salient. Primary consciousness is evolutionarily effective in directing attention and in correcting errors, enabling the organism to survive in a changing environment. It is a system possessed by most mammals, Edelman speculates, and some birds:

> Primary consciousness is the state of being mentally aware of
> things in the world—of having mental images in the present.
> But it is not accompanied by any sense of a person with a past
> and future.... In contrast, higher-order consciousness involves
> the recognition by a thinking subject of his or her own acts or
> affections. It embodies a model of the personal [or self], and of
> the past and the future as well as the present.... It is what we as
> humans have in addition to primary consciousness. We are con-
> scious of being conscious.[18]

Edelman's "higher-order consciousness" is a somewhat more technical version of what we meant, in chapter 6, by Adam being aware of himself as being in the Garden.

This higher-order consciousness, or self-concept, develops in social interaction through rewards and punishments. Such interaction enables the child to see himself or herself through the expectations of others, and also to see divergences from these expectations.[19]

The self also acts on the physical environment and is acted upon. Through memory, the environment extends into the past—the tiger in the jungle then—and it can also be projected into the future—the chances of encountering the tiger tomorrow. Such representations, against which present actions are contrasted, is facilitated by language, which, according to Edelman, depends upon developed phonological capabilities and special brain regions devoted to speech.

A symbolic memory, dependent upon the development of language,[20] creates the possibility of an inner language, or internal monologue. We can, in this sense, ask ourselves, is it wise for me to go into the jungle unarmed, if there is a good chance of encountering a tiger? Higher-order consciousness facilitates social interchange and the creation of future states through planned action, which carries a high evolutionary or survival value. Again, we can discuss the problem of the tiger with others, and perhaps go into the jungle as an armed group.

Ironically, in this scheme of thought, wholly enmeshed in process and relationship, one can see the seeds of the "permanence complex," which subverts it. How could this happen? Once experiences can be located in time, the concept of the self is no longer restricted to the present, and so could become a candidate for what Plato and others would designate the "eternal and timeless soul." The extreme example Edelman offers is that of the saint at the stake, impervious to pain and oblivious of the present. Rather than an abstraction from a complex process, the self would appear to become an independent or self-sufficient substance.

More generally, as language develops, it calls up a world of ideas, which appear stable and independent of any particular usage. Words, and the ideas they represent, are codified in dictionaries and encyclopedias, which can enhance still further the sense of the ideas' independence from experience. The assumption of common meanings in such books, or even in common practice, can create the illusion that the ideas or conceptual categories are stable. In fact, the experiences and conceptual memories which are words' ultimate sources and referents may vary widely from person to person, and from group to group; the consensual meanings of words will also change over time. But even the relative stability of language, according to Edelman, does not imply invariant ideas.[21] Moreover, the creation of a neurological basis for categories and for language is the result of evolution, embryology, and postnatal development, hardly an invariant process "made in heaven."

Stripped of their grounding in process and the environment, ideas, such as those in mathematics, *can* be considered to be a timeless, metaphysical given, and so part of the 'permanence complex.' It is at this point that Plato assigns to such ideas the role of *creating* process, indeed, of creating all reality, including the human body, in which the eternal ideas 'participate.' Ironically, the body, which has just achieved freedom with its embodied mind, loses it again, in the permanence complex, to the determinism of its own ideas, or the preestablished laws of nature, or the invariant will of God.

Rather than a permanence complex, Edelman's neurological scheme illustrates how all the categories of experience, including higher-order consciousness, are at least conceivable as neural developments through evolution, embryology, and the life of the socialized individual. Edelman has undertaken a theory of consciousness because "even if many details have to be assumed at our present state of knowledge, it would be inherently valuable to demonstrate that a cogent theory of consciousness can be constructed *solely* on biological grounds."[22]

In connecting the subjective experience of mentality with neurophysiology, or any physical embodiment, Edelman faces a set of methodological problems, which will come up again in deconstructionist literary criticism. The "content" of subjective experience may not be *clearly* knowable by the conscious subject. The experience is also not clearly definable in language, even if the experience itself were clear. And the experience is not *directly* comparable with the subjective experience of anyone else, so that it cannot be completely communicated. For example, if a person looks at a painting in a museum, what she sees may not be totally conscious. The visual image may be virtually impossible to communicate verbally, and how she feels about the painting may not be fully communicable to a friend. From a researcher's standpoint, observing the firing of a subject's physical neurons, if such specific observation were possible, then could not be fully correlated with what the subject actually "saw," or her subjective experience be compared with full accuracy with someone else's.

While it seems correct that the researcher might not achieve total clarity, I believe these problems do not vitiate the attempt to correlate neural activity with subjective experience. Neurophysiologists *can* correlate the subject's detailed statements about what he or she sees, with observable neurological functioning. They *can* also surmise by her behavior, again increasingly fine-tuned, that what the subject's statement means "operationally" is *similar* to what such a statement means if made by others.

An insistence on "clear and distinct" ideas, to use Descartes' phrase, or ideas which are invariant and totally communicable, suggests not only Descartes, but ultimately Plato. Here, a system of such ideas would seem to provide our somewhat vague and often complex perceptions with the clarity they do not have in experience. It is precisely this Platonic system which both neurophysiologists and deconstructionists are attempting to abolish (see chapter 11).

The philosopher John Searle poses another problem. In a review of Edelman's work, Searle argues, "The main difficulty is, however, obvious: so far Edelman has given no reason why a brain that has all these features would thereby have sentience or awareness.... But as so far described, it is possible that a brain could have all these functional, behavioral features, including reentrant mapping, without thereby being conscious."[23] This is, I believe, not true in principle, because with particular neural mappings we *are* conscious, and without them we are not. It is also true, however, that particular states of consciousness may be the outcome of different states of neural activity.

The relation between the subjective and objective world, or what we are calling 'embodiment,' is put poignantly by neurologist Richard M. Restak:

As I...stare out into the woods across the street, I experience a world of trees, sunlight, and the sounds of birds—sensory objects, as a philosopher would term them. Yet what I actually experience is energy in the form of vibrations from waves of different frequencies..... At this level of "reality," subjectivity does not exist.

As these waves interact with the receptors in my ears and eyes, they trigger neural codes which upon relay to the brain result in the brain's creation of a model of the external world. Since it is the brain that does this, our individual brains, the model assumes a subjective character: It is *our* world. Yet we don't think or speak about it as subjective; on the contrary, this mixture of the objective (waves of energy) and the subjective (our brain's construction via neural codes of a model), we refer to as the "objective world." But it is not objective in the sense of being known independently of the brain.[24]

Clearly, Edelman and his colleagues have a lot of work to do to nail down this relation between neurological process and subjectivity—for example, which particular or alternative mappings are involved, and what it is about them that makes them conscious. This is a suggestion for further research, not a theoretical objection, as Searle admits.[25]

No one is more conscious than Edelman himself of how much is left to be done, and of just how thin and controversial his sketch is. But filling it out and achieving what accuracy is possible, rather than reverting to philosophical ideas of permanence, which dismiss embodiment altogether, would seem to hold the strongest promise for arriving at the true relation of mind and body.

What seems undeniable is that our mental images and symbols—indeed, what William James called the whole 'stream of thought'—are neurologically embodied, and that, considered in either of their aspects, as neural activity *or* subjectivity, they guide our action. It is also clear that if subjective consciousness is achieved, it depends on the growth of complexity in the organism, and results in an extraordinary increase in freedom, which seems most evident in social and cultural experience.

Edelman's scheme depends on a narrow Darwinist analysis of process. What it omits is the kind of thinking Stuart Kauffman has provided in basic biology: that natural selection, restricted to the survival value of traits induced by accidental genetic change, may not be able to explain the emergence of complexity and regular forms of order, or the pleiotropic reconfiguration of organisms after random genetic changes. This conflict will, I suspect, become increasingly clearer in biology in the early decades of this new century.

Artificial Intelligence and Cognition

We turn next to the contribution that computers and artificial intelligence make to the framing of our new paradigm. Developed after World War II, not only have computers and artificial intelligence offered increasingly sophisticated models of mentality and physical processes, and so greatly influenced science and philosophy, they have also radically changed the world in which any new paradigm must operate.

By focusing on the notion of information processing, the inventors of artificial intelligence, and a growing body of the scientific community, derived three hypotheses which can be summarized as follows: (1) Information processing is a fundamental means of understanding what is happening in the world, from nuclear particles to human minds. (2) *What* is happening in the world is *itself* information processing. (3) The material or energetic "substrate" of information processing is a variable, so that no particular physical system, such as the brain for human-like mentality, has a privileged position. The last fifty years has seen an uneasy testing out and, for their proponents, a validation of, these three hypotheses.

An early, though inadequate, attempt to state this set of claims, known as the Church-Turing thesis, was first enunciated independently in 1936 by artificial intelligence founders Alonzo Church, an American logician, and Alan Turing, his British counterpart. The Church-Turing thesis states that a computer can simulate any "algorithmically calculable system" using a general symbol system. Such a general symbol system might be Boolean algebra or symbolic logic. An algorithm is a sequence of rules and instructions setting up procedures to solve a problem or set of problems. As Jack Copeland, a philosopher at the University of Canterbury, New Zealand, explains: "If the Church-Turing thesis is true (as everyone thinks) and if our own cognitive processes are algorithmically calculable, then it follows that in principle a computer could give an exact simulation of the mind."[26]

Despite initial obvious differences between the brain and the early computers (the brain was wet, the computer was dry; the brain used neurons, the computer used circuits), the similarity between the two seemed clear enough. For example, the firing and quiescence (non-firing) of neurons could be represented by the opening and closing of circuits. But the Church-Turing thesis implicitly went further. It suggested that if thinking could be considered as calculation, and if a computer's programmed language could be considered as a medium of thinking, a computer's operation could be seen as mimicking, if indeed not replicating, human thought.

However, at the dawn of the computer age, many researchers viewed this analogy with suspicion. Experimental psychologist Karl Lashley, for example, writing in the late 1940s, cautioned against any such simple analogy between the human brain and what is known as the von Neumann serial computer. This computer, with its on-and-off switching, its binary language of 0s and 1s, its processing of all information through a single track, and its invariant lexicon, is still the basis of most of our present generation of personal computers. Lashley's objection was that, because millions of neurons were involved in any action, any particularly neuron was dispensable. This meant that the brain, unlike a computer, was an "analogical," not a digital, machine, and that analysis of its activities would need to be in statistical terms.[27]

Francisco J. Varela, a cognitive psychologist; Evan Thompson, a philosopher; and Eleanor Rosch, a psychologist, writing in 1991, expressed other objections. A von Neumann computer, they argued, runs its entire program through one path. This kind of symbolic information processing is based on sequential rules, applied one at a time. Accordingly, this "'von Neumann bottleneck' is a dramatic limitation when the task at hand requires large numbers of sequential operations..."[28]

However, as computers have developed further, they have become major factors in research, from cosmology to microbiology, to neurophysiology and cognition. Increasingly, these fields have relied on computerized models, and have been seen as being *about* information processing. Where von Neumann computers have, indeed, seemed too simplistic to model many phenomena, particularly human thought, new computers seem able to replicate natural processes of all types, based on radically different principles.[29]

Psychologist Howard Gardner reports on such "massive parallel processing systems" (M.P.P.S.). These, he tells us, simulate visual perception by using physical or virtual machines involving millions of independent processors, which carry out many processes at the same time. Gardner writes:

> In these M.P.P.S.'s, memory and perception occur in a distributed fashion: that is, instead of there being a single central control, or the complex passing of information between modules, many units operate simultaneously and achieve their effects statistically. The multiple connections allow much of the knowledge of the entire system to be applied in any instance of recognition or problem solving.... No information inheres in a specific locus; thus, even though many units (or cells) may be destroyed, the relevant memory or concept continues to exist.... These properties seem closer to the kinds of search and decision organisms must carry out in a complex and often chaotic natural world.[30]

Using the most advanced computers, many cognitive psychologists and neurophysiologists, such as Edelman, are testing out hypotheses about human mental functioning which cannot be performed experimentally on the human brain. These researchers are devising models which are honing in on replicating actual mental processes, such as calculation, imaging, categorization, and decision-making.[31]

If a computer could actually physically replicate the brain, or by some other physical means could pass beyond some critical margin of emergent process, there would seem to be no reason why it could not think. This is to state, in terms of the third hypothesis with which we began this section, that brains and human bodies are not necessary for "true" thought. Rather, the physical computer could be substituted for the embodied mind.

Here we must consider the objection of philosopher John Searle, that computers fail to experience subjectivity and meaning, not that they have different mechanisms than a brain or are unable to carry out mental functions.[32] But is subjectivity a useful criterion?[33] Searle maintains that humans, as opposed to computers, *know* what our words mean, whereas the symbols used by computers have no semantic meaning whatsoever for the computers themselves. This lack of subjective experience would seem to be as true for a pocket calculator, as it would be for "Deep Blue," the international computer chess champion. For this reason, Searle maintains, one cannot design a mind simply by providing a program. However, the argument seems time-bound, and may not apply to computers of the future (see below).

Ray Kurzweil, a writer on computers and a computer inventor, tells us that as computers develop in the new few decades, they will predictably blur the distinction between mind and mechanism, and between life and non-life. According to Kurzweil, computer development is moving at exponential speed, so that by 2020, modestly priced computers will be capable of "20 million billion neural connection calculations per second, which is equal to the human brain." In 1997, they "could [only] perform around 2 billion connection calculations per second."[34]

Kurzweil, like others we have discussed, sees evolution as increasing our capacity to process and organize information. He views computers, and, more generally, technology, as a predictable phase of human evolutionary development, rather than an extrinsic or synthetic addition.[35]

However, where natural evolution took hundreds of millions of years to develop biological computational capacity, technological innovations occur far more rapidly. For example, what is known as "Moore's Law," named after Gordon Moore, chief executive of the Intel Corporation in the 1960s, states that computational capacity is doubling every two years. Put alternatively, the size of a transistor on an integrated circuit chip is being cut in half every twenty-four months. In 1971, there were 3,500 transistors in the latest computer chip; in 1997, there were 7.5 million.[36]

Using such increased capacity, computers are now under development that understand and respond to natural languages, visualize real-time speech for the deaf, translate from one language to another, and serve as highly interactive personal assistants. Although these developments are based primarily on neural nets which mimic the computing system of the human brain, they are still within the provenance of what can be called "machines," and what can be considered to lack life or subjectivity.

Going a step further, Kurzweil confidently projects the creation of "free-standing," self-replicating intelligence that can compete with and ultimately exceed ours. It is at this point that computer development would fully realize the third hypothesis posed at the opening of this section: the consideration of the material or energetic "substrate" of information processing as a mere variable, with the brain having no special status. This would mean the full replication of human intelligence through alternative physical means, or other forms of artificial intelligence equal in status to ours.

Intelligence, life, and subjectivity are not, Kurzweil contends, tied to the specifics of our animal bodies, and specifically to our brain. Even within our own biology, however, he argues that the material substratum is not unique: We constantly change atoms, and most of our cells (outside the brain), as well.

Eventually, Kurzweil predicts, we will be able to scan human brains and download them into physical systems which are not subject to the organic problems faced by DNA-based tissue, which expends much of its capacity in life maintenance. *"We will be software,"* Kurzweil exclaims, *"not hardware."*[37]

A far more limited projection of artificial intelligence is made by John Rennie, editor-in-chief of *Scientific American*. Rennie relates that "from the 1950s through the early 1970s, most artificial intelligence researchers were smoothly confident of their ability to simulate another organ, the brain. They are more humble these days: although their work has given rise to some narrow successes, such as medical-diagnostic expert systems and electronic chess grandmasters, replicating anything like real human intelligence is now recognized as far more arduous."[38]

Such sobriety seems justified. Generally, in any projection into the future, unforeseen theoretical and technical problems, and lack of funding for research or development, often pose unpredictable limits. In the late 1950s, for example, researchers in the U.S. outer space program were confidently predicting the development of ion propulsion of space vehicles and planetary space stations within a couple of decades. Due to unforeseen technical difficulties and staggering costs, these advances have still not occurred as of this writing. Controlled nuclear fusion and a general cure for cancer were considered imminent in the 1950s, and have still eluded discovery. More generally, the extraordinary increase in productive capacity released by the Industrial Revolution has yet to eliminate world poverty. The fact that advances seem theoretically possible do not mean that they can be quickly actualized, or that they will be replicated to the extent that they transform the reality of significant segments of the population.

Kurzweil, however, and other visionaries of the computer age, seem undissuaded by such considerations, and eagerly anticipate the next technical breakthrough. In predicting lifelike artificial intelligence,[39] they see the model in living organisms themselves, which build information-processing appliances (life forms) atom by atom, a process which, when artificially initiated, is known as *nanoengineering*. With nanoengineering, Kurzweil believes, human beings will be capable of building intelligent forms at the atomic level. This capacity will grow, he argues, until we can create forms whose intelligence exceeds ours, and which begin to replicate themselves, and which experience in lifelike ways.[40] These forms would then theoretically make themselves up out of extremely small, intelligent units, called *nanobits*, which are at the order of magnitude of a billionth of a meter, or five carbon atoms.

Kurzweil thus projects a world to be realized in this century in which human beings will have alternative or virtual copies or variants of themselves and could theoretically live forever, thus solving a major problem dealt with by the permanence complex. This is also a world in which alternative intelligent forms, with rapidly increasing capacities, will inhabit the world with us. He writes:

> Machines, derived from human thinking and surpassing humans
> in their capacity for experience, will claim to be conscious, and
> thus to be spiritual. They will believe that they are conscious.
> They will believe that they have spiritual experiences. They will
> be convinced that these experiences are meaningful.[41]

While one can strenuously argue with Kurzweil about the accuracy of the dates he assigns to his predictions, and the extent to which such developments will penetrate to the earth's entire population, the predictions themselves carry a sense of credibility. The world he projects, if not ours or our children's, might well be that of future generations—unless they destroy themselves, or their creations do the job for them.

In this century, human beings will need to think hard about what to do with the almost limitless power we will have to meet physical needs, create alternative minds, and constitute new realities. We will also need to consider to what extent what we value in human experience is tied to the frailty and specificity of our animal bodies, and to the reality of our experiences in this world, as opposed to alternative worlds created solely by information.

Finally, we will need to ask ourselves if we wish to accept the solutions to problems of permanence which computers may offer us, such as downloading ourselves onto less frail materials substrates than our bodies.

Already, it is evident that some people deeply resist the possibilities outlined by Kurzweil and others. At a conference on "Extended Life, Eternal Life," held at the University of Pennsylvania, a number of philosophers and theologians stated clearly that extended life, or even an eternal life offered by computers, would differ metaphysically from eternal life with God. As such life would defer this blessing indefinitely, it would be undesirable.

Rev. Diogenes Allen, a professor of philosophy at Princeton Theological Seminary, had this to say:

> The contrast between seeking to perpetuate myself and what
> Christianity has to offer can be seen in a Moravian daily text from
> July 19, 1999. The prayer says, "O God, we ask for a long life, and
> you gave us eternity. We ask for healing, and you prepare us for
> the glory of Christ's risen body. How can we return enough
> thanks or praise?" That is different from a craven fear seeking to
> perpetuate a selfish life.[42]

Today, many people simultaneously hold doctrines of permanence and embrace modes of thought in which those doctrines do not appear. This ambiguity has created deep confusion. As crises mount, many people turn back to permanence, despite its increasing lack of credibility. For many people, the sciences themselves are too abstract, too removed from the human condition, to be convincing. What is necessary to humanize these new advances? As we will see in the next chapter, this is precisely what a group of twentieth-century thinkers has attempted to do, by creating a human paradigm for their century and for ours.

Chapter Ten

Toward a Human Paradigm

In our cognitive as well as in our active life we are creative. We add, both to the subject and to the predicate part of reality. The world stands really malleable, waiting to receive its final touches at our hands. Like the kingdom of heaven, it suffers human violence willingly. Man engenders truths upon it.

William James[1]

Writing history is like watching a multi-ring circus. All the acts seem to be going on independently, and yet, if one looks closely, the tightrope walkers, jugglers, and clowns are closely watching each other, taking notes, and passing on their information to their colleagues.

If there is a center ring in the history presented in this chapter, it encircles a group of thinkers who have attempted to imagine how the different elements of modernity can be integrated into human experience. Although many others could be cited, I have selected the social psychologist George Herbert Mead, the philosopher John Dewey, the psychiatrist Harry Stack Sullivan, and the ego psychologist Jane Loevinger. Together, they suggest the elements of a new human paradigm which places us in a contingent world without the props of permanence, but with a deep sense of interrelationship and consequent responsibility. Rather than seeing human beings as static essences, they view us as participating in a multi-faceted dialogue between autonomous identity and environmental and social dependence, between growth and action, and ultimately between our inner satisfactions and our outer commitments.

This new paradigm is the social counterpart of advances in the physical and biological sciences, and draws directly upon some of this work. Later, in our conclusion (chapter 12), I will attempt to spell out what implications this paradigm has for an activist stance in today's rapidly changing world.

A Social Preamble

This new view of the human condition has been developing over a period of more than two hundred years. Any point in time to begin our analysis would be artificial, but the publication in 1776 of Adam Smith's *The Wealth of Nations*[2] is a reasonable place to start.

In 1776, when political power in England still belonged exclusively to the male landed gentry, Smith describes the urban commercial market as a venue of unimpeded opportunity. Such a system had already begun to operate in some opposition to the virtually totally fixed classes of the medieval period. In Smith's market economy, self-interested men (entrepreneurship and labor mobility were still then largely limited to men), without reference to the ancient privileges of nobility or of land ownership, need have only various combinations of brawn, brains, and capital in order to participate. That the working class could not generally raise the capital to be entrepreneurs does not entirely vitiate the formal openness of Smith's system.

Smith is clear that privilege has nothing to do with natural ability. For Smith, the nobility and the landed rich are not intrinsically smarter than anyone else. Human intelligence, according to Smith, is indifferent to social distinctions. Today's class-, race- and ethnicity-biased intelligence tests, which, to some extent, have helped maintain these distinctions, were a long way off.[3]

Once people enter the market, as entrepreneurs or workers, they operate with impeccable logic to maximize their interests. Even lapses in individual logic are compensated for: If one business charges too much, for example, others will lower their prices to secure the market. Entrepreneurs, then, invest or start businesses where there is a favorable gap between prices and costs. Workers, with whatever skills and mobility they have, take jobs where wages are highest.

Here is a system which renders human beings and their products commodities or interchangeable units, much like the self-contained atoms of the Newtonian world. Rather than community, the market fosters an atomistic selfishness and a reliance on "objective" material facts, valuing human activities and goods according to a single standard, or "bottom line."[4]

Notice that, like Newton's universe, this system works without state (or divine) intervention, a reaction, in Smith's time, to the earlier interventionist role of monarchically controlled mercantilism. As everyone is equally endowed with God-given reason, and the rules of the game are clear, each person can make a maximally intelligent decision. The same absolute and singular rationality which pervades the heavens and the mechanics of bodies on earth, with their blind following of God's laws, as Newton articulated them, pervades Smith's economic sphere, with its "invisible hand." This means, for example, that the demand for goods will invariably stimulate production to the point that only the most efficient producers will be left in the field, enjoying a profit only marginally above costs.

This system, however, is man-made, an autonomous product of social life which has the look of an organism. In this sense, it is not deducible from physical laws, but clearly subsumes them in some higher order. Its results are neither attributable to God nor to fate, nor to deliberate political decisions. While the Industrial Revolution would radically subvert Smith's notion of small, atomized producers, and trade unionism his idea of the isolated worker, this is a system in which, with major modifications, we are still living, and which has now been extended to the furthest corners of the earth (see chapter 11).

One form of rebellion against Smith's economic units or market, and against the earlier system of closed classes, was the growth, in the nineteenth century, of romanticism. While the romantics fought for democracy at the political level, at the personal level, they asserted the uniqueness of their individuality, and their capacity and obligation to act directly and organize their lives according to personal feelings and values.

The romantics pursued this agenda with an energy and confidence which have perhaps never been equaled. The romantic hero of the nineteenth century did not act to fulfill the code of aristocratic honor of the *ancien regime*, nor, in the more modern mode, act to maximize profits. Nor did the romantic hero or heroine, contrary to Locke or Hume, act simply to enhance pleasure, seeking out the net total of potential pleasurable sensations with invariant reason. Rather, the romantic hero or heroine acted because of passion for another person, or outrage with social injustice, or desire for self-expression or personal fulfillment.

While romanticism attacked social authority, including traditional religion, in the name of individualism, religion also came under attack because of the general growth of secularism and the new status of science, particularly in continental Europe as opposed to the United States and England. In the United States, particularly, the pull toward secularism was somewhat offset by the growth of revivalism and of popular sects of Christianity, such as Baptism and Methodism, as well as other fundamentalist and evangelical sects, which were particularly attractive to the lower-middle and working classes. As these forms of Protestantism developed, they tended to rely more on direct religious experience, as opposed to religion mediated by clergy, and community consensus as opposed to church authority. In this way, they remained more active than their continental European counterparts. In addition, as Americans moved into the western frontier, they relied heavily on their religious groups for solidarity and support, as did immigrant groups of all denominations as they made their new home in America.

At least in western Europe, with the authority of the churches identified with older ways of thought, and with men and women increasingly preoccupied with secular affairs, traditional notions of God and the soul suffered a partial eclipse. If Friedrich Nietzsche (1844–1900), perhaps the last of the romantic philosophers, was still considerably in advance of general social mores, in proclaiming "God is dead," he was also correct in assuming that secular modes of thought and action were permissible in ways which would not have been countenanced a hundred years before.[5]

As opposed to the cult of rational empiricism, the market, and the slowly fading influence of religion, the romantic hero raised the standard of fiction, the imagination, the spontaneous event, and, most importantly, the individual. This "cult" of the individual—of the lover, genius, or revolutionary—became the theme of the life histories of this period's outstanding persons, and of its literature, particularly the novel, and its musical counterpart, the opera. This is what unifies such highly disparate people as Napoleon Bonaparte, John Keats, Ludwig von Beethoven, and Giuseppe Garibaldi, Mary Wollstonecraft, Margaret Fuller, George Eliot, and Sarah Bernhardt; and their fictional counterparts, such as Stendhal's Julien Sorel in *The Red and the Black*, and Giacomo Puccini's operatic heroine, Tosca. Each of these individuals sought to realize an image of himself or herself which had the timeless look of a work of art, and yet was enmeshed in a particular history.

Romanticism revolted not only against the norms of traditional society, but against the notion of a single or uniform rationality pervading the world. Eighteenth-century Enlightenment thinkers like François Voltaire, Étienne Condillac, and Jean Jacques Rousseau believed that human reason could discover the rules of rational life implicit in the universe. In this respect, morality and political science were the same to them as the physical sciences. In the end, truth would be discovered, not invented. Just as scientists would discover the laws of nature, and the invariant mathematics which those laws followed, so reason, if left unfettered by prejudice, could uncover the laws of morality and human history leading to the one true society. Ironically, this generation of thinkers fully endorsed an ahistorical basis for human life on the eve of an event—the French Revolution—which would make such thinking inconceivable.

For the post-Revolutionary romantics, truths and ideals were, in William James's phrase, "engendered" by human beings, not discovered; as contingent, historical products, they were far from inevitable. In the words of the Oxford philosopher Isaiah Berlin:

> Romantics . . . said something wholly new and disturbing: that
> ideals were not objective truths written in heaven and needing to
> be understood, copied, practiced by men; but that they were cre-
> ated by men. Values were not found, but made; not discovered, but
> generated. . . . A Russian thinker, Alexander Herzen, once asked,
> "Where is the song before it is sung?" Where indeed? "Nowhere"
> is the answer—one creates the song by singing it, by composing it.
> So, too, life is created by those who live it, step by step.[6]

Economic results, then, for the romantic thinker, should not be automatic, as Smith had declared, the predictable result of the interaction of individual economic "units" with fixed characteristics of rationality and economic self-interest. Rather, the romantics believed, economic results should emerge from understanding coupled with empathy, from freely chosen values and visions for the future. Such free choices should provide not only the basis of economics, but of art, politics, and life.

Romantics would also lash out against the objective and automatic character of science, at least as it applied to human beings. While scientists from Isaac Newton to Hermann von Helmholtz (d. 1894) would seek to establish an objective system of energetic reactions of bodies in space, the romantics would see such a system's patent inadequacies as an explanation of human experience. As Wordsworth would say, "We murder when we dissect."

While Kant would proclaim the separate realm of the aesthetic, romanticism would, for the most part, see art emerging from life, and revel in its very lack of uniformity. If art in the age of industrialism was held to be "gloriously useless," this was a result of the facts of social power and organization, not a metaphysical statement about the detachment from life of either art or romantic ideals.

Some romantics fully embraced individualism, but others, pioneered by Johann Gottfried Herder (d. 1803), promoted the idea of collectives which subsumed the individual. Whether the "folk" or the nation, these collectives were seen as forming their own sets of rules. Each culture was considered to have its own inner dynamics and emergent values, and was justifiable in its own terms. Although the romanticism of the group could end in nationalism or racism—"my country right or wrong"—it also created a way of looking at cultures as free, autonomous creations. While Herder himself believed that certain common humane values bridged different cultures, the idea of culture as a free creation could easily support full cultural relativism.

The dominant view the West held of other societies generally differed from this romantic ideal. Until roughly the middle of the nineteenth century, the West had, for the most part, possessed little consciousness of other societies except to know that they existed, that they were curious, and that they were "backward," a belief which is still held today in some quarters. For practical and imperialistic politicians, such "exotic," "primitive," or "backward" societies offered the possibility of colonization and exploitation, which could be accomplished with little understanding of those societies' structure or culture. Often viewed as positive at the time, colonialism, as the "white man's burden," promised to spread European enlightenment, which presumably embodied the fullest advance of universal, human reason to subject and presumably "less advanced" peoples around the world.

Initially, archeologists and observant travelers carried out the investigation of contemporary cultures, and the excavation of ancient sites and translation of texts, within the framework of a Hegelian universal history. Such a history represented the necessary path on which, it was thought, all societies must travel in erecting a social order which best elicited man's invariant soul, or the equally invariant World Spirit or Reason. After Darwin, cultural evolution would be seen as a complement to biological evolution, with the West at the evolutionary apex.

By the end of the nineteenth century, and increasingly in the early decades of the twentieth, a new anthropology, based on more romantic or relativistic ways of thought, attacked the prevailing idea in the West that its culture, with its religion, values, and science, had some privileged metaphysical justification, or necessarily represented humanity's highest development. Like Herder, the new anthropologists, epitomized by the German-American Franz Boas (1858–1942) and the Polish Bronislaw Malinowski (1884–1942), saw other societies, radically different from our own, as responses to conditions in their particular environments. More profoundly, they viewed them as integrated systems with histories, internal values, and meaning structures which should be understood on their own terms, without reference to or invidious comparison with Western civilization. Reciprocally, they saw human beings as increasingly endowed with similar genetic capacities, which permitted a wide range of cultures and, within these cultures, highly disparate roles.

Sensitized by the new anthropology, with its emphasis on collective culture, French sociologist Émile Durkheim maintained in *The Division of Labor in Society* (1893) and *Suicide* (1897), that the social order of the West could be seen in a state of disintegration. The mechanisms of its destruction were precisely those identified by Adam Smith. Durkheim, however, saw the key elements of Smith's system in a far less favorable light—its emphasis on the socially disengaged, rational, self-seeking individual, rather than the community; the impersonal market, which tore people away from their homes and villages; and the division of labor, which alienated them from their work by breaking it up into numbing, repetitive processes. (Smith, for example, had identified over twenty steps in the making of pins, each performed by different workers.) In such a system, people experienced a profound depression or anomie, which could lead to suicide. The analysis of Karl Marx (d. 1883) in his multivolume *Das Kapital* was not dissimilar, although he emphasized the vast inequalities of compensation between owners and workers. Heavily influenced by Hegel's *thesis-antithesis* analysis of history, Marx argued the inevitability of open class warfare.

At the same time that Marx was predicting the inevitability of the proletarian revolution and the classless society, political democracy was on the rise, at least in the West. This manifested itself in two related ways—the diminution of the power of the monarchy, the prevalent form of government in Europe, in favor of a democratically controlled administration; and the gradual widening of the franchise. In America, much of this development took place at one stroke with the American Revolution, leaving, at a legal level, some property franchise issues for a decade or two, race franchise discrimination until just after the Civil War, and gender franchise discrimination until after World War I, when suffrage became virtually universal, despite some lapses in practice. But throughout most of Europe, parliamentary democracy and the widening of the franchise only came about through armed revolutions, starting with the French Revolution of 1789 and continuing well into the nineteenth century. In England, after the Glorious Rebellion of 1689, democracy was advanced by progressive extensions of the franchise throughout the nineteenth and the early twentieth centuries.

As democratization spread, the counterpart of the autonomous economic man became the independent voter. However, the production units, contrary to Adam Smith, far from being atomized, grew increasingly larger, sometimes to the point of becoming monopolies, setting prices and working conditions, eliminating competition, and engendering a vast amount of social misery. The political arena began to look like the economic, with political campaigns appearing more and more like marketing ventures fostering politicians controlled by large financial interests. The extent to which the mass of voters could resist manipulation and vote in their own interests, that is, operate with the logic they were once believed to have had in the economic sphere, became a major focus of debate throughout the nineteenth and twentieth centuries, and has continued to the present day. This issue was fought out, for example, by the German socialist Eduard Bernstein and the Russian revolutionary Vladimir Lenin in a series of virulent polemics. Bernstein maintained that, with the increase of the franchise and the growth of labor parties in Europe, a violent revolution would be unnecessary. Needless to say, Lenin denied this, and vilified Bernstein as a compromiser.

Socialist agitation throughout the nineteenth century, and the opportunity to curry votes from newly enfranchised groups, as well as the clear inefficiencies and breakdowns of the classical market economy, sparked a reconsideration of the extent to which the market could be left to function automatically. In the 1880s, the conservative chancellor Otto von Bismarck initiated a set of sweeping government programs for a united Germany, including sickness, accident, and old-age insurance; limitations on female and child labor; and maximum working hours. Increasingly, the state, empowered by the growing franchise, began to intervene to insure a better functioning economy and to provide for social welfare. In the United States, such legislation came in waves, from the Progressive era prior to World

War I, to the New Deal, and then has been essentially continued, amended, or eroded since then. The redistribution of social benefits, and even the partial shaping of society which this implied, were taken by some as a democratic option. Others, on the political right, continued to believe that such matters were best left to God or to the unhindered workings of the economy, and have striven to cut back government-provided benefits.

BS

Beginning around the turn of the twentieth century, a group of American thinkers in highly disparate fields began to develop a radically new line of thought, influenced by and partially reacting to European social and political philosophy, and events both in Europe and the United States. While embracing the romantic notion of values and truths as created rather than discovered, they emphasized, more than had the romantics, the enmeshment of individuals in social structures. They believed that democratic choices should be reached through accurate empathy created through situational involvement and through historical and scientific understanding. Accurate empathy, they held, should replace reliance on impersonal rationality and "objective" laws, on the one hand, or on romantic intuition and sentiment, on the other.

At bottom, these thinkers saw human beings not as static products determined by an eternal soul, invariant reason, or automatic systems, such as the market, or as pure individuals entertaining their own romantic sentiments, but as agents in contingent development and in a constant dialogue with the equally evolving orders of nature and society. For these thinkers, the purposeful situation, both social and environmental, became the basic unit of analysis, as opposed to the soul, God, and eternal ideas, or invariant laws of nature or history. Purposeful situations became the matrix of physical relations, personal morality, social policies, and art. Out of these situations would emerge the individual and social decisions, and the arts and the sciences, which would create the future. These thinkers represent a view of humankind which suggests a new paradigm for Western thought.

George Herbert Mead

George Herbert Mead (1863–1931), a social psychologist who had been a student of William James and a colleague of John Dewey at the University of Chicago, conceived important elements of this paradigm. Although barely read today, Mead pioneered in aligning the social sciences with interactive and relational modes of thought advanced in the physical sciences.[7]

For Mead, the task of social psychology is to explain how the self-conscious individual develops in a social setting. In order to do this, not only does Mead dispense with the substantive soul, but in stressing the need for showing how thought evolves, he also disposes of the invariant Kantian forms, such as space, time, and causality, as well as Kant's notion of invariant reason. Equally expendable for Mead is Watson's behaviorism, as it pretends consciousness and symbolism do not exist.

Mead is clear, as Descartes is not, that mentality is embodied in the central nervous system, which can be seen objectively as neurons and experienced subjectively by the individual. Unlike many modern epistemologists, who are preoccupied with *qualia*, Mead focuses on the act. Like Edelman (see chapter 9), he sees *qualia*, objects, and ideas (or concepts) as integrated parts of continuing actions in which the individual seeks control of his or her environment. Mead writes, "What I am insisting upon is that the patterns which one finds in the central nervous system are patterns of action—not of contemplation, not of appreciation as such, but patterns of action."[8] For example, for Mead, the *quale* of brown, as opposed to green, indicates that firewood will burn, and achieves prominence in the action scheme of making a fire.

Verbal language, evolved from more basic gestural language, seeks a response from others, such as the word "tiger," which elicits either flight or fight. A gesture or word becomes a significant symbol "when it has the same effect on the individual making it that it has on the individual to whom it is addressed or who explicitly responds to it..."[9] Meaning thus emerges primarily in the context of a social act.

The meanings of verbal symbols become standardized or "universal" over time with the relative uniformity of response to their use. For Mead, there is no preexisting system of Platonic ideas or universals, but rather simply the development of such standardized socialized meanings.[10]

Finally, the environment itself is not simply given, but to a large extent is selected by its role in our developing action schemes. This is what William James meant by "selective attention"—seeing in the environment what is important for us to see in a particular scheme of action. Thus, if we are about to carry a stack of books, we will notice their size, but ignore their contents. As the schemes develop into action, and we receive "feedback," what we attend to will also change. Thus, as we begin picking up a stack of books, we will attend to the fact that larger books should be placed on the bottom.

For Mead, as for Edelman, the transition from consciousness (Edelman's "primary consciousness") to self-consciousness (Edelman's "higher-order consciousness") takes place when we become objects to ourselves. This, Mead says, occurs when we internalize the expressed attitudes of others toward us within a social environment.[11]

Locke, for the most part, postulates fully realized individuals or selves as existing prior to the social process, and sees the State as a contract between such individuals. Mead turns this around; he sees self-conscious individuals emerging from society. Mind is not a congenital endowment, but the result of a process of socialization, and behind it, of historical, social, and physiological evolution.

The composite attitudes which others take toward the individual, Mead calls the "generalized other" and is the base against which the individual works out a particular version of himself or herself. The "generalized other" carries specific characterizations and value judgments and so represents a substantial amount of control, although there is still room for individual self-assertion.

The individual can also choose to change or expand the social group of reference, that is, the group to whose reactions he or she habitually responds. Some may see their primary social group as a particular class, or the nation-state; still others, the globalized economy, or all humankind. As we saw, the choice by a section of the Jesus movement to appeal to the larger world of gentiles in Roman times wholly changed the nature of Christianity, and reciprocally the typical Christian self.

Mead's view of individuality and its relation to society relies on a model of the world shaped in part by the field physics of the late nineteenth and early twentieth centuries. According to Mead, each individual sees the world from his or her perspective, or, in Mead's use of Whitehead's phrase, as a particular "prehension." (A prehension, we will remember, can be seen physically as a spatio-temporal field with a locus at the individual, and, cognitively, as an individual's perspective on the world.) It thus includes other individuals, who will have *their* own prehensions. In this sense, there is no *noumenal* world, or world in itself, outside these prehensions. And yet, as we have already noted, a prehension is not a purely subjective response, as it is a focus of a field in which the things perceived are contributing.

Mead spells out how individuals enter into the perspectives of other individuals, or the generalized perspective of a group, by acquiring a social self. The group shares an evolving common perspective, or generalized prehension, reflected in part in a common culture and a common language. This perspective expresses not only particular sensuous qualities and objects which the culture or group distinguishes, but the group's ethics, scientific laws, logics, and other modes of thought. These perspectives are not absolute—as, in different ways, Plato and Kant say they are—but are evolving social products. In a society as complex as ours, these are changing rapidly, and, at any given moment, the group may not reach consensus. Nevertheless, there is a substantial area of agreement on what fits within the prevailing perspective, or, what scientific historian Thomas S. Kuhn would call the "prevailing paradigm."[12] For example, those *outside* our society's prevailing perspective might include people under the influence of drugs; those who believe in Ptolemaic astronomy; or those who embrace mass murder as a political option.

Mead relates the prevailing social perspective to schemes of action which project the participating individuals into the future.[13] For example, if the prevailing social perspective is that the stock market is weak, an individual may decide to wait out the recession by holding on to her stock. Her sense of the future, and those of other investors, is, of course, subject to change, and will affect how she and others act.

Perspectives also include moral judgments, which also affect the creation of the future. Where Adam Smith discounted morality as irrelevant to an analysis of the market, Karl Marx saw it as the central issue, for example, that workers were paid less than the value they contributed to the product. Such a view for Marx justified the Communist Revolution.

According to Meade, history exists *only* as it is prehended from the point of view of the present. Thus, the very nature of the French Revolution will change depending on whether it is interpreted from the point of view of modern libertarian or of Marxist politics. The introduction of new evidence and changes of perspective, including the prevailing rules for interpreting that evidence, create that freedom which any society has in interpreting its own history. How that freedom is carried out has today become an angry debate between modernists, relying on "objective" means of securing evidence and constructing history, and postmodernists, relying more on subjective or class orientations (see chapter 11).

Mead's position is to reject a fully objective notion of history, which he describes as "the picture of reality as a four-dimensional continuum of space-time, of events and intervals, forever determined by its own geometry, and into which we venture with our own subjective frames of reference..." In this sense, Mead emerges as the first postmodernist.[14] For Mead, minds are embodied. We prehend the universe from our perspectives, which includes our societies; and these societies construct their past as causal preludes to their present and future. History is then a construction of mind enmeshed in body, in society, and in time.[15]

As in the physical sciences, prehensive thought provides Mead a bridge between appearance and reality, and between subjectivity and objectivity, as it did for Whitehead. With Mead's contribution, the social sciences become a working part of the new paradigm.

John Dewey

American philosopher and educator John Dewey (1859–1952) provided major philosophic support for Mead's social psychology. Read today, Dewey still seems one of the wisest voices of the twentieth century, uniting a vibrant core theory of knowledge with aesthetic and political concerns.[16] How many philosophers today seek contemporary relevance as avidly as did Dewey? How many would ask of their work, as did Dewey, "Does it end in conclusions which, when they are referred back to ordinary life-experiences and their predicaments, render them more significant, more luminous to us, and make our dealings with them more fruitful? Or does it terminate in rendering the things of ordinary experience more opaque than they were before . . ?"[17]

Like Mead, Dewey sees the purposeful, interactive, experiential situation involving individuals in nature or society as the basic unit of existence, and secondarily of discourse and philosophy. All other notions can be derived from Dewey's understanding of this primary process, as he spells out its implications for the physical and social sciences, education, aesthetics, and politics. (In this chapter, we will be taking up primarily his core theory of knowledge. For his vital theories of education and politics, see chapter 12.)

For Dewey, having the interactive, purposeful situation or field as his fundamental unit of knowledge does not mean self-enclosure or solipsism. Dewey presumes that nature exists independently of us, but that it is not an object of knowledge before it enters our field as an object of action or inquiry. Dewey writes, "I am not questioning as a fact of *knowledge* that certain things *are* the stimuli of visual and auditory perception. I am pointing out that we are aware of the stimuli only in terms of our response to them and of the consequences of this response.... When color is perceived, it is in order to paint..."[18]

As in modern physics, we conceive realities as information, which is the product of a field in which we are a part. For Dewey, as for Mead, information or physical existence in isolation from such fields is not meaningful.[19] Nature coerces, but it does so within the interactive situation in which we live and attempt to meet our needs.

For Dewey, knowledge is an abstraction from a process which he calls "knowledge-getting." In knowledge-getting, we interact with an environment which exists beyond us; it is not just a series of events taking place in the cortex. Thus a perceived stone is not just a neural event in the brain, but part of the environment of the perceiver. Interacting with an object means interacting with the object in its environment, for example, not just lifting a stone, but lifting the stone out of the water.

Dewey's "situation," it should be clear, is very close to Whitehead's "field" or "prehension." Life is inseparable from its environment, thus providing a physical argument against the notion of self-sufficiency. He writes, "An organism does not live *in* an environment; it lives by means of an environment."[20]

For Dewey, needs and goals are as much a part of the field as are objects and facts; they are not some extrinsic matter or separate metaphysical categories introduced into situations. As organisms progress, their complex organization allows them greater sensitivity to their environment, and more capacity for feeling needs and satisfying them, themes further developed by Harry Stack Sullivan and Jane Loevinger.

Although Dewey lacked Whitehead's expertise in physics, his thinking, like that of Mead and Sullivan, was grounded in physical field theory. His epistemology, however, was devoid of any hint of Whitehead's Platonic metaphysics of permanence, which I have called Whitehead's "second explanation." Thus, Dewey is not concerned with discerning the mind of God or God's "judgment" of any specific occasion. In social situations, Dewey holds, an individual should better spend his time understanding the needs of a fellow individual in a particular situation, than attempting to apply God's preexisting ethical laws. Dewey's epistemology, devoid of Whitehead's Platonic metaphysics of permanence, would form the basis of his well-developed social theories.

Dewey's intense focus on the situation means that there can be no split between experiential reality (means) and ethics (ends). Ethics will become more sensitive or developed as situations and their implications for action become better understood. What Dewey has in mind is what is meant by "situational ethics," but ethics which are informed by as broad a sweep of experience and scientific and social research as is possible.

But Dewey, like Whitehead, holds that each situation reflects its specific history and its involvement in a larger field. In addition, terms and meanings change as the situation develops. When science is freed from the contemplation of invariant Being, Dewey writes, it becomes "an affair of time and history intelligently managed."[21] This represents Dewey's nominalism, a theory developed in medieval scholasticism which said that the particulars of the world, rather than their class characteristics or generalized essences, are the realities.[22]

For Dewey, ideas are "operational" *within* a goal-oriented situation. Dewey writes, "Ideas are operational in that they instigate and direct further operations of observation; they are proposals and plans for acting upon existing conditions to bring new facts to light and to organize all the selected facts into a coherent whole."[23] This epistemology roots even the simplest proposition in a purposeful context.

Facts are equally instrumental within this ongoing, interactive experience. For example, for a medical researcher seeking a cure for a disease, the destruction of certain cells is evidence of the existence of the bacteria. This, in turn, alerts the researcher to look for further confirmatory evidence before finally deciding on the appropriate form of treatment, say, an antibiotic.

A similar analysis applies to Dewey's concept of truth, which he takes from William James. As James writes, "Truth *happens* to an idea. It *becomes* true, is *made* true by events. Its veracity *is* in fact an event, a process: the process namely of its verifying itself, its *veri-fication*. Its validity is the process of its valid-*ation*."[24]

Equally, cause and effect become parts of a single connected history or ongoing situation. Dewey writes, "The conception of 'effect' is essentially teleological; the effect is the end to be reached; the differential means to be employed constitute its *cause* when they are selected and brought into interaction with one another."[25]

For Dewey, all the terms that we use to describe reality have their origin in the interactive, experiential situation; any breakout from that process is an abstraction. Equally, distinctions of subjective and objective, mental and physical, or the world of qualities and Galileo's and Newton's world of matter-in-motion (the distinction Locke makes between secondary and primary qualities) are all abstractions or constructions from the primary, experiential situation of goal-reaching or inquiry.[26]

All these elements can be identified and expressed by language, which is a product of social relations in which human beings communicate together to achieve common objectives. Like Mead, Dewey is clear that language does not map a previously existing system of eternal Platonic forms or Aristotelean essences. Rather, language is the vehicle which identifies those elements which achieve prominence within a developing social context of mutual assistance and direction. Thus, the word "tiger" means what is to be mutually hunted.

Abstracted from their situations of origin, words can enter into new situations, generating new meanings. For example, "tiger" can be taken out of the purposeful situation of its origin in hunting, to characterize an aggressive man. It also can be used to depict all animals with similar characteristics. Only in this way, Dewey says, does language achieve its generic or universal character, which grooms it for its unjustified use in classical philosophy as the lexicon of invariant, eternal ideas.

For Dewey, ideas do not exist in themselves as Platonic ideas or invariant Aristotelean essences. They are not the supreme reality of which the specific and less real partake. The idea of a tiger is, for Dewey, an abstraction of *experienced* tigers, not an eternal essence of which the specific and less real existential tigers of the world partake.

As we have seen, for Dewey, language has an important social as well as epistemological dimension. Like Meade, Dewey sees the experience of language, either gestural or verbal, as what might be called empathic reflection. It is perceiving how one's words will be understood by the person to whom they are addressed, as well as what they mean for oneself. He provides the follow example:

> *A* requests *B* to bring him something, to which *A* points, say a flower.... *B* learns that the movement *is* a pointing; he responds to it not in itself, but as an index of something else.... [B] responds to the thing from the standpoint of *A*. He perceives the thing as it may function in *A*'s experience, instead of just egocentrically. Similarly, *A* in making the request conceives the thing not only in its direct relationship to himself, but as a thing

capable of being grasped and handled by *B*. He sees the thing as
it may function in *B*'s experience.[27]

Such social experience is the genesis of mind, as it is for Mead and Edelman, and, as we shall see, for Harry Stack Sullivan.

Thus, Dewey sees the interactive and collective social process as primary. The individual is a later development, both in the culture and in the family. Failure to recognize the social nature of mind leads to the primacy of introspection in philosophic thought, dramatized by Descartes. It also allows for a belief in fully competent individuals as the *antecedent* condition of the social contract, as in Locke, as well as the notion of pure or transcendental reason, as in Plato, Kant, and Hegel.[28] Dewey's philosophy offers a comprehensive attack on permanence in virtually every manifestation in which it has appeared in Western thought. He writes:

> The permanent enables us to rest, it gives peace; the variable, the changing, is a constant challenge.... Philosophy, thinking at large, allows itself to be diverted into absurd search for an intellectual philosopher's stone of absolutely wholesale generalizations, thus isolating that which is permanent in a function and for a purpose, and converting it into the intrinsically eternal, conceived either...as that which is the same at all times, or as that which is indifferent to time, out of time.[29]

Every principal notion of permanence in Western thought comes under attack: a supernatural being, the eternal soul, eternal ideas, and invariant laws of nature and history.

Dewey's answer to the problems of philosophy is strict adherence to the full implications of contingency and interrelationship. "To see the organism *in* nature, the nervous system in the organism, the brain in the nervous system, the cortex in the brain is the answer to the problems which haunt philosophy. And when thus seen they will be seen to be *in*, not as marbles are in a box but as events are in history, in a moving, growing never finished process."[30] What Dewey did was reexamine every major field of thought, and give to modern life a sense of relationship and adventure which seems implicit in the very nature of the experienced world. With Whitehead, Mead, and Sullivan, Dewey recreates the world in process, and provides a philosophy for his century, and perhaps beyond.

Harry Stack Sullivan

George Herbert Mead's interactive and embodied theory of social psychology, and John Dewey's philosophy of interaction, find their counterpart in Harry Stack Sullivan's interpersonal theory of psychiatry. Sullivan (1892–1949), an American psychiatrist, while grounded in Freudian psychology, made a sharp break with Freud by basing his psychology on a view of the world which drew on the new physics, as opposed to the mechanistic world of Newton. Essentially, Sullivan used the field model to place the developing child in a physical and social environment, and then explained psychic disturbance as malfunctioning interactions within that system. This work fitted well into the developing paradigm of Whitehead, Mead, and Dewey.

Since Descartes, Western thought had been dominated by the model of a fully conscious, innately rational person, who knew his or her own interests. This model was essentially the secular version of the eternal, rational soul, metaphysically separate from the body, which had been developed by Greek thought and appropriated by the Christian Church. The model was questioned by nineteenth century writers from Johann Wolfgang von Goethe to Fyodor Dostoyevsky and by philosophers such as Sören Kierkegaard and Friedrich Nietzsche, who showed man's underside and irrationality, but the model continued to dominate Anglo-American philosophic thought well into the twentieth century.

However, psychiatry, beginning in the last decade of the nineteenth century with the work of the Viennese Sigmund Freud (1856–1939),[31] would discard the exclusive concern of the psyche with consciousness and rationality. Freud would dominate American psychiatry until well after World War II, forming a curious counterweight to Watsonian behaviorism.

Freud's early preoccupation was with the effects of trauma on "normal" sexual maturation, which he equated with heterosexual, genital sex.[32] According to Freud, trauma, such as incest, fixes libidinal or sexual energy in infantile forms of sexual expression, which are contemporary with the trauma. Energy may also be fixed by "constructive traumas," for example, in which the child *imagines* the incest.[33] Because infantile forms of sexual expression are unacceptable in adult life, we repress them, and the libidinal energy attached to them appears in covert forms, such as verbal slips, dreams, and neurotic symptoms.

Freud, whose thinking was dominated by the Newtonian deterministic science of his day, maintained that nothing can enter the psychic sphere, indeed, the world in general, for which there are not clear causes. Libidinal energy, equivalent to physical energy, is always conserved. The libido's transformation from its original form, for example, infantile sexuality, into neurosis or dream constructions corresponds to energy's transformation from motion to other forms, such as heat, light, or sound. Neurotic fixation of libidinal energy can also be seen as corresponding to kinetic energy's transformation in physics to *potential* energy. At the same time, however, Freud is never completely reductive. In his theories, energy or force is always displayed or altered by meaning, and meanings are only changed by psychic forces.

Neurosis occurs because a person may not be able to release fixated and excessive libidinal energy in acceptable ways. The agent that prescribes and limits these ways is the superego. Originally the censoring voice of the parents, which is internalized, the superego becomes the censoring and normatively prescriptive voice of society, as the individual emerges into the adult world from nuclear-family life.

By mastering the "reality principle," that is, the way the world works, the ego, in early Freud, becomes the broker in that world for the "pleasure principle," by finding outlets for the libidinal drives. These outlets are direct, as in sexual relations, or indirect, taking sublimated forms, as in art. The "pleasure principle" was a fairly direct appropriation from the thinking of Locke and Hume, which ultimately reduced human motivation to the seeking of pleasure and avoidance of pain. Psychoanalysis, which consists of the patient reliving earlier traumas (or "constructive" traumas) by talking with a therapist, allows at least some of the trapped libidinal energy to be released. This process is also facilitated by the patient learning appropriate adult forms of relationships, or of sublimation.

As his work developed, Freud began to see that the ego's task is far more complicated than merely finding outlets for sexuality or aggression. In his later writings, the ego, seen as directly concerned with achieving "mastery," takes on the autonomous functions of personality construction. As the ego matures, it becomes increasingly developed, or complex.

In his study of dreams, Freud found a close approximation to works of art, which demonstrate psychic integration. (In surrealism, there would be virtually a direct transcription of dreams.) In his later writings, he begins to speculate on the fact that there are two sources of libidinal energy, Eros and Death. Eros, according to Freud, naturally integrates energy and the psychic content to which it is attached; death naturally decomposes such material. To the extent that Eros can work without conflict, it creates increasingly complexity, which is the basis not only of the integration of dreams and artworks, but of an increasingly complicated and differentiated ego. These latter writings, which was largely lost on the general public, who associated Freud with his earlier "drive theory," provided the basis for the next several generations of psychiatric theorists, such as Erik Erikson and Jane Loevinger.[34]

When Harry Stack Sullivan began his work in the 1920s, he went beyond his Freudian mentors in associating psychiatry with scientific thought which questioned the duality of soul and body. His work is allied specifically with the social psychology of Mead (Sullivan was a medical student at the University of Chicago during Mead's tenure), and with the philosophy of Whitehead and Dewey. Sullivan was also influenced by the anthropologists Ruth Benedict and Edward Sapir, who emphasized the role of the cultures they studied in shaping their members.[35]

Sullivan's mature thought is defined in a posthumous book, *The Interpersonal Theory of Psychiatry*, culled from his later lectures and writings.[36] It provides no less than a modal biography of a developing individual, describing how an infant constructs the world from his or her earliest experiences, and then develops into a mature human being. Here Sullivan shows how our earliest mental processes are one with our physical needs, and how these needs are defined in complex relations between the young organism and its physical and social fields, a mode of thought which shows Sullivan's reliance on field theory.

Far from having prescriptive, genetically determined instincts, or a rigidly prescribed path for psychosexual growth, a human being, Sullivan finds, is extraordinarily susceptible to social influence.[37] One reason the infant is so receptive, in addition to an open-ended genetic inheritance, is the infant's extraordinary helplessness and dependence on what Sullivan calls the "mothering one" to supply his or her physicochemical needs. The infant experiences periodic tensions which can become life-threatening and terrifying, due to lack of oxygen, sugar, water, or adequate body temperature. Gradually, the infant develops foresight as to how to meet these needs. Sullivan, like Mead, embeds objects and *qualia*, like "warm" or "pink," in these developing action schemes. Sullivan writes, "The whole philosophical doctrine of representation might, if one wished, be wrapped up in this statement that successful action creates or is identified with...foreseen relief."[38]

The infant starts with instinctive actions like crying, which evoke reactions from the mothering one. The infant's notion of cause and effect develops from the efficacy of those actions. The mothering one's nipple becomes a *sign* that satisfaction of hunger will follow.[39] From this, it is clear to Sullivan that signs are elaborations of sentient experience, or what he, like Whitehead and Mead, calls "prehensions," and that they exist " 'in' experience and not outside in objective 'reality,' "[40] or independently as Platonic ideas. The similarity of Sullivan's reconstruction of infantile experience to Dewey's purposeful action could not be clearer.

This is well-illustrated in Sullivan's description of the infant's earliest interactions with the environment. According to Sullivan, the infant transacts his or her needs through specific zones of interaction with the environment, such as "the nipple-investing, nipple-holding, and sucking apparatus.... The zone of interaction may then be considered to be the end station in the necessary varieties of communal existence with the physicochemical world, the world of the infrahuman living, and the personal world."[41]

Sullivan further shows how physical relations transform themselves into social symbols. The infant begins to form concepts of the "good nipple," which provides satisfaction, and the "bad nipple," which provides anxiety. (There is also the useless or "wrong nipple," which for one reason or another does not produce milk.) The infant, by combining many experiences from different zones of interaction, arrives at the concepts of a "good" and "bad mother," associated with the "good" and "bad nipples."[42]

From the infant's social involvements will come the basis of his or her personality.[43] Like Mead, Sullivan defines personality in relational terms, as *"the relatively enduring pattern of recurrent interpersonal situations which characterize a human life."*[44]

The infant personifies three phases of what eventually will become "me." According to Sullivan, these are the "good-me," the "bad-me," and the "not-me," which are all related to the body. He explains:

> *Good-me* is the beginning personification which organizes experience in which satisfactions have been enhanced by rewarding increments of tenderness, which come to the infant because the mothering one is pleased with the way things are going.... *Bad-me*, on the other hand, is the beginning personification which organizes experience in which increasing degrees of anxiety are

associated with behavior involving the mothering one in its more-or-less clearly prehended interpersonal setting.... When we come to...the *not-me*, we are in a different field—one which we know about only through certain very special circumstances.... The personification of not-me is most conspicuously encountered by people who are having a severe schizophrenic episode...[45]

"Not-me," then, is the awful, dreadful unknown, which has been dis-associated from the body and the "good-" and "bad-" me's by extreme anxiety, and which forms the basis of nightmares, uncanny experiences, and psychosis. Sullivan believes that the "not-me" occurs when severe anxiety paralyzes the infant's capacity to fit experience into any developing pattern of cause and effect or control, that is, any scheme of purposeful action.

Sullivan's self-system is created negatively, to avoid anxiety. But Sullivan also says that there is a positive reason for its creation, which is to gain gratification. Here the infant, interacting with the environment, and particularly the mothering one, establishes a set of interrelated schemes for achieving gratification. It is this set of schemes which constitutes the infant's self-system or personality. Unlike the soul, the self-system is constantly developing.

Sullivan makes clear that the self-system is not the incorporation or introjection of the mothering one, who as a mature adult, with a complex and developed ego, is radically different from the part she plays in the infant's schemes of interaction with her. In subsequent stages, however, the self-system will develop into the mature adult, and will achieve a complexity *comparable* to that of the mothering one.[46]

I've chosen to concentrate on Sullivan's discussion of the first few months of life because it demonstrates most powerfully his general philosophic orientation, and sets up the developmental scheme which carries the infant into maturity. In this way, Sullivan, extending the work of Sigmund Freud, serves as a bridge between the social psychology of Mead and the philosophy of Dewey, to the developmental psychology of Jane Loevinger.

Our central concern has been with how Sullivan's view of psychiatry reflects a larger orientation to the world. Sullivan's enmeshment of the newborn organism in a social and physical environment; his stress on the continuum between the physical world and the mind, and between what is conventionally called "nonsymbolic" and "symbolic" behavior; and his description of the development of the self-system, all challenge philosophies based on notions of permanence from Plato through Hegel. Here there is no independent soul, no preexisting set of eternal ideas, no invariant reason, but enmeshment in the physical and experiential world.

The Developmental Psychology of Jane Loevinger

Like Harry Stack Sullivan, the contemporary American psychologist Jane Loevinger sees her human subject as participating in an ongoing dialogue between a developing ego structure and its social environment. As she depicts it, the evolution of the ego structure in the lifetime of each individual shows the same tension between inner self-organization and outer relationship that we have seen in every field of thought reviewed in part II.

Loevinger uses empirical testing, principally sentence-completion tests, rather than the psychiatric interview, as her main source of evidence. From these data, she has constructed a scheme of classification which shows that human beings, rather than having invariant souls, follow a line of development along a route of increasing complexity.[47] By her emphasis on complexity, Loevinger suggests the work of Alfred North Whitehead, the American philosophers J.T. Fraser and Alexander J. Argyros, and others we have examined. She also represents the full realization of Freud's later view that the ego achieves autonomous complexity.

Loevinger believes that her work emerges logically out of the mainstream of post-Freudian thought, and particularly from the work of Harry Stack Sullivan.[48] Loevinger writes, "Sullivan's conception of the self-system, his version of the ego, is a process, it is social, and it is a structure; that is given in his very terminology. It is also purposive and concerned with meanings. It operates holistically to the same extent that the ego does in much of psychoanalytic theory..."[49]

According to Loevinger, each developmental stage of the ego incorporates and transmutes the previous one, and prepares for the next one. The stages are invariant in their order, that is, a person must pass through each one to reach whatever final stage she achieves. Barring illness, deep trauma, or senile regression, the stages are irreversible.

Loevinger's claim that ego development is nonreductive means that it is not a function of some simpler factor—as human motivation was a function of seeking pleasure and avoiding pain for Locke and Hume; and as it was, for the most part, in the early Freud's "pleasure principle." Nor are Loevinger's developmental stages completely correlated with or dependent upon intelligence or cognitive development, as in the work of Piaget. Although Loevinger confirms that more intelligent or cognitively developed people are more likely to reach higher stages of ego development, she believes that they do not necessarily do so. Nor is ego development directly correlated with or dependent upon age, as people of radically different ages will reach different terminal stages. (The age groups, however, *will* show a typical typology or set of characteristics for each stage.) Also, the extent of progression through the stages is influenced by heredity, but not wholly determined by it.

The following description of Loevinger's stages draws directly on her own summary.[50] To read it most usefully, imagine people you know, of different ages, exhibiting these characteristics. As the stages proceed, the important issue is the increasingly complexity of the ego structure; its implications for how the person processes and deals with information (as in Fraser and Argyros); and how he or she conceives and functions in purposeful, social situations (as in Mead, Dewey, and Sullivan). In each stage, the world expands, as it achieves greater differentiation and complexity.

Presocial Stage. The infant dwells in an egoless or autistic state, where the self is undifferentiated from the world of sensations and objects he or she experiences.

Symbiotic Stage. There is object stability, but a symbiotic relation with the mother. A bottle is the same bottle it was a moment ago, but the child has not fully differentiated itself from its mother.

Impulsive Stage. Differentiation from the mother has occurred. Impulses—"No!," "Do it myself!"—are curbed by rewards and punishments that the child believes are immanent in things. For example, a child, like a cat, will be afraid of a rolled-up newspaper that has been used for spanking. The child experiences other people as "bad" or "good" *to me*, with little existence in their own right. The vocabulary of older children will contain words like "sick," "high," "turned on" and "hot," referring to bodily, not mental, states. There is present-time orientation; motives, causes, and logical justifications are confused. A child remaining in this stage may be called "uncontrollable" or "incorrigible," and sees his troubles as located outside himself.

Self-Protective Stage. Impulses are controlled by anticipation of rewards and punishments. There are rules, but the main rule is "don't get caught." The cause of blame is still external; the fault lies with "other people," "my eyes," or "my figure." Older people remaining in this stage see life as a zero-sum game; work is generally considered to be onerous; the good life is the easy life.

Conformist Stage. People have "internalized" the values of the group, or of principal people in their lives. They identify their welfare with that of the family or group; they accept group rules, with disapproval being a potent sanction. "Right" and "wrong" are defined by compliance with rules rather than by the real consequences of acts. People are expected to be similar within broad groupings—boys and girls, or whites and blacks. Niceness, helpfulness, and cooperation are valued. Inner life is seen in terms such as "happy," "sad," and "glad." Moral clichés are common; there is concern with appearances, social acceptance, reputation, and material things.

Self-Aware Level: Transition from Conformist to Conscientious Stage. Loevinger says that this is the modal level in U.S. society, the society on which her study is primarily based. The level is characterized by an increase in self-awareness, including some allowable differences from social norms, and the appreciation of multiple possibilities in situations. Words for feelings, which reflect the individual's relation to other persons or to the group, include "lonely," "embarrassed," "homesick," "self-confident," and often, "self-conscious." Persons at this level still do not fully see other people as having a rich internal life, but continue to see others in relation to themselves. Nor do they see moral rules as primarily creating better conditions for a group or society, but rather as the rules within which one is expected to live.

Conscientious Stage. This stage is characterized by long-term, self-evaluated goals and ideals; differentiated self-criticism; and a sense of responsibility for self and others. The self is now a discernible entity differentiated from the world; the world is seen as independent, with needs separate from the self. This stage is rarely reached before thirteen or fourteen years of age. Loevinger writes: "Where the Self-Protective person obeys rules in order to avoid getting into trouble and the Conformist obeys rules because the group sanctions them, the Conscientious person evaluates and chooses the rules for himself." The person differentiates between appearances and reality, and social expectations and moral standards; and more complex polarities—trivial versus important, lust versus love, dependent versus independent, and outward appearances versus inner life. One also finds at this stage more accurate empathy and mutuality in interpersonal relations.

Individualistic Level: Transition from Conscientious to Autonomous Stages. At this transitional level, the person is sensitive to emotional dependence and problems of individuality, and better able to recognize individual differences and the complexity of circumstances. One also finds here a greater interest in relationships, less moralism, a better ability to tolerate paradox and contradiction, and more understanding of psychological causality and development. Thus, in interpreting a play like Sophocles' *Oedipus Rex*, an audience member at this stage would carefully weigh the circumstances to see if Oedipus knowingly killed his father or slept with his mother, and might go further and see the drama, as did Freud, as a playing out of unconscious wishes. Despite such increasing subtlety, the viewer at this stage, as opposed to someone at the next one, might still see Oedipus's basic conflict as being with the laws of the state, rather than with his own unconscious wishes.

Autonomous Stage. The autonomous person is capable of dealing with inner conflict, and sees the world as nuanced and multifaceted, rather than consisting of polar opposites. She or he also has higher toleration for ambiguity; is willing to allow others autonomy; and cherishes personal ties. An interest in psychological causation and personal fulfillment partly supplants a need to achieve. There is accurate expression of feelings, such as sensuality, sorrow, and existential humor, appropriate to different roles. There is also a realistic view of the self; and the holding of broad, abstract social ideals, such as justice.

Integrated Stage. This stage manifests the transcendence of inner conflict, and self-actualization. At this stage, people achieve a full sense of who they are in relation to the world, and pass beyond indecision and unreconciled views to a full integration. Perhaps the earliest model of a fully integrated human being we have in literature is *Oedipus at Colonus*, in which Sophocles gives us the portrait of a man who has resolved his inner doubts and achieved the peace of a higher understanding. Shakespeare's Prospero in *The Tempest* is perhaps another example.

Each one of these stages, as Loevinger's collaborator, Augusto Blasi, points out, constitutes a self-maintaining structure or organization the individual establishes in relation to the environment. The aim is not just survival, but "the desire to satisfy one's needs more adequately, to become more competent, to grasp the world more fully..."[51] Such a notion looks very much like the concept of 'organism' advanced by Whitehead, Kauffman, Margulis, Mead, Dewey, and Sullivan. The organism actively selects from the environment, though it doesn't totally control it. In Piaget's terms, the individual or organism "accommodates" to the environment and "assimilates," by altering its own internal structure.

What drives the system forward toward greater consciousness and more autonomy or freedom? Blasi, rightly, I believe, distinguishes logical possibility, provided by Piaget's cognitive development, from personality development. An example of the former would be knowing someone's feelings through role playing; of the latter, being someone who will *act* on that knowledge. Clearly, cognitive development is generally a necessary but not a sufficient condition for personality change, and represents an abstraction from the full involvement in the purposeful situation which implies action.

Loevinger points out that ego development usually takes place when the individual is exposed to what she calls "pacers." These are people and social situations which provide higher-level models, and so urge the individual forward.[52] Such people may be mentors, or teachers, or more advanced peers. Schools, businesses, or voluntary organizations can create "pacer" situations by training their members to handle tasks which require increasingly higher levels of ego development.

Although culture may not be entirely responsible for personal development, it is clearly a necessary condition. Indeed, one can imagine that certain cultures might not have sufficient space for Loevinger's "higher" stages at all. A clear example would be paleolithic hunting and gathering societies, with quite simple languages. The different handling of gender roles in cultures, for example, would also influence a person's attainment of different levels. Cultures and subcultures might also determine the specific *nature* of the stages, and, despite Loevinger's disclaimer here, even to some extent their *sequence*. In a culture that values conformity, such as traditional Chinese culture, conformity would play a different role than in a somewhat more individualistic culture, such as we find in contemporary western Europe or the United States.[53]

Despite Loevinger's necessary failure to construct a universal sequence of stages, the individual's urge toward greater freedom and consciousness across a broad spectrum of cultures suggests that the urge is indeed autonomous and universal, though culturally embedded. This urge would then be allied to what Whitehead calls the "creative advance" by including a notion of complexity free of specific cultural biases, and particularly that of the population upon which her work was normed.

Ego development, however, need not be an end in itself. Various schemes of self-actualization, which stop with a sense of personal fulfillment—the "wonder of me"—leave one with a hollow sense of inadequacy. Beyond personal fulfillment, and as a result of full involvement in social situations, lies the moral notion of responsibility. Loevinger writes:

> Since responsibility, by definition, consists in establishing relations of consistency between self and actions, the structure of responsibility must be related logically to the basic rules presiding over the definition of oneself as a person and determining the meaning that one has for himself and that the world has for him. Those rules correspond to what this book [*Ego Development*] has called ego structure. Because a person understands himself to be essentially and unequivocally thus and so—his self-definition, he also understands the actions that are related to his essential characteristics to be necessarily his—his responsibility. The obligation to act may come from different sources such as authority, social pressure, his conscience, or the person herself; responsibility, nonetheless, is ultimately always a response of the ego (or of the person) that defines him as necessarily related to that source of obligation.[54]

Each of the principal authors discussed in this chapter, George Herbert Mead, John Dewey, Harry Stack Sullivan, and Jane Loevinger, has sought to construct the relationship between the environment and the individual. Each sees this relationship as a dialogue in which the individual's concept of the world progresses with his or her growth in personality or ego. In imbedding the notion of responsibility in this developmental process, Loevinger makes the "ought" a decision of character. In chapter 12, we will return to responsibility as a central notion, following a review of the present situation, which establishes the milieu in which that responsibility must be exercised.

Chapter Eleven

In This Moment

By the rivers of Babylon, there we sat down, yes, we wept,
       when we remembered Zion.
We hanged our harps upon the willows in the midst thereof.
For there they that carried us away captive required of us
         asong; and they that wasted us required of us
         mirth, saying,
Sing us one of the songs of Zion.
How shall we sing the Lord's song in a strange land?

Psalm 137[1]

During the 1980s, my wife and I participated in several fact-finding delegations to embattled Central American countries—Guatemala, El Salvador, Honduras, and Nicaragua, the latter then in the throes of the *contra* war. Our hosts, representatives of labor, human rights, and peasant organizations, often began their talks with the phrase, "*En este momento, la situación...*" ("the situation in this moment..."). They would then describe the present difficult conditions in which they were working to bring their country to where they felt it should be.

This is our time to take stock. We make our assessment at a time of crisis, in which, after a century of wars, we face still more conflicts, as well as a limitless war against terrorism. We will begin by considering our changed views of science and of history which deny us the kinds of assurance afforded earlier generations. We will assess the globalization of the economy, with its promises and pitfalls, and the new society which has arisen as a result of radical changes in technology. We will also discuss the decline of political participation, and analyze how deconstructionist thought attempts to deal with the modern world, and how, in my view, it fails to offer a solution.

This chapter thus addresses our "situation in this moment." Then, in our final chapter, we will see if the ideas we have discussed in part II come together to offer a viable paradigm for understanding our world and dealing with its problems.

An Uncertain Nature

A loss of certainty has infected virtually every area of our lives. One such area has been our relations to nature. For the ancients, the natural world had existed for eternity and would so continue, and so offered an eternal receptacle or container for mortal human beings. In the science of Aristotle, the continuity of nature included not only the eternal celestial bodies, but all the species of plants and animals, whose essences he believed were also eternal and invariant. This sense of the continuity of nature was strongly upheld by Galileo and Newton, who viewed nature as ruled by eternal laws, prescribed by the Creator, extending to the furthest reaches of the universe. Even if human beings and their fate were no longer as unquestionably at the center of the world as they had been in the Age of Faith, the natural world itself could be relied upon to continue on its basic course forever.

In the nineteenth century, as we have seen, this assurance began to dissolve. After Darwin, it became increasingly difficult to believe in the stability of species, or in a moment of creation in which these species were formed once and for all by God.

In the twentieth and now twenty-first centuries, uncertainty about the stability or even continued existence of our world has come from a variety of sources. Quantum mechanics has severely questioned the notion of determinism, which had provided the ultimate certainties of Newtonian physics. Scientists across a number of disciplines have also brought forward evidence that matter, and particularly organisms, in their pursuit of complexity, make up their own laws or systems of organization and thereby evade predictability. From cosmology, we learn that the universe may well have a beginning and may well have an end, although such considerations are still speculative. We also learn that we are quickly eroding the natural resources of the planet, particularly its atmosphere, forests, soil, and oil and water supply. We can no longer fully entertain that ultimate sense of stability, that at death we will return to the eternal one-ness of a stable universe.

This new view in no way mitigates science's increasing capacity to in-form us about the infinitely interesting world we live in; to provide us a sense of community with the natural world and even with the derivative, artificial worlds of human invention; and to furnish the intellectual base for meeting human needs. Nor does the lack of scientific certainty, including the impermanence of the system which it describes or the lack of a unified or stable means of its description, detract from the wonder which it un-folds. Indeed, for many scientists this sense of wonder rivals in its profun-dity earlier feelings allied to religion or God. Rather, the lack of certainty in science means simply that we must learn to live with the contingent and changing nature of our existence.

But for some people, such a loss of certainty about nature has been alienating. For them, the world has become estranged, if not hostile, and no longer the generative source or final secure resting place for their lives.

An Uncertain History

In the twentieth century, history also failed to provide the sense of permanence and certainty we lost in science and the natural world. On the contrary, the history of the last hundred years has provided us with a series of disquieting disasters. In the first years of the twenty-first century, there is little assurance that historical certainty is on the way.[2]

In the past, a confidence in history was a conviction that, despite dis-ruptions, civilized life would continue, and groups to which one was loyal or attached—family, tribe, church, society, city, or civilization—would endure. Wars or social upheavals would disturb but not destroy this continuity. At death, one would be held and preserved in the collective memory of these groups, and, though no longer an active participant, one would persist as an influence, thus guaranteeing one's "immortality." Equally important, works of science, scholarship, or art would survive their creators, granting them continuity forever as the works joined their respective traditions.

Such beliefs are perhaps less gratifying than the absolute metaphysics of permanence, in which souls or even bodies achieve immortality and dwell forever with God; or the conviction that the ideas of civilization will survive without historical condition in the timeless Platonic world or in

God's mind; or Hegel's view that civilization will inevitably achieve the fulfillment of divine purpose. But beliefs in the mere continuity of history are not without their satisfactions. Such was the message at the end of *The Epic of Gilgamesh*: The hero will die, but the city or civilized life will go on forever. That message was also an important component of the idea of the People in Judaism: Individuals would perish, but the People would continue as a sanctified group.

Western civilization has wavered back and forth between this sense of continuity and the threat of annihilation. Ancient history is a chronicle of fallen cities and nations, with the attendant fear that one's city or state will be the next to be lost. The Book of Lamentations in the Hebrew Bible, with its agonizing depiction of the sack of Jerusalem, is the great biblical poem of such an apocalypse. For Jesus, and for his followers for several hundred years, the end of the world was imminent. For Saint Augustine, in the fifth century, the fall of the Roman Empire could only be balanced in the scale of certainty by the eternal City of God. Throughout much of the Middle Ages, intermittent fear of annihilation from barbarian raids, invasions, plagues, or a divinely sent apocalypse, haunted Europe, although such anxiety was relieved by the hope of ultimate immortality.

By the Renaissance, fears of total destruction on this earth had receded. Wars continued, but they were, for the most part, fought by relatively small, professional armies and governed by codes of etiquette, with limited territorial objectives. Indeed, they were frequently more concerned with shows of strength than with massive slaughter, much less wholesale destruction of cultures. Civilization, it was believed, was not at risk.

At the same time, living standards increased, life expectancy improved, and technology began its exponential growth. Human beings embraced various secular forms of belief in progress, whether that progress was to be measured by the inevitable triumph of reason in the Enlightenment, the elimination of all poverty through the Industrial Revolution, the establishment of the democratic state through the "blessings of democracy," or of the "classless and just society" through the Communist Revolution. A belief in the teleology, or a necessary endpoint to history, such as Hegel expresses, replaced for many the earlier notion of the eventual Kingdom of God, or the second coming of Christ.

This last century has not been kind to any of these beliefs. World War I began to approach "total war," involving whole populations. Taking full advantage of a new technology, it wiped out a generation of young men on both sides, and, particularly through protracted trench warfare, subjected the survivors to forms of mental and physical torture which, for many, permanently disrupted their faith in civilized life. Historians and others felt that an era had passed, that the form of civilization which Europe had taken since the Renaissance had ended.

Similarly, in World War II, which was even more destructive, many who had directly experienced the trauma of combat, military occupation, saturation bombing, or the concentration camps never fully believed in the reality of their subsequent lives, although they went on living, and frequently did not fully face these doubts until old age.[3] Certain articles of faith, such as beliefs in the goodness of human beings or that humankind was on a track of progressive enlightenment, were seriously eroded.

At the end of World War II, the explosion of atomic bombs at Hiroshima and Nagasaki initiated an age in which, for the first time, the end of all civilized life seemed a real possibility. Those of us who are middle-aged or older still remember how, for more than forty years, the world lived in the presence of a doomsday aggregation of nuclear bombers and ballistic missiles; of dire warnings and war games with their ghastly scenarios ("Will the living envy the dead?"); and of the prospect of clouds of nuclear waste and polluted land beyond redemption (the "nuclear winter"). A monstrous level of military preparedness also helped focus the mind on the continued possibility of disaster.[4]

With the fall of the Berlin Wall in 1989, the cold war began to pass into memory. The horrors of the Stalinist state had already been clear for some decades, particularly after the death of Joseph Stalin in 1953. Those in the West who still believed that, after the Russian Revolution of 1917, the Soviet Union had taken the road to achieving its inevitable goal of the humane, classless society, were, for the most part, disillusioned.

With the end of the cold war, the world entered an uneasy period of conflicts, which collectively involved millions of people—wars in Cambodia, the Balkans, Somalia, the Congo, Colombia, and other areas. As the world's surviving nuclear superpower, the United States, though intermittently involved in some of these conflicts, seemed itself invulnerable. What was particularly shocking about the terrorist attacks on the Pentagon and World Trade Center on September 11, 2001, was not merely the extent of the death and destruction, but that the United States was far more vulnerable to attack than virtually anyone had imagined. Many Americans, who had complacently stopped following foreign news, began to understand the world as a far more dangerous place than they had imagined.[5]

Although the attack of September 11 had not involved chemical, biological, or nuclear weapons, nor a sophisticated delivery system, there is now no assurance that such weapons will not be used in the future, and little confidence that if they were, this country would have adequate means of defense. With deadly biological weapons relatively easy to produce, and antidotes uncertain, how long will it take for some terrorist or rogue state to unleash them? Or for nuclear weapons, floating on the international black market, to fall into the wrong hands?[6] Or for more states to achieve nuclear capacity, and the era of nonproliferation, that dates from the international pact of 1968, to end?[7]

In this present period of uneasy U.S. hegemony, we cannot avoid asking ourselves how long it will take for dictators as devious and monomaniacal as Hitler or Stalin to rise to power again, with regimes as vicious and suffocating, and with a military technology more advanced and dangerous. Perhaps our generation, or even that of our children, or theirs, will avoid military destruction, but can it be avoided for millennia, or forever? Such thoughts disrupt our sense that history has any kind of dependable continuity, or that it illustrates values whose continuance is independent of our efforts to maintain them.

World War II, we remember, was also the time of the Holocaust, with Nazi Germany's deliberate murder in concentration camps of eleven million civilians, including six million Jews, which revealed an unexpected depth of nihilism at the heart of Western culture. Ironically, Karl Marx had predicted that the Communist Revolution would take place first in Germany because he considered it the most capitalistically advanced country in Europe, and, indeed, in the period before World War I, Berlin was arguably the cultural capital of Europe. Yet this "advanced" or "civilized" country unleashed the Holocaust.

The possibility, almost realized, that the continuity of an entire people, European Jewry, could be ended by the deliberate action of a reputedly civilized nation has, for many, called into question God's role in history, or whether there is any certainty in historical progress. What was the use, people have asked, of writers like Friedrich von Schiller, Goethe, and Thomas Mann; of the German universities and learned societies; of the timeless gift of German classical music and philosophy; or of the sheer cultural wonder of a Munich or a Berlin, if the country which nurtured them could also produce the mass orgy of National Socialism and the Holocaust? If such a civilized country could do what Germany did, what does "civilization" mean?

The sense that the Holocaust was an "aberration" loses credibility as cases of genocide or genocide-like atrocities mount. Stalin's killing of millions of Soviet citizens during the five-year plans and the purges; the Khmer Rouge "killing fields" in Cambodia; the destruction of hundreds of Mayan villages in Guatemala; "ethnic cleansing" and the use of mass rape as a weapon of war in Bosnia and Kosovo; and the destruction of the Tutsi people in Rwanda—all challenge our belief in human goodness and progress, or that a benign Providence oversees the universe. How many of us still believe that people are "really good at heart," as a young Dutch Jew, Anne Frank, told her diary before her family was betrayed and shipped to a concentration camp? Hasn't the twentieth century provided us with too many examples of gratuitous humiliation, torture, and killing to leave us with any confidence in human goodness as an invariant essence of human nature or the human soul, or to imagine that civilization is following some sure upward path of progress?

"All men seek the good," Plato had said, a notion which was reinforced by Christian theology, which, despite the reservation of original sin, saw the soul as ultimately pure and divine; and by the Enlightenment, which saw human beings embracing the rationality of justice and social progress. Yet in the last century, as in all previous periods, human beings have looked their fellows in the face, and starved and tortured them into agony. It is also a fact that, in this period, as in those before it, nations, many of whose citizens live in incomparable opulence, have let other nations sink into misery or starvation without lifting a hand. A particularly poignant example is the worldwide epidemic of AIDS. Here the means exist to contain the epidemic and to prevent massive death and suffering, but the developed world, which can afford the cost of the necessary life-saving medicines, has failed to offer adequate aid.

Globalization and the New Society

The post–World War II era has created a growing realization that the world is rapidly outstripping and simultaneously destroying its capacity to sustain life. At first blush, the situation looks tolerable. While the world population has increased by a factor of four in this century, the world economy is seventeen times larger. But as *State of the World 2003* makes painfully clear, a crisis confronts us:

Global population now exceeds 6.2 billion, more than double
what it was in 1950, and is currently projected to rise to between
7.9 billion and 10.9 billion by 2050. Nearly all of that increase
will occur in the developing world, where resources are already
under serious strain. In these countries, nearly 1.2 billion people—
almost a quarter of the world's population—are classed by the
World Bank as living in "absolute poverty." These people are surviving on less than the equivalent of $1 a day, and they are gener-
ally very vulnerable to additional misfortune—whether in the
form of disease, drought, or food shortage.[8]

As this report makes clear, standards of living in the developing world
are falling, most notably in Africa. There are two sets of problems, ecological and political. Ecological issues pose problems both for the developing
and the developed world. The Western economic model, including reliance
on fossil fuels, which so dramatically raised living standards in what is now
the developed world, is now highly questionable as these fuels begin running out. Indefinite expansion is also made problematical by deteriorating
ecosystems on which the global economy depends. Fresh water, forests,
rangelands, oceanic fisheries, and the atmosphere are steadily eroding.
With world population continuing to grow, available resources simply will
not be enough to sustain the population even in poverty.[9] Finally, levels of
pollution in some areas, particularly eastern Europe, are already lethal, and
disasters, such as the nuclear meltdown and diffusion of nuclear radiation
at Chernobyl, or possible destruction of nuclear facilities through terrorist
attack, continue to pose serious risks.

The globalized economy offers the promise, if not the present reality, of
economic relief for the billions still in poverty, although, as we have noted,
the world is fast approaching an economic and ecological crisis. However,
in substantial parts of the developing world, such as the Middle East, most
of the gains from globalization have gone to the economic elites who have
reaped immense advantages, both economic and political, by trading national resources to the transnationals. Despite some exceptions—mostly in
Latin America—crass dictatorships and token democracies, dominated by
self-interested classes or the military, are still the rule in the Third World.
The result is that hunger and disease run rampant among all but the elites
of these countries, cutting lives to half their natural length, given the present state of medical knowledge.[10]

At the geopolitical level, the globalization of the world's economy has not thus far fostered any complementary growth in a system of effective world government, despite the growth of some transnational economic authorities, such as the European Union (EU) and the World Trade Organization (WTO). In recent decades, the United Nations has even lost strength, with sharp cutbacks in its financing and its peacekeeping operations, and with the rejection of its authority by the United States in the Iraq war.[11] Lacking a ready deployment force, the world organization has not taken collective responsibility for stopping recent massive human rights violations, as defined by the U.N. Universal Declaration of Human Rights, in countries such as Bosnia, Rwanda, Sudan, the Congo, and Afghanistan, and has proven ineffective in a number of recent peacekeeping operations.[12]

The unmistakable conclusion of this historical evidence is that progress cannot be assumed, as in earlier centuries. History, as never before, seems contingent on human effort. Yet it is sometimes claimed that the globalized economy is creating a planetary consciousness and, through computerized communications, the means by which the world will mobilize its resources to respond to environmental pollution, overpopulation, poverty, genocide, and war. Globalization, for some people, carries the teleology of history, the sure realization of the good society, through a linear process. In this sense, they see it as the successor to the Enlightenment, the Industrial Revolution, democracy, or communism.

If we consider the present state of the world, however, we must conclude that the world's problems are still with us, and some are growing worse. We also find that globalization is producing a culture in which human experience seems increasingly abstract, disengaged, and, for some, only speciously real.

Globalization can be seen in two ways, either as a continuation of trends begun in the Industrial Revolution, and so its ultimate fulfillment, or as a sharp break with the earlier economy, which was based on the self-contained nation-state.[13] This latter position is argued by political scientist Stephen J. Kobrin of the University of Pennsylvania, who points out that the system of single-state authorities commanding clear geographic areas, a system signaled in Europe by the Treaty of Westphalia in 1648, has now given way to a system of multiple authorities with overlapping jurisdictions. In addition to the nation-state, these authorities now include the transnational corporation, which operates in quasi-independence of state authority; the multilateral organization, such as the European Union and World

Trade Organization; the World Wide Web; the international financial market; as well as an increasingly powerful group of nongovernmental organizations (NGOs), such as Greenpeace or Amnesty International, which comprise what is known as "civil society." Kobrin compares the new economy to the shifting borders, ambiguities of authority, multiple loyalties, and transnational elites of the Christian Commonwealth of the Middle Ages, as opposed to the nation-state system which succeeded it.

While Kobrin is right in pointing out the new features of globalization, it is also useful for us to think of many aspects of globalization as a continuation of the Industrial Revolution. One advantage of doing so is that analyzing how the Industrial Revolution transformed human experience can still provide us insights for the present and future. Understanding both the features which globalization shares with the Industrial Revolution, and those which seem distinctly new, creates the basis for devising social policies which minimize globalization's defects while taking advantage of its economic efficiencies.

THE ALIENATION OF WORK

As Adam Smith and, later, Karl Marx, pointed out, the division of labor and specialization of economic functions that began with the Industrial Revolution meant that the worker could no longer trace, in a meaningful narrative, the object of his or her labor from its raw materials—for example, a piece of uncut leather—to the finished product—a pair of shoes. Rather, a worker performed a limited function, such as the gluing-on of heels or processing of orders, and then lost the product in the void.

Although repetitive industrial labor, at least in the postindustrial West, has been almost eliminated in favor of computerized production and service jobs (factory labor is increasingly done in the global South), the alienation of work has in some ways, at least, increased.

Kobrin points out that workers today have even less sense of the total process of the production of goods, if they are actually engaged in such a process, than did their eighteenth- and nineteenth-century predecessors. Goods today are frequently assembled in three or four places, and financed and marketed in others. As components of products or information are assembled from plants in several countries or garnered from centers which are virtually unaware of each others' existence, loyalties based on personal contact or national allegiances tend to disappear. As information replaces goods, a sense of the product's tangibility also diminishes.

COMMODIFICATION

Industrialism over the last two hundred years has created a value system which reduces human effort to "bottom line" accounting. In this sense, a worker is "nothing but" a unit which adds to the value of a product; he or she otherwise has no interest for the employer. Two systems of values thus compete, one based on the profit motive and the other on humane considerations, sometimes supported by religion or metaphysics, with the latter system constantly on the defensive. One example occurs in the current trend of "downsizing," where workers who have devoted decades of their lives to a specific company may be laid off to protect or enhance the financial position of owners and high-level managers, who may have little or no loyalty to the workplace or the workers. Another is the planning of cities and suburbs, where historic sites, farmland, and traditional neighborhoods compete unequally with apartment complexes, urban sprawl, and shopping malls.

CULTURE AS PRODUCT

Commodification has also affected our sense of culture. When Marx spoke of culture, including religion, as "superstructure," justifying the economics of the class system, the "products" of culture, such as plays and books, were largely restricted to the ruling bourgeois class. Today, in the West, a major sector of the economy, reaching every layer, consists of "cultural" commodities, including information on the Web; images on television and films; and advertising and product design, so that economics and superstructure would seem to merge.[14] In many publishing houses, for example, as marketing hype invades the body of books hustled out to catch momentary peaks of celebrity or notoriety, books themselves begin to look suspiciously like other commodities. As English critic Steven Connor writes, the "images, styles and representations are not the promotional accessories to economic products, they are the products themselves."[15]

At the same time, our sense of the increasing disjunctions, absurdities, and surrogate realities of life since World War II has been heightened by art and fiction, which mimic the prevailing culture. Critic Alan Wilde writes: "[A]n indecision about the meanings or relation of things is matched by a willingness to live with uncertainty, to tolerate, and even, in some cases, to welcome a world seen as random and multiple, even, at times absurd..."[16] This sense for uncertainty and absurdity can be seen in playwrights like Samuel Beckett, Harold Pinter, and Edward Albee, or a novelist like Thomas Pynchon.

THE DISRUPTION OF COMMUNAL AND FAMILY LIFE

In the United States, the mobility of workers and managers has constantly increased in the more than half century since World War II. Lifelong residence in the place of one's birth is becoming a rarity, as is the continuity of practicing the profession of one's parents.[17] This migration and mobility is partly the result of the spreading corporate culture, and partly of economic displacement in the global South, and loss of manufacturing jobs in the industrialized North. The effect has been the loss of the continuity of generations living in proximity to each other and sharing their lives, and the longevity and shared histories of stable communities, professions, and workplaces.

Rather than engaging in communal activities or personal relations with their families or friends, workers or managers today spend much of their free time—whether it be in Singapore, Guatemala City, or suburban Detroit—immersing themselves in the multiple realities of the mass media, which seem perhaps more engaging, if less substantial.

As the corporate culture has directed its advertising and entertainment to separate age groups, it has heightened the split between generations. A deep connection to the certainties of place, history, and social ethics has been disrupted, as the young immerse themselves in "peer culture," and, perhaps even more than their parents, are preoccupied with mass-marketed products, computers, and the media. The children, particularly of the poor, because of the effects of deindustrialization on inner-city communities, may be increasingly immersed in a growing street culture, with its attendant problems of delinquency and drugs—although drugs and disaffection are prevalent in middle-class suburbs as well. I once asked students in a class at MIT what their fathers did for a living. The answers were disturbingly vague—"Something in a chemical plant," one student reported.

THE DESTRUCTION OF LOCAL CULTURE

As globalization spreads, it penetrates to areas of the world which, a few hundred years ago, were only peripherally related, if at all, by colonization or trade with the West.[18] In so-called "First World" countries, standardized chain stores, managed by personnel often having no local connections, displace traditional family-owned businesses. In the developing world, integration into the global economy, involving the importation of goods and cultural products, including their lifestyle messages, destroys local economies and cultures, often mixing high-tech with continued

207

poverty. A sense of cultural threat pervades much of the world today, particularly in Islamic areas, where it provides some of the emotional basis for resistance to U.S. hegemony and for terrorist attacks.

THE INFORMATION REVOLUTION

In times past, one's life was the product of locally available information provided by family, friends, and members of one's village. This relation to localized information was what defined a traditional society.

As the availability of information increased, as in an empire like Rome, with its regular couriers and mail; its body of literature, including translations; and its opportunities for travel, one's world expanded. Prosperous citizens knew about the Parthians living in what is now Iran, administrative problems in Rome, wheat shipments, new styles of house decoration, Greek philosophers, and theologians from North Africa.

As the localism of the Middle Ages gave way to the modern age, the scope of available information began to include the entire world, so that today it takes in every conceivable aspect of it, scientific, sociological, and political. Information, whether from the mass media or computers, seems ubiquitous and overwhelming.

Received in fragmented units, and increasingly less from printed material or communal human contact, such information, particularly transmitted through the mass media, is often decontexualized and impossible to trace to a localized source. As the duration of the unit diminishes from narrative to soundbite, so does the individual's capacity to integrate this information into some unified view of a situation or, more generally, of life.

At the same time we gain increasing "access" to multiple realities, we often feel atomized and disconnected. As we sit behind a computer or television screen, we identify ourselves less and less as engaged members of a social group or communal project. (Although "list-serves" and "chatrooms" have some of the appearance of community, they distinctly lack the directness and familiarity of a face-to-face group.) Finally, as mass media, and particularly computers, gain the ability to provide alternative realities, the virtual and the real fuse. With the loss of a sense of reality, our enmeshment in life or commitment may diminish.

On the other side of the ledger, to those, almost exclusively still in the "First World," who have the resources, access to information through the Internet and other sources offers the possibility of a heightened global consciousness, and connection with potentially allied interest groups all over the world. The same computers that foster atomization have thus helped the growth of social movements, most notably through the revolutionary changes in communication made possible by e-mail and the World Wide Web. In just a few decades, one can see a significant growth in global awareness, buttressed by a vast gain in crosscultural contacts; the enlargement of school curricula to include other cultures; and a deepening concern for a wide range of planetary issues, most notably the environment.

All these factors—the alienation from work, the commodification of workers and the goods of life, the destruction of local cultures, the transformation of art to product, and the insidious effects of the information revolution—are now part of the package of globalization, as are its benefits of economic efficiency, and its possibilities of dealing with economic problems on a global scale. Globalized capitalism, as Nobel laureate economist Joseph E. Stiglitz writes, in his *Globalization and Its Discontents*, is also subject to abuse by the major economic powers, as it can be used to maintain or increase the huge gap between advanced and developing countries.[19] As *New York Times* journalist Paul Krugman has pointed out, the system in the First World also operates to increase the gap between the rich and the rest of society, including the middle class.[20] These problems, however, should not simply be assumed; rather, we must combat them by a progressive, engaged social policy. Globalization, with its huge economic potential, represents a set of opportunities, not an insurance policy. Saving civilization, or rather transforming it so that it deepens and enriches human life, is the acute challenge of our time.

The Decline of Political Participation in the United States

Although the need is acute, the will to effect change in the United States through the political process has been eroding. Many people simply do not feel part of the decision-making process, and have become passive spectators of politics. Despite the emergence of antiglobalization, animal rights, and other social movements, a sharp decline in visible protest movements since the 1960s has been one of the fallouts of a political system which today looks more and more like the economic market. For many people, the sense of achieving eventual fulfillment or satisfaction through the linear progress of democratically sponsored legislation no longer seems a likely option.

In the United States, popular sovereignty and the rise of progressive legislation and of state-sponsored social welfare policies, together with the immense energy of the industrial economy itself, fostered a considerable spread of benefits. Starting in the late nineteenth century, disparate groups, such as labor, farmers, women, ideological leftists, and sometimes racial and ethnic minorities, worked together for reform, demanding political representation; consumer, child, and labor rights; social welfare assistance; and racial, ethnic, and gender equality. To do so, as philosopher Richard Rorty points out in his *Achieving Our Country*, they joined coalitions, such as the Farmer-Labor Party, the Progressive Movement, and various political substructures, whose efforts culminated in the New Deal and its successors. Since the 1960s, Rorty indicates, such alliances have considerably weakened, and a reaction against these earlier gains has begun. Unlike in Europe, where the welfare state was initially introduced by conservatives like German chancellor Otto von Bismarck, in the United States, welfare benefits were associated with the New Deal, and consequently never gained full acceptance from conservatives. On the other side of the political spectrum, many intellectuals today have abandoned economic activism in favor of issues of multicultural fairness or, otherwise phrased, the "politics of difference."

Washington Post columnist E.J. Dionne sees the effects noted by Rorty as part of a more general decline of political interest in the United States. In his *Why Americans Hate Politics*, he writes:

> After two centuries in which the United States stood proudly as
> an example of what an engaged citizenry could accomplish
> through public life, Americans view politics with boredom and
> detachment.... Election campaigns generate less excitement than
> ever and are dominated by television commercials, direct mail,
> polling, and other approaches that treat individual voters not as
> citizens deciding their nation's fate, but as mere collections of im-
> pulses to be stroked and soothed.[21]

Dionne finds the distance widening between whites and African-Americans, between the inner city and suburbs, between social classes, and between ethnic groups. The notion of a working alliance between such groups, united by common interests, looks less and less likely.[22] Rather than engaging the mass of voters, both parties, according to Dionne, have become "vehicles for upper-middle-class [and upper class] interests." The percentage of voters has declined markedly in the last few decades. The most disaffected group has been the poor, which has seen an ever-widening gap between itself and the rich. Ironically, as the poor slip into Third World levels of consumption and services, their alienation increases and with it, their voting frequency, which, in turn, leaves them increasingly disenfranchised.[23]

The numbers tell the story: In the 2000 presidential election, 54.7 percent of the population reported voting, but only 28.2 percent of those with family incomes under $5,000 did.[24] But the numbers also indicate just how much political disaffection has touched the entire electorate. In 1964, 67 percent of women and 71.8 percent of men voted. By 2000, these numbers had declined to 56.2 percent of women and 53.2 percent of men.[25]

One crucial reason for political disaffection in the last few decades may be found in the political system's radically increased dependence on substantial amounts of money. With Congressional campaigns currently running in the millions of dollars, primarily because of huge media bills, candidates and parties have become far more dependent than they were on corporate and other special-interest capital.[26] With access to mass media, that is, with sufficient funds, candidates are confident that, within broad limits, whatever the message, they can prevail. Edward S. Herman and Noam Chomsky point out that the media, notably television and the press, generally not only take *positions* which best serve the people who own or pay for them, but also use *methods* to the same effect: the decontexualization of information; appeals to individuals as opposed to organized groups; a lack of reference to new means of organizing social action, such as the Web; and the absence of messages concerning what to do about social problems.[27]

The alignment of corporate and special-interest capital with the interests of the affluent segments of society, with their capacity to control the political agenda, is not difficult to trace. The affluent voters who oppose active government and higher income taxes ally easily with corporations seeking lower corporate taxes, preferential government contracts, and protective or nonintrusive legislation. Without effective legislation, as in Europe, to limit political contributions, corporate and special-interest capital continues to dominate the political system. As a result, collusion between industry and government has never seemed more pervasive.[28] Finally, as Dionne points out, this alliance has been able to attract the working class by exploiting "wedge" issues, like abortion rights and gun control, at the expense of their economic or class interests.

Along with the poor, the other group which is most alienated from the political process is youth, lacking as it does, for the most part, membership in political or social movements. Of all groups, youth appears most vulnerable to a mass-mediated culture, and as the culture and the economy merge, there is pressure through every avenue of communication to be what the economy demands—a consumer with as little social conscience as possible. In the 2000 election, only 32.3 percent of 18–24-year-olds voted, a figure which has ominous implications for the future of our democracy.[29]

Deconstructionist Thought

Alienation from politics has, if anything, been enhanced by an influential school of philosophic and aesthetic criticism, called deconstructionism, or poststructuralism, which surfaced in the 1960s. This school of thought has served to erode the sense of reality that culturally attuned people of earlier eras achieved through artistic experience or philosophy. Yet, by directly attacking notions of permanence, deconstructionist philosophers, primarily French, such as Claude Levi-Strauss, Roland Barthes, Michel Foucault, Jacques Lacan, Jacques Derrida, and Jean-Francois Lyotard, have played an extremely influential role in developing the vanguard of modern thought.

In going about their work, deconstructionist philosophers have attacked the permanence complex at a number of key points. Notions such as the permanent essence of human nature, the soul, eternal ideas, God, the laws of history or its inevitable outcomes, and invariant standards of morality or aesthetics, have all been laid waste. These philosophers, however, generally have failed to provide any acceptable alternative, leaving their followers, for the most part, unable to achieve philosophically guided commitment.

DECONSTRUCTING LITERATURE

Literary criticism has been a prime target of deconstructionist thought. Literary historian Terry Eagleton tells us that, in the period following World War I, "modernist" literature was seen not only as an aesthetic adventure, but as a vehicle for understanding fundamental questions of human existence—human relationships, personal identity, and our place in society. Postwar society also idealized literature as an answer to a numbing commercial world.[30] It was for this purpose that literature needed to represent life, although the life it represented was far more complex than that depicted in the literature of an earlier day. Modernist writers described the multiple layers of the psyche; the embodiment of history and mythology in the present; the varied viewpoints which collectively constitute awareness of a social situation; and the multiple meanings and allusions of language. Writers as disparate as Marcel Proust, Virginia Woolf, Gertrude Stein, Franz Kafka, Thomas Mann, and James Joyce heightened the reader's sense of this complex reality, a reality which the reader was called upon to believe existed "out there," and which was sensitively seen by the writer, whose vision it was the reader's task to share.

By contrast, the post–World War II deconstructionist philosophers have argued, for the most part, against the notion that language "represents reality out there," or specifically, the writer's vision of it. Rather, the meaning of literature is whatever the language "signifies" for the reader. Hayden White, for example, writes that Foucault "denies the concreteness of the referent and rejects the notion that there is a 'reality' which precedes discourse and reveals its face to a prediscursive 'perception'."[31]

This body of critics also sometimes argues not only against the identity of the individual writer, but of the individual reader. A work of art, they claim, is neither created nor understood primarily in individual terms, but reflects the views of the prevailing culture, and, particularly, its dominant classes.[32]

To be sure, individuals are not isolated, and it is true that we and our languages are socialized, as our review of thinkers like Whitehead, Edelman, Mead, Dewey, and Sullivan has shown. But these thinkers, for the most part, make clear that individuals are best conceived as foci of their social and cultural fields. As such, individuals achieve a measure of independence which is a factor of their capacity to integrate their fields from their particular standpoint. It follows that to reject an individual's direct relations to these fields, or that person's capacity to express or understand those relations in an idiosyncratic way, however mediated by socialization, including a socialized language, denies the individual any sense of responsibility for his or her perceptions, expressions, or acts.

Here, it might be helpful to take up in more detail an aspect of postmodernist criticism, its now-notorious attack on the authority of the author, enunciated with considerable bravura in 1968 by the philosopher and critic Roland Barthes. He writes:

Classical criticism has never been concerned with the reader; for that criticism, there is no other man in literature than the one who writes. We are no longer so willing to be the dupes of such

213

antiphrases, by which a society proudly recriminates in favor of precisely what it discards, ignores, muffles, or destroys; we know that in order to restore writing to its future, we must reverse the myth: the birth of the reader must be requited by the death of the Author.[33]

This attack on the author contains a number of important qualifying truths. If the purpose of reading is to distill the author's intentions, deconstructionist critics question whether the author can actually *know* those intentions, or, given the multiple meanings of language, that what the author writes can accurately *reflect* them. As French psychoanalyst Jacques Lacan points out, this is particularly true if that motivation is not consciously accessible. Deconstructionists maintain that language contains multiple meanings, even for its user; that ambiguity is built into linguistic or imagistic systems; and that consciousness may represent the opposite of what someone intends—although, we should point out, that opposite is usually delicately related to the unconscious motivation. Another real difficulty, some deconstructionist critics identify, is that the reader necessarily reads with the mind-set of his or her time rather than with the author's mind-set. These difficulties, as we saw in chapter 9, are similar to those in relating first-person subjective experience to third-person neurophysiological observations.

But here again, the reader's difficulty in understanding the author's intention, as the author's difficulty in understanding his or her own, cannot argue away the residual usefulness of understanding the writer's intentions and world. Whatever the difficulties, it seems worth attempting, even if full understanding is only an approachable limit, just as it is worth attempting to connect subjective experiences with neurophysiology, and, in real social relations, it is worth attempting to understand another person, or gain what is called "accurate empathy."

The act of constructing accurate personal narratives is also the process by which we understand ourselves and configure our own identities. The psychiatric work of Heinz Kohut, for example, which bases personal therapy on the construction of such narratives, illustrates just how important they are for achieving stability and personal identity.[34] Even if the picture of ourselves which emerges is complex, with far less than a unified and stable configuration of qualities, but rather a tension of competing, changing, and contingent elements, it is nonetheless achievable and useful. It will provide an historical explanation for how we tend to see the world, our built-in biases or characteristic modes of interpretation, our areas of concentration, and our blind spots.

DECONSTRUCTING HISTORY

Not only has modernist culture been subjected to philosophic attack, but so has modernist history. Following the precepts of the German historian Leopold von Ranke (1795–1886), modernist history has been an attempt to use exhaustive research, particularly into contemporary documents, to reconstruct historical periods as a set of events in space and time, and as they were experienced by the people who lived them. The strategies of the deconstructionist attack on this kind of history can be seen as virtually identical to those which postmodernist scholars and critics have mounted against the modernist critical approach to art, and particularly to literature.

The first, and most basic, has been an attack on the assumption that the entire aim of history is to "represent" the way things were in the past—that is, a past "reality." If the novel needn't represent the "reality" of its characters, or the subjective life of its author, history needn't represent either a set of events in space or time, or the subjective experience of the people who lived them—although here the argument is even less convincing.[35]

Similar to a novel, what history presents is a "text" rather than a "reality," the deconstructionist critic declares. The "signified" is the interpretation, not some objective reality or set of events. The postmodernist historian is not obliged to seek out the data and construct a picture of the past, following rules of evidence, as in a courtroom. Rather, stated broadly, he or she constructs a story which has internal coherence, and uses as its interpretive framework the historian's (and the reader's) position or mindset in the present. This is a mindset which reflects the historian's class and what Thomas S. Kuhn would call the "prevailing paradigm." The historian, as well as the reader of history, is considered then to be inescapably trapped in his or her own time, ethnicity, race, gender, and age, so that "objectivity" or "truth" is unobtainable.

The conservative, modernist historian Gertrude Himmelfarb makes clear that the historian's task is not easy. "Historians, ancient and modern, have always known what postmodernism professes to have just discovered—that any work of history is vulnerable on three counts: the fallibility and deficiency of the historical record on which it is based; the fallibility and selectivity inherent in the writing of history; and the fallibility and subjectivity of the historian."[36] The difference between historians in the past who, through the practice of their craft, have partially overcome these difficulties, and historians in the postmodernist style, is, according to Himmelfarb, "the presumption that because it is impossible to attain such truths, it is not only futile but positively baneful to aspire to them."[37] Here, again, the gains in overcoming the difficulties seem, as they are in neurophysiology or in the interpretation of the literary author, worth the rigors of the historian's craft.

DECONSTRUCTING SCIENCE

An attack similar to that on literary representation and the author, and on history, has been launched in the post–World War II period on the objectivity of science. The French philosopher Jean-Francois Lyotard, for example, claims that in recent years, science has broken up into a plethora of self-contained fields, each with its particular "language game," including its own lexicon, laws of evidence, and legitimation procedures. Lyotard discounts the notion that "truth," or any standard independent of its culture, is involved in modern science, a position which parallels that of Foucault, Derrida, and other deconstructionists.[38]

Although the breakup of the unity of mathematics, and the use of mathematical modeling without full experimental confirmation, as we saw in chapters 7 and 8, lends some credence to the postmodernist position, it radically overstates the problem. Demonstrability through rigorous experimentation, and not just the technical ability to create a model for hypothetical data, is still the ultimate ground of reliability in contemporary science. The acknowledgment of the observer's role in the uncertainty principle, for example, qualifies but does not destroy the "objectivity" of science. Also, the difficulties of obtaining experimental verification in some aspects of quantum physics and cosmology, which have put added emphasis on mathematical and computer modeling, do not eliminate experimental verification as the ultimate grounds of proof.

A related but more muted attack comes from Thomas S. Kuhn in his widely read *The Structure of Scientific Revolutions*. In writing scientific history as a succession of paradigms with their own self-contained scientific methods and standards, Kuhn can be interpreted as saying that each paradigm is an arbitrary cultural expression, which would imply that it is only as good as what it succeeded. Contemporary science would then have no more valid a claim to truth than the Copernican-Newtonian paradigm.

Kuhn exaggerates the differences between the Newtonian and modern physical sciences to the point that he sometimes implies there is no commonality of method or overlap in their views of the world. Quite the contrary. Modern physics fully credits Newtonian mechanics with usefulness for larger masses, and has maintained a fair amount of continuity in method. As physicist Steven Weinberg suggests, there was a considerably greater break between Newton and Aristotlean essentialism (see chapter 3) than between Newton and modern physics.[39] Rather than a decisive break with Newtonian science, modern physics, according to Weinberg, represents a closer approximation to the truth, not an arbitrary excursion into simply another cultural paradigm.

The postmodernist critique of science, I believe, creates more uncertainty than is warranted. Although contemporary science presently lacks a deterministic rationale, and although there are clearly problems in securing a unified or adequate theory of all observable phenomena, science is demonstrably successful in explaining a great deal of the world. This success has been heightened in recent decades by a considerable growth of multidisciplinary cooperation, as exemplified by the integration of biology into the physical sciences (see chapter 8). While science no longer serves to describe how the world demonstrates permanence, and no longer provides traditional forms of certainty, it is nonetheless a comfort to know that, day by day, the secrets of the natural world are being better known, and that with knowledge, we can achieve greater familiarity with our natural home.

MULTICULTURALISM AND THE WESTERN CANON

While globalization has extended the economy and commercialized culture of the West throughout the world,[40] ethnic, racial, and sexual minorities have fought with some success for greater inclusion in the institutions undergirding and reflecting Western culture. This fight was originally part of the struggle, culminating in the late 1960s, to extend civil rights to women and minority groups in the United States, and, in Europe, to question the hold of the *haute bourgeoisie* on the structures of power. It has also been supported by demographic changes whereby the dominant ethnic group—whites of western European background—are becoming a minority. Although the civil rights movement has lost much of its momentum in recent decades, and the European student "revolution" of 1968 failed, and even the longer-lasting feminist movement has lost some of its edge, on the cultural side they have resulted in various groupings in society establishing their legitimacy in relation to a previously somewhat monolithic white, male culture.

One point of postmodernist attack has been on the "canon" of great books, or the "Tradition," as T.S. Eliot haughtily called it, which was standard in the universities of the West.[41] The abandonment of the canon as the sole source of great writing has, in some cases, opened the curriculum to new cultural influences, and enlarged our minds beyond the circle of traditional legitimacy. Such readings may now include the Koran, the *Sundiata* of Mali, the *Ramayana* of India, or *Genji-Monogatari* of Japan. Not only are students now rightly asked to read such works, but they are also reading more works by women, who have documented a long history of prejudicial male domination, including the exclusion of female artists and writers, and by authors belonging to ethnic and racial minority groups within the West.

Finally, like literature, particularly in the period starting in the 1960s, history has radically expanded its scope to include the lives of members of the working class, women, ethnic groups, and colonized peoples. Again, there has been an immense gain. For example, it will now be impossible, I hope, to write of Britain's occupation of India with the same smug assurance of virtually divine providence that we find in G.M. Trevelyan's traditional account,[42] or to blindly accept the virtual ignoring of women, Native Americans and African-Americans, and the working class, among others, which vitiated American historical texts until well in the 1970s.

Contemporary history, like literature, however, does not always reflect acceptance of the legitimacy of such works on their merits, but rather a begrudging acquiescence in the power politics of academic life. Academia has broken up into a variety of separate turfs, each defended by its own constituency, so that an unfortunate corollary of a desirable enlargement of the curriculum has been an artificial immunity from criticism for any group which can stake a cultural claim. Each of its works must then be approached on its own terms, as would a diffident cultural anthropologist studying a new culture, and criticism is only considered valid by a member of the group.

RELATIVITY OF CRITICISM, RIGHTS, AND MORALITY

As the French student revolution of 1968 came and failed, thinkers such as Jacques Derrida and Michel Foucault worked to break down any preexisting structures which might be considered to undergird philosophy, seeing in such structures the ideology of the ruling classes or the ghosts of Platonism. The proliferation of competing styles since the 1960s has reflected a lack of one overarching aesthetic or historico-critical theory, or the conviction, on the part of those advocating multiculturalism, that such a theory is even possible.

Similar problems to those in cultural or historical interpretation, with its defense of relativism and separate turfs, also appear in issues of morality. Here, cultural relativism and criticism of any single metaphysical base for human rights can take the form of a refusal to oppose any culturally sanctioned practice. An example would be the refusal of certain United Nations members to oppose the practice of clitoridectomy in other nations, which by Western standards, and those of some members of those societies, seems physically cruel, and a violation of women's and girls' right to bodily integrity. As with cultural products, would it not be useful to attempt to establish some metastandards by which, within a wide compass of multicultural receptivity, such moral issues might be judged? It would seem here that such a standard could be the U.N. Universal Declaration of Human Rights.[43] In the last chapter (chapter 12), I will suggest one possible way such standards might be grounded.

AN EPISTEMOLOGY OF NONACTION

When one turns to political theory and action, the effect of deconstructionist thought has too often been to deflect commitment from any consistent line of action, by questioning whether there is any truth or meaning which can be pursued.[44] While other influences have been at work, such as the effects of a mass-media culture and the power of unlicensed money, the deconstructionist stance has not been without effect, at least in academic circles. English Marxist critic Terry Eagleton writes:

In one of its developments, post-structuralism became a convenient way of evading . . . political questions altogether. The work of Derrida and others had cast grave doubt upon the classical notions of truth, reality, meaning and knowledge, all of which could be exposed as resting on a naively representational theory of language. If meaning, the signified, was a passing product of words or signifiers, always shifting and unstable, part-present and part-absent, how could there be any determinate truth or meaning at all?[45]

Richard Rorty writes of this period:

We are told over and over again that Lacan has shown
human desire to be inherently unsatisfiable, that Derrida
has shown meaning to be undecidable, that Lyotard has shown
commensuration between oppressed and oppressors to be impossible, and that events such as the Holocaust or the massacre
of the original Americans are unrepresentable. Hopelessness
has become fashionable on the Left—principled, theorized,
philosophical hopelessness.[46]

In describing such hopelessness, Richard Rorty and other commentators, it seems to me, ignore the growing role of civil society, including the
increasing impact of nongovernmental organizations (NGOs) and the de-
mocratizing opportunities offered by the Internet, which many activist
groups are using to bypass the corporate-owned media and to build global
networks. Protest in this country, and worldwide, continues, as exemplified
by the Tiananmen Square uprising (1989); the Zapatista uprising (1994);
general strikes and demonstrations in Africa, South America, Asia, and the
United States, including the protest in Seattle (2000) against structural adjustment programs and other policies of the World Trade Organization, International Monetary Fund and World Bank (2000-03); and massive public
protests against the war in Iraq (2003).

Nevertheless, if we consider the last few decades, the challenge to permanence, with its sustaining certainties, and the effects of the global economy and its associated mass culture, have worked together to create a
stance of cynicism and passivity in the United States, in comparison with
the more activist 1960s and 1970s. In the intellectual community, which
might have provided leadership during the last three decades, this stance
has been reinforced by deconstructionist thought. With such a stance, we
can neither face the very real dangers of this period, nor seize the opportunities of enormous gains in economic power, knowledge, and communications which are offered in today's globalized world. In this situation, such
a stance seems nothing less than tragic.

This chapter has attempted to survey briefly "the situation in this moment." The problems before us are formidable. Without some considerable
input of motivation, it is doubtful they will be solved. Our "moment" occurs
at the edge of a new millennium, a crucial time of opportunity for the task

we have undertaken in this book—that of considering our four-thousand-year history, and evolving a new worldview. This is the time in which, with a new sense of purpose, we must act.

In our final chapter, we will attempt to answer several key questions: How can a different epistemology better prompt us to action? How can we forge community, and create a sense of our own identities, while meeting the problems raised in the preceding pages? And finally, how can we work together as responsible individuals, to build a world we want to live in without the props of permanence?

Chapter Twelve

Toward a New Activism

*It belongs to the goodness of the world, that
settled order should deal tenderly with the faint
discordant light of the dawn of another age.*

Alfred North Whitehead[1]

*Let your "yes" mean "yes," and your "no" mean
"no."*

Jesus of Nazareth[2]

The end of the twentieth century left many of us numb, indifferent, and self-
concerned. If there were glimmerings of another age, we had to look hard.
What happened on September 11, 2001, did not create a new world. The
basis of today's world lies in the world we already had, in its deeper meaning; its future is still ours to create.

The Argument

Let us take a look at where we have come so far, and see if we can
discern, in Whitehead's phrase, "the faint discordant light of the dawn of
another age." In part I, we took up notions of permanence in Western
thought. As we saw, these ideas, which achieved an early expression in *The
Epic of Gilgamesh*, were developed in Judaism and even more strongly in

Christianity, which united theology with the classical thought of Plato and Aristotle. The core of this set of beliefs was also expressed in various forms in the philosophies of Descartes, Locke, Kant, and Hegel, and, mostly in reaction, by Hume.

The main ideas of permanence have been:

- A divine being or beings, as the generative source and ultimate focus of the universe;
- Human beings as eternal entities or souls;
- A world shaped forever by a set of interrelated Platonic ideas;
- A final redemption beyond the contingencies of the historical world;
- Invariant essences and laws of nature; and
- A predetermined end to historical process.

These notions are all highly interrelated, and are part of what we have called the "permanence complex." Behind this complex, we can discern the controlling motive of security: our deep need for comfort, protection, and solace in a threatening world, and in a state of being which ends inevitably in death.

It has been the task of part II to show how developments in highly disparate modes of thought—in science, history, psychology, and philosophy—have attacked the permanence complex from every angle. Although we may not have found an "answer" to the problem of impermanence or death, which earlier ages answered unquestionably by religious faith and philosophy, we have attempted to describe the world as it is, and not, perhaps, as we would like it to be. But with this description, we can discern an energizing convergence of ideas, which indeed looks to a new paradigm. This new way of thinking about the world, which corresponds to what has been learned about it, particularly in the last 150 years, differs markedly from the mind-set of permanence:

- Rather than looking to a generative source and ultimate focus of the universe in a divine being or beings, the new paradigm sees the world as responsible for creating its own forms, forming its own laws, and determining the outcome of its own history.
- Rather than holding that human beings have eternal souls, it conceives of human mentality as the world's evolutionary creation.
- Rather than believing in a world fixed forever by a set of interrelated ideas, it sees concepts as evolving social creations.
- Rather than conceiving of a fixed order of nature, it sees the natural world in full evolution and self-determination.

- Rather than conceiving of humankind as separate from the world, it embeds us in our brains and bodies, and in the surrounding world. The new paradigm implants us in an evolving ecosystem in which we are codependent beings, responsible for ourselves and for the biological environment which supports us.
- Rather than seeing human beings as self-sufficient entities pursuing our self-interest, it positions us in the social order, sees us as shaped and nurtured by others, and lays the basis for deep loyalties to the social basis of our being.
- Rather than believing that human history has a fixed endpoint or teleology, it gives us responsibility for historical outcomes.
- Rather than believing that human history has a fixed endpoint or teleology, it gives us responsibility for historical outcomes.
- Rather than believing in a final redemption or salvation beyond the contingencies of the historical world, it looks to this world to give us whatever feelings of continuity or satisfaction are possible.

Finally, we should briefly review the aspects of "the situation in this moment" which erode our sense of certainty:

- Nature, which we had thought was eternal, now seems historical and contingent.
- Today, not only the teleology of our history seems questionable, but also, with the experience of the last century, history's very continuity, as well as the essential goodness of human beings.
- Globalization and the information revolution, while offering immense promise, provide no certainty that they will solve many of the world's problems, and have weakened a number of traditional social contexts, leaving a sense of unreality and political passivity.
- Postmodernist culture and deconstructionist thought, while attacking major aspects of permanence, seem to fail to offer an adequate explanation of the world, or a basis for social or political involvement.

At the very time that we need a new paradigm of thought, we are beset by uncertainties which arise from our current situation. Accordingly, we must deal with these, as well as with the problems of permanence, if we are to achieve a different orientation, and a capacity to act.

In this final chapter, we will try to meet the challenge we set for ourselves at the onset: If we can better understand Western culture, can we use such knowledge to create a sense of personal purpose and involvement in today's world?

I believe that if we act with increased awareness, accurate empathy, disciplined inquiry, energized purpose, and good humor, in cooperation with others, we *can* make changes which will improve our lives and the lives of a widening circle of others. If we cannot live forever—as, in our imaginations, do the gods—we *can* act, as Gilgamesh learned, heroically and responsibly. I believe that if we take the implications of part II seriously, we can transform the rootless selfishness of the present period can be transformed into a new sense of social involvement.

Acting in the Present Situation

The first step in using the new paradigm is to change the emphasis in our perception of meaning from contemplation to action, as Mead, Dewey, and others reviewed in chapter 10 suggest. Essentially, this shift would mean seeing the primary purpose of language as being engaged in real work, and taking responsibility for the results. Literary critic Terry Eagleton puts it this way:

> Meaning may well be ultimately undecidable if we view language contemplatively, as a chain of signifiers on a page; it becomes "decidable," and words like "truth," "reality," "knowledge" and "certainty" have something of their force restored to them, when we think of language rather as something we do, as indissociably interwoven with our practical forms of life.[3]

If the ultimate end of both art and thought is to help the individual become a better, more effective person, that end must include centering and reconstructing of the self as an agent in society and politics. Such a centering can be achieved, as Dewey points out, by locating the individual at the center of a field of perceived needs and possibilities. In this empathic situation, active engagement, enhanced by interpretive thought, initiates meaning. We can also pursue a line of development, such as suggested by Jane Loevinger, in which the ego or personality matures to achieve its full capacity for dealing imaginatively and responsibly with the world's situations.

Such engagement means that the individual takes an active responsibility for dealing with these situations, and, ultimately, for history. Just as the laws of the natural world are the responsibility of the world's physical constituents, so history is the responsibility of human beings. The eighteenth-century Enlightenment, and the liberal and Marxist accounts of how history must turn out, simply have not proven true. The world is *not* ruled by reason or by the laws of history; poverty is rampant; state socialism, at least of the Soviet type, has proven a bust; and globalization poses innumerable problems. Today we know that we cannot appeal to history as an autonomous and predictable force apart from the contribution of the people who live it.

From the sciences, we have learned important lessons about interdependence. Just as particles prehend, or are foci, of their physical fields and achieve their qualities through interrelationship within these fields; just as individual species exist in mutual interdependence and together produce a viable biosphere, in the twenty-first century we must see our task as maximizing our connection with others. We must understand their situations and needs, and our own, and maximize our cooperation in order to meet these needs.

If we adapt the relational frame of mind suggested in this book, we will increasingly emphasize the public character of our past and potential acts—that is, their effects on others, and the effects of others' acts on us, and the mutuality of our interests. If we accept a progressive notion of responsibility, that our perception of mutual needs is sensitized by the development of our egos or personalities, we will act as a characterological issue, because of who we are. And if permanence can no longer provide a fixed set of objectives, say, through a divinely ordered set of moral laws, we must seek the basis for action through involvement, character, and the widest resources of thought and experience.

In *The Public and Its Problems*, John Dewey defines a "public" as those who share interests. For Dewey, the state ideally is "the organization of the public effected through officials for the protection of the interests shared by its members."[4] In the modern context, this refers not only to community, state, or federal governments, but also to multilateral organizations like the United Nations, the Worldwide Web, and civil society—that is, the entire network of overlapping jurisdictions which now characterize this period.

As a framework for action, Dewey maintains that we must see ourselves as existing within situations, each of which can be considered a public, and then improve our effectiveness within them. Reconceiving publics as the matrices for effective social engagement is the political counterpart to the interactive physics and biology we have reviewed. Including new publics within our sphere of involvement is one result of the telecommunications revolution that characterizes our digital age.

The field in which we operate is our democratic society. The ideal democratic system includes, of course, the various levels of government, but it also encompasses every other organized part of society, including the neighborhood, family, workplace, political party, voluntary or nongovernmental organization, transnational corporation, Internet, and a variety of multilateral organizations. Operating within such a spectrum of responsibility progressively demands the most that individuals can give. Instead of requiring full mastery at the outset, this system establishes conditions under which human beings can achieve their full potential, through their participation, their education, and their receipt of the benefits which the system can produce.[5]

What does this reassessment of democracy mean in practical terms, and how can it restructure political life? Taking Dewey's notion of multiple publics, we can begin to identify various situational matrices that need to be restored or established to effect social ends.

THE NEIGHBORHOOD

One such group which comes immediately to mind is the neighborhood. Here is a natural physical community, but one which, for many Americans in the post–World War II period, no longer works. There are numerous reasons why this is so, such as the atomization of individuals by the mass media and the computer, the growth of the suburbs, and the continuous dislocations of the economy. "I hardly know my neighbors" is a common refrain.

Yet the neighborhood can be the crucible of democracy, whether it be an apartment complex, a collection of city blocks, or a rural township, where neighbors can meet face-to-face and work for common objectives. The neighborhood is also where the direct pull of daily life still can be felt, in opposition to the inferential constructions of life offered by the media or computer. This is not to denigrate their uses as purveyors of information or providers of opportunities for social involvement, but it *is* to urge strongly the importance of direct contact with neighbors, and the possibilities this offers for common endeavors. Here is where the skills of joint action can be developed—skills of listening respectfully, bringing expertise to bear on local situations, compromising, planning, organizing, and implementing. Here keen awareness, accurate empathy, disciplined inquiry, energized purpose, and good humor can have immediate, tangible effects. Here is where the political process can begin, not in the grandiose schemes of the Enlightenment or the Communist Revolution, but in the day-to-day problems of citizens working together to secure better police protection, schools, or community facilities.

THE FAMILY
The social, economic, and technological changes of the postwar period have often worked destructively to break affective ties between members, to isolate generations and age groups, and to numb communication through excessive involvement with media and computers. But the family also can be a field for aggressive activism to reestablish communication, increase ties, and forge common purposes; and, alternatively, to resist acquiescence in alienation or depression. The family, considered as a public, is the area of life which is, potentially at least, most free of the block on empathy placed by the "bottom line." In its nurturing of beloved children, ideally, the family is an area in which progress clearly can be identified with education, ego development, and increasing capacity. Here parents, particularly, can work for the perceived mutual benefit of all.

THE WORKPLACE
Where the neighborhood may be disrupted by constant turnover, and both the neighborhood and family by the isolating effects of mass culture, effecting change in the workplace must take into account the fact that it is organized to maximize programmatic efficiency. Profit-making institutions, in addition, geared to making money, are the product of a hierarchy of ownership and management which may be oblivious of the interests of employees and the consuming public. Particularly in the case of national or transnational corporations, the interest of management in workers, and in the local culture, may be minimal.

In changing the working situation from alienation to cooperation, the keys are information and organization. From management's side, better information about the product and its use will help workers cultivate a sense of responsibility by making clear how their labor fits into a larger picture. From the workers' side, organizing into labor unions can serve as the basis of securing better benefits, working conditions, and pay. A reinvigorated labor movement can provide not only benefits but camaraderie and meaning.

At bottom, both workers and managers need to see how their organization belongs to the field of its operation, and to act in that moral context. Owners and managers can identify more with their consuming publics and their workforce, and thus give priority to the social purpose of their product or service. For this to happen, given the prevailing ethos of profit-making and self-interest, a whole set of pressures will need to complement voluntary action. These can include the possibility of government regulation or public ownership, if sectors of the economy fail to deliver. Other inducements include tax incentives, consumer and shareholder activism, corporate codes of conduct, and worker organization.

In the developing world, oligarchic leaders are just beginning to learn that they may need consumers with enough purchasing power to sustain economic prosperity, in order to maintain their own income levels, although *maquiladoras*, sweatshops, and union-busting are still the rule. Multilateral institutions like the International Monetary Fund are beginning to find that reducing poverty is a necessary component of creating viable economies, although IMF policies are still geared to protecting the interests of the investing groups. Both domestically and abroad, transforming the profit motive, or properly constraining it, will be one of the most difficult tasks of the new century.

THE POLITICAL SYSTEM

The purpose of the democratic systems established between the seventeenth and nineteenth centuries in the United States and western Europe was, initially, primarily defensive. It was to constrain the greed of self-interested rulers or of a special subsection of the public, the "king's friends," and, more broadly, the landed aristocracy. Hence the creation of such political forms as popular and frequent elections, and constitutional guarantees of individual rights.

Phrases such as "to secure these rights," from our Declaration of Independence, emphasized that the primary justification of government was the protection of individual rights, such as free speech and physical security, rather than the advancement of a widening range of citizen interests. The object of our Bill of Rights was to constrain government from infringing on those rights, which, as Locke had suggested, were thought to exist prior to government and even society.

The protection of individual rights has been immensely useful in securing individuals and institutions from the harassment and persecution of the state, and in providing those rights a space in which to flourish.[6] But the doctrine has been used in some cases to proclaim immunity from any consequences of their exercise. An individual's "right to bear arms," for instance, whatever its questionable historical or Constitutional basis, has served as a rallying cry to reject social responsibility for the violent consequences of virtually unregulated ownership and use of guns.[7]

The theme of limiting government to the protection of rights, and to securing the country from external threats, also has been used to inhibit government from providing social services or otherwise playing an active role in society.[8] A positive role for government, such as the provision of social and economic services, was not on the American agenda until well into the twentieth century, although, as we have seen, it was initiated in Europe half a century earlier. During the New Deal, when the United States government first played this role, some sectors of society resisted it on the grounds that the public could not legitimately act through its government to deal with social problems, however dire. This criticism has increased in the present. The argument that the government's legitimate role is to protect rights and its citizens against external threats, and otherwise not interfere in the economy or society, means, for instance, that poverty is not considered a political issue, but a personal problem. People who are poor, this line of reasoning implies, lack the will to extricate themselves from the situation which they have created. As a partial consequence of this criticism, the United States tolerates higher levels of poverty, ill-health, and poor education in its population than does any other country in the developed world.

As we have seen, one reason the New Deal was able to gain national support is that a wide range of overlapping groups, including disparate social classes and ethnic communities, could unite because of the stress of the 1929 depression. As E. J. Dionne notes, however, the idea of an "inclusive and fraternally associated public" would seem less likely today than it was during the New Deal. As we noted, the effect of late-industrial society, including the media, is to isolate the individual consumer and voter, reinforcing the sanction of individual rights at the expense of communal involvement.

If the political system is to meet its public obligations, the first step, then, must be to redefine democracy from a legal guarantee of rights, to the heart of the matter: the sharing of interests and the creation of cooperative programs, by and for a wide range of publics.[9] The second task is to reinvigorate public participation so that democracy can be truly representative.

Democracy formally requires that government include the interests of the full range of the electorate, rather than only a sector of society which is roughly of the same economic class as those in office. With media control and virtually unlimited funds, it is not difficult for this class to disguise legislation which reflects its sole interests.

As we saw in chapter 11, many Americans today believe that the political system no longer represents their interests, and have withdrawn their participation, even to the point of not voting. Yet that system still holds the promise of providing a vast range of needed protections and social services. While competing, in some respects, with transnational corporations, multilateral organizations, and NGOs, the traditional form of the nation-state is still quite powerful.

Putting political power back into the hands of the greater public will require new means of communications, provided by computers, and more sophisticated use of less-expensive media to supplement traditional methods of organizing, publicizing, petitioning, and lobbying. Achieving this end will also require legislation, particularly to limit campaign financing and political contributions, which will restore power to voters.

Influencing their national political system remains the most important means by which citizens can exercise control over transnational corporations and determine their nation's participation in multilateral organizations and international treaties. Control over the transnationals is one of the most complex problems facing the modern world, and will require the most sophisticated coordination of national politics, workplace pressures, and the work of civil society.

Equally, reengaging the United States in multilateral organizations and treaties, including those in arms control, vitally affects our survival. As the United States pulls out of its multilateral obligations, it sows the seeds of nuclear anarchism and the proliferation of other weapons of mass destruction. Unilateralism also downplays crucial multilateral efforts to protect the environment and achieve other socially desired ends, such as to protect children, control diseases, and maintain human rights. Reversing this trend, and achieving multilateralism and the other political objectives mentioned above, will require a concerted citizen effort, working through the political system and civil society.

CIVIL SOCIETY

When the young French statesman Alexis de Tocqueville visited the United States over 165 years ago,[10] he identified voluntary associations as the particular genius of this country, and a necessary balance to the formal political system. Voluntary associations, such as Rotary or Sierra Club chapters, continue to provide a network of involvements today through which members of a democratic citizenry cooperate to achieve meaning and social purpose outside the formality of official politics and the impersonality of the market. Such associations also enable citizens to compensate partially for the lapses and social injustices of our political-economic system, by directly providing social services.

As in all political activities, effective volunteer work requires learning a variety of skills: how to recruit members and choose officers; to account for and budget funds; to conduct discussions and meetings; and to resolve conflicts and reach decisions in ways that respect the sensitivity and interests of both the majority and minority, in order to achieve the closest approximation to the group's informed views and interests, and to realize them in the world. Today, new skills such as establishing and using Web sites and computerized networks are necessary, particularly if groups are to operate over considerable distances, and create common cause with people who are otherwise strangers.

The network of voluntary associations or nongovernmental organizations together that comprise what is called "civil society" has been a primary vehicle for the post–World War II world's attempt to achieve economic, social, and cultural rights, in addition to civil and political rights.[11] Voluntary organizations often work to secure these rights within the particular context of a local society and culture. In addition, civil society is involved in helping to secure international peace, a sustainable world economy, and a nurturant global environment.

As *State of the World 2003* notes:

> Because of their scale and because of the politics that surround
> them, governments and international institutions are often influ-
> enced by archaic ideologies or beholden to entrenched economic
> interests. Outside groups with fresh ideas and representing new
> political pressures are often required to overcome the momentum
> of the status quo.... This example of NGOs stepping in to fill a
> gap left by governments [at the World Summit on Sustainable

Development in Johannesburg in 2002] provides guidance for how the world can one day get beyond the sort of impasse that has blocked international progress on many economic, social and environmental issues in the past decade.[12]

In *Religion in the Making*,[13] Alfred North Whitehead shows how travel throughout the ancient world enlarged the traveler's thoughts from concern for his tribe to all humankind, thus providing the basis for world consciousness which underlies world religion. Today, this consciousness, achieved not only through travel but through tools like the World Wide Web, includes vital matters on the agenda of survival: to end environmental degradation, develop a sustainable economy, eradicate world poverty, and create the conditions for a lasting and nurturant peace. This is the challenge of civil society, which, as it achieves increasing power, may well realize Richard Rorty's dream of a united reform movement—but on a global scale.

Vision and Activism

Purpose emerges through involvement in situations, as one understands one's condition and the condition of one's associates and the surrounding world. Yet involvement in specific situations is not enough. Ultimate effectiveness requires vision, or, put another way, the development of an effective personal philosophy.

In my view, such vision or philosophy must be informed not only by the specific situations in which one is immediately involved, but by a continuous dialogue with the lessons of more generalized experience available in one's society and culture. In the end, we must unite our conception of progress toward biological, cultural, and characterological complexity, with accurate empathy in specific situations. Human beings achieving this unity will include the vast world and infinite time in their experience; see that world as nuanced and multifaceted; respect the right of all sentient beings to develop in a nurturant environment; and interact with others to make this a reality.

While various paths or configurations of complexity are possible, a sense for what promotes complexity and integrated development emerges as a crosscultural, foundational value. This value must supersede the bottom line of commercialism on the one hand, and the anarchic aspects of deconstructionist thought on the other. It can emerge as a guiding vision in our situational involvements, which can energize and inform our specific goals.

Complexity by itself is not enough. Without accurate empathy for others, that is, without full situational involvement, an individual's complexity may represent a capacity to do damage. Smart dictators may be more dangerous than crude ones. It is also important to realize that emotionally rich involvements may well have more to offer than arid intellectualism or insensitive ideology. Here, detachment does not represent superiority. Finally, it is clear that no single culture has any monopoly on quality, or any right to exploit others for its own advantage.

Education for Democracy

Democracy offers a vital check to abuses based on self-interest or a single standard which ignores the values or cultures of other individuals or groups. In a genuine democracy, every aspect of social process—including vision, the identification of specific interests, and the choice of effective tactics—is subject to debate, and to adjustments which take opposing ideas and interests into account. At each step, democracy must work through informed persuasion. We cannot presume that our own ideas are necessarily correct. That is the great lesson of Aristotle, one that belies his sometimes authoritarian politics: Persuasion should triumph over force. In a democracy, that is the ultimate challenge of one person, one vote. If the system works effectively, each person must be persuaded, not forced, to vote in response to a person seeking office presenting his or her case. The person holding or seeking office must, in turn, be open to persuasion by his or her constituents. Democracy can also offer the more refined challenges of heightening sensitivity or wisdom, so that an increasingly sophisticated set of interests are on the table. The interests of minorities, as well as the majority, are part of a final solution, and reconciliation of differences is superior to any short-term triumph.[14]

In the United States, is there a mechanism which can help prepare citizens for the obligations of democracy? Can it help produce the "democratic" man or woman? Can it unite knowledge and vision, with the techniques of effective action? Can it help produce people with the required maturity to meet the challenges of a system which relies on all of its members?

The answer, which has been suggested from Thomas Jefferson to John Dewey, is education. Dewey writes:

If there is especial need of educational reconstruction...it is because of the thoroughgoing change in social life accompanying the advance of science, the industrial revolution, and the development of democracy. Such practical changes cannot take place without demanding an educational reformation to meet them, and without leading men to ask what ideas and ideals are implicit in these social changes, and what revision they require of the ideas and ideals which are inherited from older and unlike cultures.[15]

Education's special task in a democracy, in addition to its traditional role of imparting knowledge and technical skills, can be divided into several components. The first has to do with preparing students to play an effective role in purposeful, social situations involving a variety of "publics." The second has to do with promoting students' characterological or ego development so that they willingly see their responsibilities, and meet them with wisdom and humanity. The third involves enlarging students' understanding to include a vision that informs their participation.

Dewey, and a host of progressive educators who followed him, stressed that the most productive incubator of education, the most emotionally engaging and memorable, is the involved situation. In this simulacrum of the real world, the student experiences what Dewey calls "learning by doing."

Publishing a class newspaper or maintaining a class Web site, for example, engages students in the accurate empathy involved in sensitive reporting; the mathematics of business and production; and the cooperative and democratic processes of joint decision-making and management. At the same time, these projects provide opportunities for learning specific facts about real situations; inferring principles from these experiences; applying those principles to other situations as working hypotheses; and relating these findings to standing bodies of thought. In such projects, students learn skills which prepare them for work with varied publics in a responsible life.

Beyond this, schools should be encouraged to teach the techniques of political organizing used in both formal politics and voluntary associations. Such training should include member recruitment, petitioning, lobbying, running meetings, establishing computerized groups, and operating a Web site. "Civics" curricula should provide specific information about how the present political system actually works, including its counterparts in the voluntary sector, as opposed to its merely formal operations.[16]

To promote ego development, schools should provide what Jane Loevinger calls "pacer" experiences, that is, exposing children to people, materials, and situations which urge them toward progressively higher levels of ego development (see chapter 10). Schools should also involve students in conflict resolution, communication, and other social skills to increase students' ability to operate effectively within a group.

How should we measure educational progress? The question is important, as criteria for progress inevitably influence practice. In complementing standardized knowledge and problem-solving tests, we need to develop ways to assess social effectiveness if the schools are to maintain a situational focus.

Up until now, schools have relied heavily on intelligence tests to help determine student placement. In addition to class and ethnic biases, not only do such tests say little about situational effectiveness, but the test scores remain fairly constant despite school experience. As a useful supplement, ego-development tests, perhaps revised to take ethnic and gender differences more sensitively into account, might measure change. By discerning such capacities as the handling of complexity, empathy, and ambiguity, they would help teachers assist students in becoming increasingly more effective in social and political situations.

If education is to attempt to increase students' capacity to deal with the real world, this must affect not only what students do in class, but what they read. Textbooks which present a synthetically created "subject," such as physics or American history, as the final truth about these fields, will fail to reveal how these fields develop in time—how they are the product of countless individual contributors, and how these specific contributions solve particular problems or reflect particular historical preoccupations.[17] If students see these fields as experiments at truth, they will see physics or history as the result of a social effort to which someday they may want to contribute.

But education, like politics, must also look beyond the immediate situation. At the vocational level, of course, its task is to prepare students not only to obtain jobs, but to enable them to assimilate new vocational demands in a future economy. Beyond that, education's task is no less than to prepare citizens to be able to be effective members of society, working in a variety of publics—the neighborhood, family, workplace, political system, and civil society. This suggests that institutional education should be available throughout the entire lifespan, particularly if early education has been inadequate. The ultimate contexts in which human situations are embedded are evolution and historical progress, and, reciprocally, the structure of the ego or personality. If an individual's vision is to be based on an understanding of evolutionary, historical, and developmental advance, education must provide this knowledge. This will mean learning how the physical and biological worlds advance into greater complexity and integration; the various means by which history progresses toward increased complexity, or breaks down; the expressions of philosophers, writers, and artists who have created their own integrated visions; and how the individual moves through stages of increasing complexity or integration, to achieve maturity.

It is here that science, history, the humanities, and psychology each have their special place. The excitement of history comes in sharing the experience of others in different places and times, whose lives are captured in the clutch of immediacy. It is to know with the intimacy of historical detail the full context of their experience, including the relevant personalities and circumstances. In the story of Mohandas Gandhi, for example, a student can learn how Gandhi's combination of will, idealism, and craft interacted with his time to contribute to Indian independence. For the historian or reader, history is not a self-referential story, an excursus into fiction or ego, as deconstructionists suggest. Rather, it is an attempt to reconstruct the experience of other people in other times in as vital a state of accuracy as the historical record and skills of the historian and reader allow. This understanding, then, becomes part of a growing body of wisdom which sees the story of humankind in terms of personal development and public politics, and which can inform present action.

Science provides the same insight into the adventure of matter and organisms in their immediate occasions and in the development of the world. The Harvard chemist George Wald once observed that, in his practice of chemistry, he tried to "feel like a molecule." To know science is to reconstruct the situation of the particle, molecule, or organism, and to see its action or development in its environment or prehensive field, with the same accurate empathy that one can bring to history or personal relations. It is to attempt to construct the laws or uniformities which generalize specific results, and to create the history of galaxies, the earth, life systems, and organisms.

Literature and art provide their own inimitable insights. In Shakespeare's *Macbeth*, for example, we see the birth of a dictator in a way which is more poignant, and perhaps more revelatory, than sometimes can be gleaned from history or biography. In all works of art, we see the subtle, intricate play of forces which mimic the organic and historic development of personality and the world.

Finally, psychology reveals the individual in the grip of a personal history, and the particular way that individual develops an irreducible personhood within his or her environment—a personhood which displays the same sense for organic composition as one finds in science and art. Here, as we have seen, psychologists such as Freud, Sullivan, Piaget, and Loevinger have created a vision of development which can inform how we understand ourselves and others, and how we can feel a moral connection to them.

But the *end* is not knowledge or vision. Perhaps the ultimate answer to Plato and Aristotle is that vision, without implementation, is deficiently real. Contemplating knowledge, in the absence of involvement, lacks the richness of community and the immediacy of personal affections and loyalties. Without situational experience and its compelling affect and richness of detail, and without its achievement of results in concrete facts, vision cannot be fully realized. Nor can vision by itself create a sustaining physical or social structure through which it can be repeated, modified, or enriched.

History, science, the humanities, psychology, and philosophy, the latter with its special task of generalization, are not ends which are complete in themselves. The Platonic and Aristotelean notion that society exists to support the contemplative life, contains only a partial truth. Part of the enjoyment of life is indeed contemplative. But it is also true that history, science, the humanities, psychology, and philosophy must inform socially effective action.[18]

As we saw in chapter 11, one of the difficulties presented by deconstructionist thought is that it discourages action by questioning the possibility of achieving any truth or meaning. In the universities, we saw how the aims of education are often buried under a heap of competing claims based on cultural relativism, elitism, power politics, and deconstructionist theories.

Visions change, to be sure, but if a growing complexity and sensitivity to life's demands is a worthwhile vision, they can be held as desirable ends despite competing claims. It then makes sense to work for standards of scholarship, and of artistic integration, which, within a broad range of multicultural possibilities, provide a direction for students to realize their potential as effective human beings.

At the international scale, the need for universal standards runs into the problem of local cultural or national practices. Many human rights activists maintain that certain practices diminish the fullness or complexity of life to such an extent that they are rightly condemnable by international law—for example, genocide, bodily mutilation, slavery, or blatant censorship.[19] Groups in power often impose such practices on those lacking the capacity to defend themselves.

The Universal Declaration of Human Rights, which attempts to offer an overarching set of moral standards, has been criticized as a Western instrument imposed on other societies. To be sure, each society creates its particular environment. But to prevent flagrant abuses, such an instrument which minimally defines conditions necessary for free human development seems appropriate. This calls up the need for its constant democratic review and, if needed, revision, not for its abrogation.

Art and Society

Because art is fictional, representational, symbolic, abstract, or nonobjective, it sometimes has come to be considered as offering less actuality than do "real" experiences. The secularization of life in the centuries following the Renaissance focused consciousness on factualness, just as science focused research on objects in motion, and the market focused attention on price or commodities in relation to demand. As the West industrialized, artists became marginalized producers who increasingly cultivated their isolation and idiosyncracy.[20]

It is useful to remember art's original role in collective life, in marking and celebrating clan membership, worshiping the gods, feasting and fighting, and otherwise enhancing the vividness of experience.[21] Think with what care "primitive" people embellished common objects, such as pots or spears, which now are displayed as "art" or "folk art" in museums. Or think how an art work like *The Epic of Gilgamesh* evokes its world and concentrates attention on its major themes. Philosopher Alexander Argyros writes:

Probably stemming from the rituals of early human huminids, literature offers human society the opportunity to consider those crucial decisions that affect the nature of its being, decisions concerning its gods (theology), its place in the universe (cosmology), its morals (ethics), its social organization (kinship or politics), its techniques for assigning value to objects (economics), its preferred ways of defining knowledge and of assigning the requirements of making truthful statements (epistemology), its definitions of Being (ontology), and its understanding of art (aesthetics).[22]

As society grows more complex, it continues to need art to express conflicts within its collective structure, and within the minds of its members. In an age of leveling industrialism, for example, romantic poetry pressed the claims of the spirit against those of the market, thus representing a deeply felt need. (Wordsworth writes, "Getting and spending, we lay waste our powers.")[23] Even if a work of art fails to resolve conflicts, it presents them in an encapsulated form where we can see them more clearly than in the informational chaos of daily life. If conflicts *are* resolved, the resolution often involves the kind of balance implicit in a new level of complexity, rather than in the destructive simplifications achieved by eliminating opposing forces.

Rather than considering each element as independent, with its own affective value, art shows how the meaning of the whole, and the role of each part, are achieved by interrelationship. In this way, as Whitehead points out, art parallels biological process, where molecules, cells, or organs, whether considered as physical entities or as information, achieve meaning in relation to the whole organism. Art is also analogous to the ego structures of highly developed human beings. It is what we mean when we speak of "beautiful souls"; and to sensitive solutions of problems in social or political life as the "art" of diplomacy; or to a "beautiful solution" in mathematics.

A work of art itself establishes the solution, rather than simply lifting it off the Platonic shelf of eternal ideas. The work's materiality, historic specificity, and relation to its culture, and its realization in time, *are* its reality. The work's possibility, deficiently real, is inherent in the nature of things, and suggests the beauty of Plato's world. The emphasis on the materiality of art by some modern artists, or on its production as a specific event (for instance, in "performance art"), is a subtle protest against the implication in Platonic aesthetic theory that, ultimately, art is timeless and objective, and independent of its materials or social situation.[24] For Whitehead, art is at the center of real process. What he called the "creative advance" is how the universe evolves through art.

Art also lies at the core of morality. Art generalizes the notion of 'morality' to mean whatever works to achieve balanced complexity. If art is oblivious of morals in a conventional sense, it does show the matrix in which moral values must operate. Art can then serve a moral purpose, but not by simply reiterating society's prevailing morality. Rather, its service to morality depends on the artist's freedom and independence in his or her pursuit of complexity.

The moral role of art, then, is to enhance awareness of our environment, and to heighten our capacity to see its conflicts. It is to cultivate that sense of harmony which comes with resolution, or that irony which accompanies the contemplation of incompatible elements. And it is to project futures, drawing upon the potentialities of the present. If these are, indeed, art's tasks, then art is at the very heart of a culture, and its purity of spirit must continually be reasserted.

Art provides its own standard of criticism, which questions the deconstructionist premise that beauty is a dismissible construct of society's elite. Rather, this standard says that there is a beauty in particular works, based on internal complexity and integrated relationship to the full environment, including the prevailing culture and physical environment, upon which a standard of criticism can be based. Deep similarities across cultures then make crosscultural appreciation possible. But efficacy in creating balanced complexity within its particular cultural and physical environment is the ultimate standard by which a work must be judged.

Postmodernism is sometimes called "the age of information." Without organization, information is not thought, nor art, nor life. Undigested information is the ultimate waste product of our age. The task of art is to organize information, and to suggest, through a variety of ways, the many-valued paths of cultural and personal development.

Beyond Permanence

As we review what we have said throughout this book, individual experience must be our "bottom line" of value.[25] In the end, the purpose of philosophy and history is to enhance our lives, to inform the fullest experience we can have. We cannot claim that knowledge always results in happiness, although there are, to be sure, moments or passages of intense joy which come with the fullest realization of the world. But part of knowing the world is also knowing its sadness and tragedies, its surety of personal death, its loss of loved ones, its falls from grace, including one's own, and the failures of one's efforts, however intelligent and spirited, and those of one's colleagues, to mitigate suffering and enhance life. There is no

241

insurance policy guaranteeing that our work will survive, or that our experiences will be happy ones. Even serenity, which our sages tell us is the emotional product of harmony, may not always be reachable.

Nor is value confined to the highest levels of complexity. It is simply wrong to deny value at lower levels—of sensuous pleasure, of affection, or achievement. Such experiences may be pleasurable in their own right. One cannot gainsay the primary pleasures of realizing life's values at any level at which they occur; they are also vital in the complex structure of one's life and society. What is important here is that the *experience* of such values, such as the value of sex or of physical coordination, not be at the expense of others, or significantly weaken one's ability to entertain more complex experiences.

If it is unrealistic to promise that life will be unremittingly blissful at the highest levels, complexity is no less persuasive. Plato asks the question throughout his dialogues, particularly in the *Phaedrus* and *Theaetetus*: Why is the Good better, why it is worth pursuing? His answer is that the Good is persuasive, that it offers us something in our own nature to which we respond; and that, as one gains wisdom, one can progressively see why it is best. Aristotle describes reason's continuous battle to persuade the world, in opposition to force and accident, which nevertheless may still overwhelm it. Whitehead would say that it is the very tendency in nature itself, the "creative advance," to move forward to the good of balanced complexity. And Dewey, Sullivan, and Loevinger would say that when we understand our own situation and those of others, we will act to maximize consciousness and sensitivity; that activism will follow as a natural result of accurate empathy.

To gain this wisdom, the self must choose appropriate experiences which increase its complexity, just as the educational system must provide experiences which test and expand the self's resources. Loevinger's pacer experiences, for example, offer the developing ego encouraging examples of complexity. This, indeed, was Socrates' role for his interlocutors in the dialogues. To expand the self's resources is the reason we instruct our children, teach classes, write books. Then, as the self grows in wisdom, it can enter into the service of others or of causes, such as scientific knowledge or artistic expression, or the promotion of peace or of economic well-being, which transcend itself. Philosophy consolidates such experience, and refines vision, which further develops the self and informs further experience. The purpose of philosophy, then, and of history, science, and the humanities which contribute to it, is to understand the world as it is and as it has been, and to move into the future with a compelling vision of its possibilities. As we have surveyed the world in these pages, we have found a world bereft of the sense of permanence of earlier periods. The nostalgia we might feel for such assurances is understandable, but they may not inform our vision now. Permanence has fled, but it has left a world conceived as process, contingency, and possibility. The more we understand it, the more it increases in wonder. It is a world which we can help create, or lose, by our own actions.

For our actions to be meaningful, vision must inform them. A vision of the world can then become our integrating motive, prioritizing our forces, focusing our attention, and directing our actions. Within each situation, we must be receptive to a continuous dialogue between vision and result. Outside such situations, we must discern the larger environment.

Immediacy and reflection, involvement and contemplation, swing back and forth. Internal discipline does its work in sorting and arranging our priorities on the one side, and providing composure on the other. At the furthest reach of vision, we experience an alignment with the world, with its evolutionary past, the history of our species, and with our own developing resources, and a quickening sense of possibility and responsibility. We then survey the many urgent tasks of this time, choose the appropriate opportunity for involvement, and begin to work.

End notes

Chapter 1. SUMER: GODS AND HUMANS

1. All quotations are from N.K. Sandars, *The Epic of Gilgamesh* (New York: Penguin Books, 1960). This translation, which is based primarily on tablets from the seventh century B.C.E., which the British discovered in the ancient Assyrian city of Nineveh, incorporates other sources from the preceding fifteen hundred years into a unified work. For the general reader, as opposed to the specialist, this creates a readable text, albeit at the expense of some historical purity. For an analysis of textual sources, see Jeffrey H. Tigay, *The Evolution of the Gilgamesh Epic* (Philadelphia: The University of Pennsylvania Press, 1982).

2. With Sumerian material, a note of caution is useful. Interpretation of the clay cuneiform tablets, on which epics like *Gilgamesh* were recorded, is often chancy because the tablets can be fragmented or corrupt, and because scholars have still not reached full consensus on their meaning. Once, at a conference on Sumerian literature, Samuel Noah Kramer, one of the principal founders of Sumerian studies, and Thorkild Jacobsen, a major contributor, who respected each other immensely, became embroiled in a dispute about whether or not there are verb tenses in the Sumerian language. Kramer remarked to me, "Eisendrath, where Jacobsen sees verb tenses, I see sand!"

3. Emile Durkheim, *The Elementary Forms of the Religious Life*, first published in 1912 (New York: Collier Books, 1961), p. 21.

4. For an analysis of Sumerian religion and society, see Samuel Noah Kramer, *History Begins at Sumer* (New York: Doubleday & Co., Inc., 1959) and *The Sumerians: Their History, Culture, and Character* (Chicago: The University of Chicago Press, 1960). For an alternative interpretation, see Thorkild Jacobsen, *The Treasures of Darkness: A History of Mesopotamian Religion* (New Haven and London: Yale University Press, 1976). For a fine anthology of Sumerian poetry, see *Thorkild Jacobsen, The Harps That Once...Sumerian Poetry in Translation* (New Haven and London: Yale University Press, 1987). See also Jean Bottéro, *Mesopotamia: Writing, Reasoning, and the*

Gods, translated by Zainab Bahrani and Marc Van de Mieroop (Chicago and London: The University of Chicago Press, 1992). For a depiction of Inanna in Sumerian literature, see Diane Wolkstein and Samuel Noah Kramer, *Inanna: Queen of Heaven and Earth* (New York: Harper & Row, 1983).

5.   The idea of the divine would eventually change from the set of anthropomorphic personalities in ancient Sumer to permanent philosophic essences shaping the world. This is the role that the Greek thinkers, who founded philosophy over fifteen hundred years later, would give them. Meanwhile, as we see in chapter 3, the older notion of gods who directly represent the natural forces would be maintained in the official religions of both Greece and Rome.

6.   This idea evolved easily into the notion of a permanent repository of knowledge in the soul, which Plato believed, or a permanent order of nature which reflected the mind of God, a notion held by Aristotle, Isaac Newton, and Albert Einstein.

7.   A parallel is in Genesis 2: 7 in which God forms human beings from the dust of the earth, and blows life into their nostrils.

Chapter 2. JUDAISM: MONOTHEISM AND THE PEOPLE

1.   *The Five Books of Moses*, a new translation with introductions, commentary, and notes by Everett Fox (New York: Schocken Books, 1995), Genesis 1:1–3. All quotations from the Torah (Pentateuch) are from the Fox translation. In using new translations (see chapter 4 on Christianity), my hope is to stimulate a fresh reading of the texts. In his *From Epic to Canon: History and Literature in Ancient Israel* (Baltimore: Johns Hopkins University Press, 1998), biblical scholar Frank Moore Cross argues that the text of the Hebrew Bible and the books which it included (the canon) were not fully established until about the end of the first century, probably under the strong influence of the Pharisaic rabbi Hillel.

2.   In presenting the Hebrew Bible, I am not taking up the question of its historical accuracy, which has become a major battleground in biblical scholarship. While the majority view of scholars working in the field is that there is a growing body of archeological correlatives for the biblical texts, a substantial group of revisionists attacks the idea that there is any evidence at all that the first five books of the Hebrew Bible are historically accurate.

As summarized by William G. Dever in the March/April 2000 issue of *Biblical Archeology*, which is entirely taken up with this issue, the revisionist position is that the Hebrew Bible is the product of the religious and cultural identity crisis of Judaism in the Hellenistic era, dating from the fourth to the first centuries B.C.E., and is not the story of an actual historical Israel in a much earlier period. Thus, according to the revisionists, the Hebrew Bible is literature rather than history. It is a "social construct" that reflects the religious interests and propaganda of a late, elitist theocratic party within Judaism. According to these critics, there was no "early Israel" as a distinct ethnic entity from the thirteenth to the eleventh centuries B.C.E., no Judahite state before the late eighth century, and no significant political capital in Jerusalem before the second century B.C.E.

While disagreeing strongly with these revisionists, Dever himself does not believe in the full accuracy of the Hebrew Bible. In his *Who Were the Early Israelites and Where Did They Come From?* (Grand Rapids, MI: William B. Eerdmans Publishing Company, 2003), Dever says that while the Exodus stories "may rest on some historical foundations, however minimal," the Israelites did not spring primarily from the people who fled Egypt.

Conformation for this view is provided by Israel Finkelstein and Neil Asher Silberman, who cite persuasive archaeological evidence in their *The Bible Unearthed: Archaeology's New Vision of Ancient Israel and the Origin of its Sacred Texts* (New York: The Free Press, 2001). Although they date the writing of the first five books of the Hebrew Bible much earlier than do the radical revisionists, they hold that most of it is historical fiction. Thus they say, "The historical saga contained in the Bible—from Abraham's encounter with God and his journey to Canaan, to Moses' deliverance of the children of Israel from bondage, to the rise and fall of the kingdoms of Israel and Judah—was not a miraculous revelation, but a brilliant product of the human imagination. It was first conceived—as recent archaeological finds suggest—during the span of two or three generations, about twenty-six hundred years ago." Finkelstein and Silberman date the writing of these events in the reign of Josiah, king of Judah, from 639 to 609 B.C.E.

3.   For example, in Exodus 20:3, when God commands the people "not to have any other gods before my presence," the implication is clearly that other gods exist; the people are simply told not to worship them. Or in Genesis 6:1–2, we find this passage: "that the divine beings saw how beautiful the human women were / so they took themselves wives, whomever they chose." The divine beings are not otherwise identified, but their very presence would argue that a strictly monotheistic line of thought was still in development. The persistence of nonmonotheistic thought is brought home by

Finkelstein and Silberman, when they report that literally hundreds of statues of female deities have been discovered coming from the period of Josiah.

4. For well over a hundred years, biblical scholars have been teasing out the separate sources of the Bible. A useful introduction to this effort, although one which looks more to traditional than contemporary scholarship, is provided by Richard Elliot Friedman's *Who Wrote the Bible?* (New York: Harper & Row, 1987). Again, this is an area of scholarship which has become a battleground.

5. See part I of Yehezkel Kaufmann's monumental *The Religion of Israel*, translated and abridged by Moshe Greenberg (New York: Schocken Books, 1972).

6. Job 38:4–7 in *The Writings: A New Translation of the Holy Scriptures According to the Traditional Hebrew Text* (Philadelphia: The Jewish Publication Society of America, 1982). Job appears to have been written somewhere between 600 and 400 B.C.E., at roughly the same time as drama by Aeschylus and Sophocles.

7. From "Nada" by Pierre Emmanuel, in *Mid-Century French Poets*, edited by Wallace Fowlie (New York: Grove Press, 1955), p. 273.

8. Genesis 3. Although resurrection of the dead appears in Jewish thought several centuries before Christ, it remains a distinctly minority view. See Isaiah 25:8–9 and 26:19, and Daniel 12:1–3, which reads, "At that time, the great prince, Michael, who stands beside the sons of your people, will appear. It will be a time of trouble, the like of which has never been since the nation came into being. At that time, your people will be rescued, all who are found inscribed in the book. Many of those that sleep in the dust of the earth will awake, some to eternal life, others to reproaches, to everlasting abhorrence. And the knowledgeable will be radiant like the bright expanse of the sky, and those who lead the many to righteousness will be like the stars forever and ever."

9. See R.D. Laing, *The Divided Self* (New York: Penguin Books, 1965).

10. Genesis 3:21–22.

11. This notion is totally reversed by Saint Augustine (see chapter 4), who views man's disobedience in the Garden of Eden as original sin which, transmitted through semen, infects all humankind, and destroys any possibility for the subsequent exercise of free will or moral choice. It was the acceptance of Saint Augustine's argument over the next thousand years which helped to justify an authoritarian Church and secular rule. See Elaine Pagels, *Adam, Eve, and the Serpent* (New York: Vintage Books, 1989), particularly chaps. v and vi, discussed in chapter 4.

12. Isaiah 1:18–20 in *The Prophets*, a new translation of The Holy Scriptures according to the traditional Hebrew text (Philadelphia: The Jewish Publication Society of America, 1978).

13. Here God is reported as saying to Moses: "So now, if you will hearken, yes, hearken to my voice and keep my covenant, you shall be to me a special-treasure from among all the peoples. Indeed, all the earth is mine, but you, you shall be to me a kingdom of priests, a holy nation." Exodus 19:5–6.

14. Frank Moore Cross, *From Epic to Canon*, p. 7.

15. Exodus 19:5–6.

16. Isaiah 2:1–3.

17. The object of Susan A. Handelman's groundbreaking study, *The Slayers of Moses: The Emergence of Rabbinic Interpretation in Modern Literary Theory* (Albany, New York: State University of New York Press, 1982), is to show how modern deconstructionists, with their open-ended, ahistorical approach to the "sacred" text, are continuing in the spirit of this two-thousand-year tradition (see chapter 11 below).

18. For the influence of Platonism on Philo of Alexandria, see, for example, E.R. Goodenough, *Introduction to Philo Judaeus*, 2nd ed. (New York: Barnes & Noble, 1963). For a study of Moses Maimonides, who was greatly influenced by Aristotle, see Marvin Fox, *Interpreting Maimonides: Studies in Methodology, Metaphysics, and Moral Philosophy* (Chicago and London: The University of Chicago Press, 1990). For an overview of the Kabbalah, see Gershom Scholem, *On the Kabbalah and Its Symbolism* (New York: Schocken Books, Inc., 1965). See also Gershom Scholem's seminal *Major Trends in Jewish Mysticism* (New York: Schocken Books, 1946), which covers both Kabbalistic and Hasidic Judaism, and Arthur Green's *Tormented Master: The Life and Spiritual Quest of Rabbi Nahman of Bratslav* (Woodstock, VT: Jewish Lights, 1992).

Chapter 3. CLASSICAL PHILOSOPHY: IDEAS AND ESSENCES

1. *Phaedo*, 105d–e in *The Collected Dialogues of Plato*, edited by Edith Hamilton and Huntington Cairns (New York: Pantheon Books, 1961). All references to Plato are to this edition.

2. I have chosen not to discuss other strains of Greek and Roman thought, for example, the pre-Socratics, or later, the Cynics or Stoics, because the influence of these other strains to a large extent loses its identity in the Western tradition. This leaves Plato and Aristotle, and later thinkers associated with them, most importantly Plotinus (205–270 C.E.), virtually alone in establishing a continuing relation with the thought of medieval and modern Europe.

3. *Phaedo*, 66c.

4. *Ibid.*, 80b.

5. For Plato's theory of perception, see *Sophist*, 247d–e or *Theaetetus*, 153e–154a.

6. *Phaedo*, 101c.

7. Allan Bloom writes, "The gods are a prefiguration of the ideas which are known to the philosophers." See *The Republic of Plato*, second edition, translated, with notes, an interpretative essay, and a new introduction by Allan Bloom (New York: Basic Books, 1968), p. 353. My analysis of *The Republic* is indebted to Bloom's perceptive essay.

8. *Phaedo*, 100c.

9. *Symposium*, 212a.

10. *Timaeus*, 30a–b. Although the *Timaeus* suggests that the act of creation is historic, that is, takes place at the beginning of the world, Plato can be read as suggesting that creation is an ongoing or continuous infusion of God into the world's nature, a notion which would eventually form part of the doctrine of the Trinity (see chapter 4).

11. *Ibid.*, 29c. As we shall see in the next chapter, this speculative aspect of Plato's thought would diminish his authority in the eyes of medieval Church divines.

12. The close alliance of Platonic thought to Christianity is clear in the writing of Saint Augustine. See, for example, his *Confessions*, translated with an introduction by R.S. Pine-Coffin (New York: Penguin Books, 1961), particularly books x–xii, or *The City of God*, trans. by Marcus Dods (New York: Modern Library, 1950).

13. Plato writes, "Unless...either philosophers become kings in our states or those whom we now call our kings and rulers take to the pursuit of philosophy seriously and adequately, and there is a conjunction of these two things, political power and philosophical intelligence...there can be no cessation of troubles... for our states, nor, I fancy, for the human race either." *Republic* 473c–d.

14. More thorough than Plato's dialogues, often more complex, Aristotle's works, which may be only his or his students' lecture notes, are infinitely less quotable. What follows is derived principally from *On the Soul, Physics, Metaphysics, Nichomachean Ethics*, and *Politics*. See *The Basic Works of Aristotle*, edited and with an introduction by Richard McKeon (New York: Random House, 1941). All references are to this edition.

15. When I first studied philosophy at the University of Chicago with Professor Henry Rago, a student in our class remarked, just a bit pretentiously, "You see, Professor, Plato and Aristotle are really saying the same thing, if one truly understands them." Professor Rago, an eminent philosopher and editor of *Poetry Magazine*, who had been teaching the Western classics for many years, waited a moment to collect his thoughts. Then he said, "Mr. D., I suspect you'll find that the path of wisdom here will consist of understanding their differences as completely as possible, because those differences structure a great deal of Western thought."

16. Abraham Edel, *Aristotle and His Philosophy* (Chapel Hill: North Carolina Press, 1982), p. 123. This section on Aristotle is informed by conversations with Professor Edel and by the reading of his work.

17. See *Ibid.*, particularly pp. 66 and 123.

18. The problem Aristotle posed for the rising science of mechanics was his notion that final causes, for example, for a body to fall to the earth, forms part of its essence or nature. By contrast, Newton argued that bodies fall because of their mutual gravitational attraction and that the earth has no privileged position, that is, the earth and the body *mutually* attract each other (see chapter 5).

19. My use of "man" in many of these pages reflects the fact that Aristotle, when he referred to human beings, usually meant men, as women were not citizens of the state and were considered little better than property. To the extent possible, I have otherwise tried to use gender neutral language.

20. *Nicomachean Ethics*, bk. x, chap. 7. Aristotle also holds that as God's supreme activity is contemplation, when it is practiced by men, it enables them to imitate God.

21. *Politics*, bk. iii, chap. 5.

22. Aristotle writes that "from the hour of their birth, some are marked out for subjection, others for rule." *Ibid.*, bk. i, chap. 4.

23. While Darwin himself did not deal with genetic variation, the Darwinist theory of evolution readily adapted itself to this model (see chapter 7).

Chapter 4. THE GOOD NEWS: THE ALTERNATIVE OF PERSONAL SALVATION

1. Acts 2:22–36 in *Acts and Letters of the Apostles*, newly translated from the Greek by Richmond Lattimore (New York: Farrar, Straus, Giroux, 1982), pp. 6–7. See also *The Four Gospels and the Revelation*, newly translated from the

Greek by Richmond Lattimore (New York: Farrar, Straus, Giroux, 1979). I
have used these translations, which vary somewhat from the traditional King
James, because they may help the reader take a fresh look at the texts.
Throughout this chapter, both the King James textual references and the
Lattimore translation page numbers are given.

2. *Acts* 2:37–39, p. 7.
3. The reconstruction of the historical Jesus is the subject of a mountainous
    and still growing literature, dating from Albert Schweitzer's *The Quest of the
    Historical Jesus: A Critical Study of its Progress from Reimarus to Wrede*
    (New York: Macmillan, 1910). Schweitzer spends hundreds of pages demon-
    strating how the historicity of Jesus was laboriously constructed by genera-
    tions of particularly nineteenth century French and German scholars, but at
    the end of the book depicts a mystic vision of Christ which shows as dra-
    matically as possible how belief may have little to do with history or histor-
    ical scholarship.

    Particularly in the last few decades, with the publication of the *Dead
    Sea Scrolls* of the Essene sect and the Gnostic *Nag Hammadi Codices*, there
    has been a renewed interest in the historical Jesus. For parallels with early
    Christianity in the Essene movement, see *The Dead Sea Scriptures*, with in-
    troduction and notes by Theodore H. Gaster (New York: Anchor Books Dou-
    bleday, 1976), although the relation of Christianity to the Essene movement
    has become increasingly controversial in recent years. For the texts of Gnos-
    ticism, see *The Nag Hammadi Library in English*, translated by James M.
    Robinson (San Francisco: Harper & Row Publishers, 1981). For Jewish writ-
    ings between the present canonical Hebrew Bible and the New Testament,
    which shed light on the climate in which Christianity emerged, see *The
    Apocrypha, an American Translation* by Edgar J. Goodspeed (New York:
    Vintage, 1959).

    For more recent attempts at the reconstruction of the historical Jesus,
    see Geza Vermes, *The Changing Faces of Jesus* (New York: Viking Compass,
    2001); Michael Grant, *Jesus: An Historian's Review of the Gospels* (New York:
    Charles Scribner's Sons, 1977); see also Elaine Pagels, *The Origin of Satan*
    (New York: Vintage, 1996), chaps. III and IV; *Jesus at 2000*, edited by Mar-
    cus J. Borg (Boulder Colorado: Westview Press, 1998); John Dominic
    Crossan, *Jesus: A Revolutionary Biography* (Harper San Francisco, 1995);
    and Russell Shorto's summary and bibliography of the work of a wide range
    of scholars in his *Gospel Truth: The New Image of Jesus Emerging from Sci-
    ence and History, and Why It Matters* (New York: Riverhead Press, 1997).

Endnotes

The burden of this literature is that interpretation of the historical nature of Jesus builds on the narrowest base of indisputable fact, and inevitably reflects the predispositions of particular scholars.

4. Interpretation, as well as shifts in linguistic meaning, can radically change the import of scripture. In Managua, during the Contra war of the 1980s, I heard a priest deliver this homily to his congregation regarding the miracle of the loaves and fishes through the lens of liberation theology: "Brethren, what does this passage mean? It means that Our Lord could not leave his people hungry, that they first must be fed. What is a religion which speaks only to the spirit and ignores the body? It is the religion of exploitation." See Matthew 14:14–21, p. 79.

5. See particularly John Dominic Crossan, *Jesus: A Revolutionary Biography.*

6. For an exhaustive study of the early history of Christianity, including its Jewish background, see W.H.C. Frend, *The Rise of Christianity* (Philadelphia: Fortress Press, 1984). For a description of the late Roman Empire, see Peter Brown, *The World of Late Antiquity, AD 150–750* (New York: W.W. Norton & Company, 1971). The account presented in our text focuses on the Roman Catholic church, as opposed to other divisions of pre-Protestant Christianity, particularly the Orthodox Eastern Church.

7. See *The Changing Faces of Jesus*, pp. 3, 193–202. Vermes' analysis can be taken to suggest two possibilities: that the changes of meaning from Hebrew or Aramaic to Latin or Greek were allowed to stand by virtue of an already changed theology which fit into the mythology of the Hellenistic world; or that the linguistic differences directly suggested such a different theology.

8. Isaiah 7:14.

9. Matthew 1:18, p. 50. See also Matthew 1:20, p. 50.

10. Matthew 1:1–16, pp. 49–50.

11. *The Changing Faces of Jesus*, p. 227.

12. See, for example, Matthew 28, pp. 115–16. For anticipations of this idea in Judaism, see endnote 8, chapter 2.

13. See I Corinthians 15, pp. 131–34.

14. Matthew 16:28, p. 84. See also Matthew 24:30, p. 102.

15. *Ibid.*, 24:17–18, p. 102.

16. Luke 18:22, p. 173; Matthew 5:39 and 6:1, p. 58.

17. W.H.C. Frend, *Rise of Christianity*, p. 105.

18. *Ibid.*, p. 133. However, as Christian communities, and the official Church, gained power, they prescribed codes of ethical action befitting true or orthodox Christians. Some Christians, however, abandoned their roles and re-

sponsibilities in this world to focus on their own souls through solitude, abstinence, monasticism, or martyrdom. See Elaine Pagels, *Adam, Eve, and the Serpent* (New York: Vintage, 1989), chaps. II and III.

19. *The Changing Faces of Jesus*, p. 58.

20. John 8:23, p. 216.

21. *Ibid.*, 1:10, p. 195.

22. *Ibid.*, 3:16, p. 200.

23. See Peter Brown, *Augustine of Hippo: A Biography* (Berkeley, CA: University of California Press, 1967). See also Saint Augustine's *Confessions* and *The City of God*. Augustine's preoccupation with the theology of Christianity as opposed to the life of Jesus can be seen, for example, in the fact that references to the Pauline epistles and to John in the *Confessions* radically outnumber references to the Synoptic Gospels. For the influence of classical culture on Christianity, see Charles Norris Cochrane, *Christianity and Classical Culture* (New York: Oxford University Press, 1957).

24. The doctrine of the Trinity is suggested in the preface of John, which states, "In the beginning was the Word, and the Word was with God, and the Word was God." Here the Word, or Logos, is made flesh in the person of Jesus, and is seen as God or a manifestation of God. Such a doctrine reaches far beyond the biblical notion of an historical creator. John 1:1, p. 195.

25. At the same time, the Gospel writers attempted to reduce the responsibility of the Roman authorities for Jesus' death, as epitomized by the benign portrait they paint of Pontius Pilate, a man known historically for his vicious behavior. See Elaine Pagels, *The Origin of Satan*, particularly chaps. I, III, and IV.

26. "From that day on they [the high priests and the Pharisees] plotted to kill him." John 11:53, p. 226.

27. Matthew 27:25, p. 113.

28. See Elaine Pagels' path-breaking *The Gnostic Gospels* (New York: Vintage Books, 1981), and her more recent *Beyond Belief: The Secret Gospel of Thomas* (New York: Random House, 2003).

29. Protestantism would later argue that the imposition of clergy between the believer and God could be helpful, but would, if interpreted as metaphysically *necessary*, detract from God's authority and the sanctity of God's relation to the believer.

30. *The Gnostic Gospels*, p. 169.

31. In the fourteenth-century German mystic, Meister Eckhart, we can see a medieval embodiment of essentially Gnostic thought. Two years after his death,

he was excommunicated, partly because of his doctrines, which were deeply influenced by Plotinus, and partly because he had emphasized reaching directly to his congregation in German, a practice which would characterize the Reformation two centuries later. For an anthology of his writing, see *The Best of Meister Eckhart*, edited by Halcyon Backhouse (New York: Crosslands, 1993).

32. This interpretation of Saint Augustine is based in large part on Elaine Pagels, *Adam, Eve, and the Serpent*, chaps. v and vi, and Peter Brown's superb biography. See also Augustine's *Confessions* and *The City of God*. For Biblical references, see Genesis 1–3.

33. Pagels, *Adam, Eve, and the Serpent*, p. 99.

34. *Ibid.*, p. 149

35. F.C. Copleston, *Medieval Philosophy* (London: Methuen & Co., Ltd., 1952), pp. 12–14.

36. *Ibid*, p. 92.

37. For a discussion of the medieval Christian state as a prelude to modern Europe, see R.H. Tawney's classic, *Religion and the Rise of Capitalism* (New York: Harcourt, Brace and Company, Inc., 1926), chap. I.

Chapter 5. IN THE GRIP OF PERMANENCE: DESCARTES THROUGH HEGEL

1. See Galileo Galilei, *Dialogues on the Great World Systems* (Chicago: University of Chicago Press, 1953).

2. René Descartes, *Discourse on Method and Other Writings*, translated and with an introduction by F.E. Sutcliffe (Baltimore: Penguin Books, 1968), discourse 4.

3. Descartes' emphasis on clear and distinct ideas is, I believe, misplaced. Ideas may be very clear and distinct and quite inadequate, as they may not fully describe the object they represent or map the complex environment of which that object is a part. A sphere, for example, is a clear and distinct idea, but inadequately describes a particular basketball, and the environment of air pressure and gravity which sustains it, or the part played by the ball in a basketball game. For a modern critique of clear and distinct ideas, with its Platonic origins, see chapters 7–9.

4. *Ibid.*, discourse 3.

5. *The Cambridge Companion to Descartes*, edited by John Cottingham (New York: Cambridge University Press, 1992), p. 250.

6. William James, *The Principles of Psychology*, vol. 1 (New York: Dover Publications, Inc., 1950). See also Sigmund Freud's *Project for a Scientific Psychology*, contained in *The Origin of Psycho-Analysis*, edited by Marie Bonaparte, Anna Freud, and Ernst Kris; translated by Eric Mosbacher and James Strachey (New York: Basic Books, 1954). Research on the physiology of the brain, and, in particular, the working of the neuronal system, was still mostly in the future (see chapter 9).

7. See, for example, Edmund Husserl, *Cartesian Meditations: An Introduction to Phenomenology*, translated by Dorion Cairns (The Hague: Martinus Nijhoff, 1969). See, also, M. Merleau-Ponty, *Phenomenology of Perception*, translated by Colin Smith (London: Routledge & Kegan Paul, 1962).

8. John Locke, *An Essay Concerning Human Understanding*, collated and annotated, with biographical, critical, and historical prolegomena by Alexander Campbell Fraser (New York: Dover Publications, Inc., 1959), bk. I, chap. i, par. l.

9. *Ibid.*, Intro., par. 2.

10. *Ibid.*, bk. I., chap. i, par. 5.

11. *Ibid.*, bk., II, chap. viii, par. 8.

12. *Ibid.*, bk. IV, chap. ii, par. 14; chap. xi, par. 2.

13. *Ibid.*, bk. IV, chap. xi, par. 8.

14. *Ibid.*, bk. II, chap. xxiii, pars. 17 and 18.

15. *Ibid.*, bk. IV, chap. iii, par. 18.

16. *Second Treatise of Government*, edited by C.B. Macpherson (Indianapolis and Cambridge: Hackett Publishing Company, Inc., 1980), chap. ii, paras. 7 and 11.

17. See, for example, *Ibid.*, chap. xviii, para. 202 and chap. xix, para. 212. In these and other passages, the reader can see the close parallels between Locke's political theory and the historical conditions in which he operated.

18. For Locke, as Nicholas Wolterstorff writes, "One has insight only into the existence of one's mind, into one's having of ideas and one's performing of mental acts, and into the interrelationships of these. The representatives of that long tradition, articulated powerfully already by Plato, which held that we have insight into a whole realm of necessity existing independently of us, would feel themselves profoundly claustrophobic if they thought and imagined their way into Locke's picture." See "Locke's philosophy of religion," in *The Cambridge Companion to Locke*, edited by Vere Chappell (Cambridge: Cambridge University Press, 1994), pp. 176–77.

19. For a discussion of Hume's close relation to classical scepticism, see A.H.

Basson's excellent introduction, *David Hume* (Baltimore: Penguin Books, 1958).

20. David Hume, *A Treatise of Human Nature* (Garden City, New York: Doubleday & Company, Inc., 1961), bk. I, part iv. sect. vi.
21. *Ibid.*, bk. I, part iii, sect. vi.
22. *Ibid.*, bk. II, part iii, sect. iii.
23. If one calculates for a society as whole what gives pleasure and pain, and then equates morality with this measure of social utility, the result is the utilitarianism of James Mill (1773–1836) and his more famous son, John Stuart Mill (1806–73).
24. The formation of a common body of opinion by people of breeding and good taste is the subject of Hume's essay, "On the Standard of Taste," in *David Hume Selected Essays*, edited and with an introduction by Stephen Copley and Andrew Edgar (Oxford and New York: Oxford University Press, 1993).
25. See particularly, his essay, "Of the Original Contract," in *Ibid.*
26. From Hume's essay, "Idea of a Perfect Commonwealth," in *Ibid.*
27. See, for example, Hume's essay, "On the Immortality of the Soul," in *Ibid.* See also *Hume on Religion*, edited with an introduction by Richard Wollheim, containing *The Natural History of Religion*, selections from *Dialogues Concerning Natural Religion*, and *My Own Life* (Cleveland and New York: Meridian Books, 1967).
28. Immanuel Kant, *Critique of Pure Reason*, translated by F. Max Muller (Garden City, New York: Doubleday & Company, 1966).
29. *Ibid*, preface to the second edition.
30. *Ibid.*, I, *Transcendental Aesthetic*, sect. l.
31. See the chapter, "The Mathematization of Science," in Morris Kline, *Mathematics: The Loss of Certainty* (Oxford and New York: Oxford University Press, 1980), pp. 50–68.
32. See Michael Friedman, "Causal Laws and the Foundations of Natural Science," in *The Cambridge Companion to Kant*, edited by Paul Guyer (New York: Cambridge University Press, 1991), p. 185.
33. Kant, *Critique of Pure Reason*, "Transcendental Dialectic," bk. ii, chap. iii, sect. v.
34. *Ibid.*, sect. vi.
35. See his *Critique of Practical Reason*, translated by Lewis White Beck (Indianapolis: Bobbs-Merrill, 1956); *Lectures on Ethics*, translated by Louis Infield (London: Methuen, 1930); and *Perpetual Peace*, translated by Lewis White Beck (Bobbs-Merrill, 1957).
36. Kant, *Critique of Pure Reason*, "Method of Transcendentalism," chap. ii, sect. ii.

37. Allen W. Wood, "Rational theology, moral faith, and religion," in *The Cambridge Companion to Kant*, pp. 403-404.

38. See Wolfgang Kersting, "Politics, Freedom, and Order: Kant's Political Philosophy," in *Ibid.*, p. 355.

39. See, in particular, Immanuel Kant, *Perpetual Peace*.

40. William James wrote, "Kant's mind is the rarest and most intricate of all possible antique bric-a-brac museums, and connoisseurs and dilettanti will always wish to visit it and see the wondrous and racy contents. The temper of the dear old man about his work is perfectly delectable. And yet he is really—although I shrink with some terror from saying such a thing...at bottom a mere curio, a 'specimen.'" From *Essays in Radical Empiricism* (New York: Longmans, Green and Co., 1912), pp. 436-437.

41. Peter Singer's short summary, *Hegel* (Oxford and New York: Oxford University Press, 1983), provides an immensely useful guide through the often intimidating Hegelian texts.

42. G.W.F. Hegel, *Introduction to The Philosophy of History*, translated by Leo Rauch (Indianapolis and Cambridge: Hackett Publishing Company, 1988), p. 12.

43. *Ibid.*, p. 22.

44. *Ibid.*, p. 24.

45. *Ibid.*, p. 23.

46. Karl Popper, *The Open Society and Its Enemies* (London: Routledge & Kegan Paul, 1966), vol. II, chap. 12.

47. Thus, at various times, Hegel seems indiscriminately to be exalting the state, praising the world-historical role of conquerors like Caesar or Napoleon, and dismissing the individual suffering which they caused. It is not difficult to see how a Hitler or Mussolini could see themselves as Hegelian heroes, although Hegel probably would not.

48. See Hegel's *Philosophy of Right*, translated by T.M. Knox (London: Oxford University Press, 1967).

49. Peter Singer, for example, cites the organic growth of communities suggested by the American city planner Jane Jacobs, as opposed, say, to the top-down construction of new towns outside of London in the post–World War II period, which did away with traditional neighborhoods and community structures. See Jane Jacobs, *The Death and Life of Great American Cities* (New York: Random House, 1961).

50. *The Phenomenology of Mind*, translated by J.B. Baillie (New York: Harper & Row, 1967.) For a parallel neurophysiological analysis, see the work of Gerald M. Edelman, in chapter 9.

51. See Hegel's *Science of Logic*, translated by S.V. Miller (Allen & Unwin, 1969).
52. See Joseph Margolis, *The Flux of History and the Flux of Science* (Berkeley, CA, Los Angeles, and London: University of California Press, 1993).

Chapter 6. THE PERMANENCE COMPLEX

1. See chapter 9, particularly the discussion of consciousness in the work of neurophysiologist Gerald M. Edelman.
2. For a discussion of socialization and the ego, see chapter 10.
3. *Phaedo*, 85e–86b.
4. See Émile Durkheim, *The Elementary Forms of the Religious Life*.
5. "The Theme of the Joseph Novels" in *Thomas Mann's Addresses Delivered at the Library of Congress 1942–1949*, p. 13–14.
6. The sociologist Max Weber would point out, however, that predestination might actually work in the opposite way, as it could create an almost un-bearable anxiety about whether a person had in fact been selected or not. To relieve this anxiety, he would try desperately to achieve success in this world, on the presumption that God would favor his "saints." The need to show such favor became a driving force in the growth of capitalism. See *The Protestant Ethic and the Spirit of Capitalism*, translated by Talcott Parsons (New York: Charles Scribner's Sons, 1958).
7. For a discussion of field theory and its relation to the theory of ideas, see chapters 7–10.
8. However, if God is thought of as timelessly immanent in the world, or more, the world itself, as the Gnostics, and sometimes Kant and Hegel, suggest, the world can still be seen as retaining responsibility for its own creation or his-tory (see chapters 7 and 8).
9. Isaac Newton, *Opticks* (New York: Dover Publications, 1952).
10. In a letter to the Revered Richard Bentley of December 10, 1692, Newton wrote: "When I wrote my treatise about our system, I had an eye on such principles as might work with considering men for the belief in a Deity; and nothing can rejoice me more than to find it useful for that purpose." Cited by Morton Kline in *Mathematics: The Loss of Certainty*, p. 59.

INTRODUCTION TO PART II

1. P.H. Barrett, P.J. Gautry, S. Herbert, D. Kohn, and S. Smith, eds., *Charles*

Endnotes

Darwin's Notebooks, 1836–1844: Geology, Transmutation of Species, Metaphysical Enquiries (Ithaca, NY: Cornell University Press, 1987), p. 539, n. 84E, cited by Gerald M. Edelman, *The Remembered Present: A Biological Theory of Consciousness* (New York: Basic Books, 1989), p. 3.

2. C.P. Snow, *The Two Cultures and the Scientific Revolution* (New York: Cambridge University Press, 1959).

3. In the first half of this century, Columbia University and the University of Chicago established comprehensive undergraduate programs informing students of the entire sweep of human knowledge, at least in the West. For a rationale for such general education, see Robert Maynard Hutchins' *The University of Utopia* (Chicago: University of Chicago Press, 1953).

4. I am here using the notion of a paradigm in a somewhat larger context than Thomas S. Kuhn, who confines his notion to the physical sciences. See *The Structure of Scientific Revolutions* (Chicago and London: The University of Chicago Press, 1996, originally published in 1962) (see chapter 11).

5. Margolis, *The Flux of History and the Flux of Science*, p. 90.

6. *Ibid.*, p. 11. Margolis is referring here to philosophers such as R.G. Collingwood, Hans-Georg Gadamer, Jürgen Habermas, Paul Ricoeur, and Charles Taylor, as well as Charles Sanders Peirce, Thomas Kuhn, Imre Lakatos, and Hilary Putnam. See particularly his chaps. 2 and 3.

7. Margolis lists philosophers in this century who support the invariance of human reason or the human mind as R.G. Collingwood, Carl Hempel, Karl Popper, and Jürgen Habermas. *Ibid.*, p. 22.

8. See, for example, Margolis's discussion of figures like Jürgen Habermas, Hilary Putnam, Noam Chomsky, and even Hans-Georg Gadamer. *Ibid., passim.*

9. See also John Passmore, *Recent Philosophers* (Open Court, 1991).

10. One important development which is not reflected here is the feminist movement, which has its origins in the first quarter of the nineteenth century, a time when Western women began to be heard in their own voices. Feminist authors, writing on behalf of women today, have developed a parallel track of history which deserves to be read. For introductions to this body of literature, see, for example, Simone de Beauvoir, *The Second Sex* (New York: Vintage Books, 1989); Elizabeth Minnich, et. al., *Reconstructing the Academy: Women's Education and Women's Studies* (Chicago: University of Chicago Press, 1988); Gerda Lerner, *The Creation of Patriarchy* (New York and Oxford: Oxford University Press, 1986); Elizabeth Schussler Fiorenza, *Sharing Her Word: Feminist Biblical Interpretation in Context* (Boston, MA: Beacon Press, 1998); and *A History of Women: Toward a Cultural Identity in*

the Twentieth Century, edited by Francois Thebaud, 2nd printing (Cambridge, MA and London: Harvard University Press, 1996).

11. See Richard Rorty, *Achieving Our Country* (Cambridge, MA: Harvard University Press, 1998).

Chapter 7. ALFRED NORTH WHITEHEAD: TOWARD A PHYSICAL MODEL

1. Alfred North Whitehead, *Science and the Modern World* (London: Cambridge University Press, 1925), pp. 263–264.

2. Alfred North Whitehead and Bertrand Russell, *Principia Mathematica*, 3 vols. (New York: Cambridge University Press, 1st ed., 1910–13).

3. Alfred North Whitehead, *Process and Reality* (New York: Macmillan Co., 1929).

4. Charles Darwin, *On the Origin of Species* (Cambridge, MA: Harvard University Press, 1964).

5. Darwin himself also believed in the heredity of acquired characteristics, which has been repudiated by modern genetics, and did not know of the specific role of genes, a development in biology which occurred after his death.

6. Whitehead recounted to Lucien Price, "... [T]he whole science blew up, and the Newtonian physics, which had been supposed to be fixed as the Everlasting Seat, were gone. Oh they were and still are useful as a way of looking at things, but regarded as a final description of reality, no longer valid. Certitude was gone." *Dialogues of Alfred North Whitehead*, as recorded by Lucien Price (Boston: Little, Brown and Co., 1954), p. 238.

7. Alfred North Whitehead, *Adventures of Ideas* (New York: Macmillan Co., 1933), pp. 201–202.

8. The equations of the special theory also make clear that the energy necessary to accelerate an object so that it approaches the speed of light increases to infinity. In this sense, the speed of light serves as a limit. For a general discussion of relativity, see Albert Einstein and Albert Infeld, *The Evolution of Physics* (New York: Simon & Schuster, 1966), and Robert Geroch, *General Relativity from A to B* (Chicago and London: University of Chicago Press, 1978). For an accessible review of modern physics, see Robert K. Adair, *The Great Design: Particles, Fields, and Creation* (Oxford and New York: Oxford University Press, 1987).

9. Morris Kline, *Mathematics: The Loss of Certainty*, p. 6. See also Morris Kline,

Mathematics and the Physical World (Garden City, NY: Doubleday & Company, Inc., 1963) and his *Mathematics in Western Culture* (London, Oxford, and New York: Oxford University Press, 1953).

10. Kline, *Mathematics: The Loss of Certainty*, p. 165.

11. *Ibid.*, p. 95. Even such a simple proposition as $1 + 1 = 2$ requires discrimination in its application. One match plus one powder-keg make one, not two, explosions.

12. *Ibid.*, p. 257. For a brilliantly written account of mathematics leading up to Kurt Godel's famous paper in 1932 ruling out the possibility of final systemization in many areas of mathematics, see Earnest Nagel and James R. Newman, *Godel's Proof* (New York: New York University Press, 1958).

13. For a review of psychological history, see R. J. Herrnstein and E.G. Boring, *A Source Book in the History of Psychology* (Cambridge, MA: Harvard University Press, 1965).

14. For a highly qualified defense of the behaviorist position, see B.F. Skinner, *Science and Human Behavior* (New York: Free Press, 1965), particularly chap. 17.

15. For the earlier work of Johann Gottfried Herder in the eighteenth century, which advances this view, see chapter 10.

16. For the relation of William James to Whitehead, and a general explanation of their thought, see Craig R. Eisendrath, *The Unifying Moment: The Psychological Philosophy of William James and Alfred North Whitehead* (Cambridge, MA: Harvard University Press, 1971), reissued by toExcel, 1999. For James's psychology, see, in particular, his *The Principles of Psychology* and his *Essays in Radical Empiricism* (New York: Longmans, Green and Co., 1912). James anticipated a number of developments in cognitive psychology which would not become current until the 1960s. See Ulric Neisser, *Cognitive Psychology* (New York: Appleton-Century-Crofts, 1967).

17. Whitehead, *Science and the Modern World*, p. 111.

18. For a modern neurological discussion of thirst, see chapter 9.

19. See Alfred North Whitehead, *Modes of Thought* (New York: Macmillan Co., 1938).

20. Whitehead, *Adventures of Ideas*, p. 341.

21. *Ibid*, pp. 346 and 271.

22. For a full-scale attack on these weaknesses, see Stuart A. Kauffman, *The Origins of Order* (New York and Oxford: Oxford University Press, 1993), discussed in chapter 8.

23. Whitehead writes, "Thus an originality in the temporal world is conditioned,

though not determined, by an initial subjective aim supplied by the ground of all order and of all originality." *Process and Reality*, p. 164.

24. William James writes, as if anticipating Whitehead's thought, "Yet if…we assume God to have thought in advance of every *possible* flight of human fancy in these directions, his mind becomes too much like a Hindoo idol with three heads, eight arms and six breasts, too much made up of super-foetation and redundancy for us to wish to copy it…" Jottings of 1903–1904, quoted in Ralph Barton Perry, *The Thought and Character of William James*, 2 vols. (Boston and Toronto: Little, Brown and Co., 1935), vol. II, p. 384.

25. Accordingly, in Whitehead's second mode of explanation, "proximate relevance" of eternal objects, as a guide to an organism in the process of becoming, "means relevance as in the primordial mind of God." *Process and Reality*, pp. 315 and 73.

26. See Stephen Jay Gould, *Wonderful Life: the Burgess Shale and the Nature of History* (New York: W.W. Norton, 1989).

27. Whitehead, *Process and Reality*, p. 532.

28. *Dialogues of Alfred North Whitehead*, p. 11.

Chapter 8. THE CREATIVE ADVANCE: THE NEW PHYSICS AND BIOLOGY

1. Forward to James Lovelock, *The Ages of Gaia: A Biography of Our Living Earth* (New York and London: W.W. Norton & Company, 1995), p. x.

2. Relativity physics is discussed primarily in chapter 7.

3. Robert K. Adair adds, "Energy and time constitute another set of complementary quantities; we cannot determine the exact energy of a particle or any other system at a precisely determined time." *The Great Design*, p. 163.

4. At least some physicists continue to maintain that indeterminacy is only a temporary phase, representing our lack of knowledge. See Dutch physicist and recent Nobel laureate Gerard 't Hooft's *In Search of the Ultimate Building Blocks* (New York: Cambridge University Press, 1997), pp. 11–15.

5. Richard Feynman, *QED: The Strange Theory of Light and Matter* (Princeton, NJ: Princeton University Press, 1988), p. 124. For a more technical description of quantum field theory up to 1950, see Paul Teller, *An Interpretive Introduction of Quantum Field Theory* (Princeton, NJ: Princeton University Press, 1995).

6. Murray Gell-Mann, *The Quark and the Jaguar* (New York: W.H. Freeman and Company, 1994), p. 125

7. Adair, *The Great Design*, p. 345.

8. *Ibid.*, chaps. 10–15. See Briane Greene, *The Elegant Universe: Superstrings, Hidden Dimensions, and the Quest for the Ultimate Theory* (London: Jonathan Cape: 1999).

9. The "big bang" is not a full theory of creation as it does not deal with time before the event itself. As we have seen, Platonic and Christian thought attempted to deal with this problem by positing an eternal Creator, that is, one who was outside of time. For an attempted physical explanation, see the discussion of Stephen Hawking's and Lee Smolin's theories below.

10. Up to now, observing the total amount of matter in the universe has been impossible. Much of it is in forms which have defied accurate observation, for example, "black holes," "dark matter" (matter which does not reflect or emit much light), and, until just recently, neutrinos (particles of very small or zero mass emitted during decay of other particles).

    As of this writing, current research suggests a continuously expanding universe. There is even substantial evidence, presented in a special report of *Scientific American*, "Revolution in Cosmology" (January, 1999), that expansion of the universe is actually accelerating, requiring some form of exotic energy from empty space. See also John Noble Wilford's article-length report in the *New York Times*, April 21, 1998.

11. See Hawking's *A Brief History of Time* (New York: Bantam, 1986), pp. 49 and 88.

12. The problem is that such intense condensations or black holes may also bring into play quantum mechanical forces which seriously call into question the mathematics of relativity theory which underlies the original "singularity" thesis. Thus, according to Hawking himself, the uncertain role of quantum mechanical forces in black holes questions the very notion of a big bang for the universe's beginning, or a "big crunch" for its ending—if, in fact, it will end. See also Roger Penrose, *The Emperor's New Mind* (Oxford, New York, and Melbourne: Oxford University Press, 1989), particularly pp. 302–347.

13. Lee Smolin, *The Life of the Cosmos* (New York and Oxford: Oxford University Press, 1997), pp. 36–46. The appearance of such an improbable set of parameters which creates the universe we know, or which supports life, *can* be seen as suggesting that nature is wittingly working for the production of just those parameters. See *The Anthropic Cosmological Principle* by John D. Barrow and Frank J. Tipler, with a foreword by John A. Wheeler (New York: Oxford University Press, 1986). The book, and the anthropic principles it expounds, is scathingly reviewed by Martin Gardner in the *New York Review of Books* of May 8, 1986.

14. Adair cautions, "Cosmology differs somewhat from other areas of physics in that the observations from which one draws evidence concern phenomena that usually cannot be affected by intrusive actions. One cannot do experiments, in the usual sense of the word, on the universe." *The Great Design*, p. 308. The result is that cosmology has emerged as a highly speculative field, a problem which may color Smolin's and others' work.

15. Smolin, *The Life of the Cosmos*, p. 88. Smolin's speculations have not yet achieved acceptance in the scientific community. One problem here, which immediately presents itself, is that black holes do not have enough mass to form a universe.

16. Smolin's speculations rest on the fact that only a very narrow and unlikely range of parameters could produce stars, *and* that black holes, being born of stars, will produce more universes, while universes which produce no stars will produce no black holes and no universes. Therefore, he says, there is a "Darwinist" preference for the parameters, which presumably change incrementally and at random, which produce universes with stars. Smolin proposes that, for a long time, universes will be born and die without progeny except themselves, until the parameters change to permit the production of stars. Smolin calls this theory "cosmological natural selection." Thus Smolin's speculation would solve the problem: How do we account for our system's particular parameters? His answer is that these parameters have the values they do because they make the production of black holes more likely. *Ibid.*, p. 96.

17. Roger Penrose remarks, after a couple of hundred pages of mathematics and speculation, regarding the origin or ending of the world, "What have we learnt from all this? We have learnt that our theories are not yet adequate to provide answers..." *The Emperor's New Mind*, p. 345.

18. Smolin, *The Life of the Cosmos*, pp. 116–160.

19. *Ibid.*, p. 160.

20. See Lynn Margulis and Dorian Sagan, *Microcosmos: Four Billion Years of Evolution from Our Microbial Ancestors* (Berkeley, CA, Los Angeles, and London: University of California Press, first paperback printing, 1997); Stuart A. Kauffman, *The Origins of Order: Self-Organization and Selection in Evolution* (New York and Oxford: Oxford University Press, 1993); and James Lovelock, *The Ages of Gaia* (New York and London: W.W. Norton & Company, Inc., 1995).

21. Margulis and Sagan, *Microcosmos*, pp. 39–49. See also Lovelock, *The Ages of Gaia*, pp. 69–73.

22. See Ilya Prigogine's *The End of Certainty: Time, Chaos, and the New Laws of Nature* (New York, London, Toronto, Sydney, and Singapore: The Free Press, 1997), p. 3. See also Per Bak, *How Nature Works: The Science of Self-Organized Criticality* (New York: Springer-Verlag, Inc., 1996).

23. For a general review of chaos theory, see James Gleick's popular *Chaos: Making a New Science* (New York: Penguin Books, 1988).

24. Margulis and Sagan, *Microcosmos*, pp. 49–61.

25. Kauffman, *The Origins of Order*, pp. xvi; see also pp. 285–341 and 389.

26. While agreeing with this notion, physicist Gerald Marsh points out, however, that a self-reproducing system of complex organic molecules has never been created in the laboratory. Also, Per Bak maintains that Kauffman's models do not reach what he calls "self-organized criticality." *How Nature Works*, p. 127.

27. *The Origins of Order*, p. xv.

28. *Ibid.*, p. 16. See also p. 173.

29. Thus, Kauffman writes of the self-organization of the cell: "[S]uch properties as the existence of *distinct cell types*, the *homeostatic stability of cell types, the number of cell types* in an organism, the *similarity in gene expression patterns* in different cell types, the fact that development from the fertilized egg is organized around *branching pathways of cell differentiation,* and many other aspects of differentiation are all consequences of properties of self-organization so profoundly immanent in complex regulatory networks that *selection cannot avoid that order ....* These properties may therefore reflect quasi-universal features of organisms due not to selection alone, but also to the spontaneous order of the systems on which selection has been privileged to act." *Ibid.* p. xvii.

30. *Ibid.*, p. 369.

31. To create a computerized model of the human genetic system was the object of such programs as the just recently completed (2003) Human Genome Project.

32. John Tyler Bonner writes, "It is generally agreed that the development of any animal or plant is encoded in the genes.... What is needed, therefore, is some way of understanding how genes, which are responsible for the synthesis of specific proteins, can give out protein signals in such a way that they can control all the complexities of synthesis of other kinds of substances. And the timing of all the syntheses in the embryo must also be controlled." *The Evolution of Complexity by Means of Natural Selection* (Princeton, NJ: Princeton University Press, 1988), p. 139.

33. Kauffman, *The Origins of Order*, p. 403. Kauffman's ambiguity about Platonism echoes that of Whitehead.

34. *Ibid.*, p. 537. For a classic discussion of how organisms take mathematical forms, see D'Arcy Thompson's *On Growth and Form*, 2nd ed. (Cambridge, MA: Cambridge University Press, 1966).

35. Donald E. Ingber, "The Architecture of Life," *Scientific American*, January, 1998. John Tyler Bonner also recognizes the independent role played by mathematically based patterns in biology and chemical logics. *The Evolution of Complexity*, p. 24. See also pp. 148–49.

36. Kauffman writes: "[N]atural selection is important, but it has not labored alone to craft the fine architectures of the biosphere, from cell to organism to ecosystem. Another source—self-organization—is the root source of order. The order of the biological world...is not merely tinkered, but arises naturally and spontaneously because of these principles of self-organization—laws of complexity that we are just beginning to uncover and understand." *At Home in the Universe*, p. vii.

37. Margulis and Sagan, *Microcosmos*, pp. 28–29.

38. *Ibid.*, p. 30.

39. *Ibid.*, pp. 150–51.

40. John von Neumann, *The Computer and the Brain* (New Haven, CT, and London: Yale University Press, 1958), pp. 81–82. See also Kline, *Mathematics: The Loss of Certainty*, p. 312.

41. Margulis and Sagan, *Microcosmos*, pp. 125–26.

42. Lovelock, *The Ages of Gaia*, p. 211. See also his *Gaia: A New Look at Life on Earth* (New York: Oxford University Press, 1979).

43. See J.T. Fraser, *Of Time, Passion, and Knowledge: Reflections on the Strategy of Existence*, second edition, originally published in 1975 (Princeton, NJ: Princeton University Press, 1990), p. 75. For Fraser's physical theory of time, see his *The Genesis and Evolution of Time: A Critique of Interpretations in Physics* (Amherst, MA: The University of Massachusetts Press, 1982). See also Alexander J. Argyros, *A Blessed Rage for Order: Deconstruction, Evolution and Chaos* (Ann Arbor, MI: The University of Michigan Press, 1991).

44. Argyros, *A Blessed Rage for Order*, p. 168.

45. *Ibid.*, p. 131.

46. Fraser imaginatively suggests that the feeling of a quantum mechanical particle is engendered by a painting of Jackson Pollock or by listening to the talk of an autistic child; that Freud's oceanic sense is that of a chemical; and that we feel like animals when we experience emotions with no sense of past or future. See

his *Time the Familiar Stranger* (Amherst, MA: University of Massachusetts Press, 1987), p. 292; for other examples, see Fraser, *Of Time, Passion and Knowledge.*

47. See J.P. Flavell, *The Developmental Psychology of Jean Piaget* (Princeton: Van Norstrand, 1963) and Howard Gardner, *The Quest for Mind: Piaget, Levi-Strauss, and the Structuralist Movement* (Chicago and London: University of Chicago Press, 1981).

48. Argyros, *A Blessed Rage for Order,* p. 150.

49. This mode of analysis, however, does not dispose of the key notion, found in both Locke and Whitehead, that we directly perceive causation, for example, a blow from a stick, or heat from a candle, although, as Whitehead points out, this perception is somewhat mimicked in higher organizations. Data, for Whitehead, enter the organism with a vectorial component, based on their relation to the organism in its energetic field. The organism's perception provides its sense of causality or being in the world.

50. For a more extended discussion, see chapter 11.

51. Argyros, *A Blessed Rage for Order,* p. 199.

Chapter 9. THE MIND IN NATURE

1. Some of this history is reviewed by Changeux in *Neuronal Man: The Biology of Mind,* originally published 1983, trans. by Laurence Garey (Princeton, NJ: Princeton University Press, 1997), chap. 1.

2. See Norbert Weiner, *Cybernetics, or Control and Communication in the Animal and Machine,* second edition (Cambridge, Mass.: M.I.T. Press, 1962), first published 1948. See also Weiner's less technical *The Human Use of Human Beings; Cybernetics and Society* (Boston: Houghton Mifflin Company, 1950).

3. Changeux, *Neuronal Man,* pp. 103–4.

4. *Ibid.,* pp. 78–9. For a discussion of these phenomena, see also Ilya Prigogine's *The End of Certainty,* as well as his earlier *Introduction to the Thermodynamics of Irreversible Processes* (New York: Wiley-Interscience, 1961).

5. Changeux, *Neuronal Man,* p. 115.

6. *Ibid.,* p. 137.

7. See neurologist Richard M. Restak's *The Modular Brain* (New York: Simon & Schuster, 1995), chap. 9. For a summary of the work of Roger Sperry on the differentiation of function of the two hemispheres of the brain, which won Sperry a Nobel prize, and some of the thinking and new-age speculation which it inspired, see Robert E. Ornstein, *The Psychology of Consciousness* (San Francisco: W.H. Freeman and Company, 1972).

8. Changeux, *Neuronal Man*, p. 169.

9. See Gerald M. Edelman, *Bright Air, Brilliant Fire: On the Matter of the Mind* (New York: Basic Books, 1992). For a more scholarly and ultimately more satisfying account, see Edelman's trilogy *Neural Darwinism: The Theory of Neuronal Group Selection* (New York: Basic Books, 1987); *Topobiology: An Introduction to Molecular Embryology* (New York: Basic Books, 1988), and *The Remembered Present: A Biological Theory of Consciousness* (New York: Basic Books, 1989).

10. Jerome Lettvin, a distinguished biologist at M.I.T, points out that Edelman's explanation of the neurophysiology of mental functioning is highly controversial.

11. Edelman, *Bright Air, Brilliant Fire*, p. 74.

12. Edelman explains that "three essential features [are] shared by all selection theories: variable repertoires of elements whose sources of variation are causally unrelated to subsequent events of selection or recognition, opportunities for encounter with an independently changing environment permitting the selection of one or more favored variants, and, finally, a means of differential reproduction or amplification with heredity of the selected variants in a population." *Neural Darwinism*, p. 9.

13. Edelman, *Bright Air, Brilliant Fire*, chap. 3.

14. *Ibid.*, chaps. 6–9. See also *The Remembered Present*, chap. 3

15. Edelman, *The Remembered Present*, chap. 3.

16. Edelman, *Bright Air, Brilliant Fire*, pp. 100–101.

17. *Ibid.*, p. 120. For a more detailed explanation, see *The Remembered Present*, chap. 9.

18. Edelman, *Bright Air, Brilliant Fire*, p. 112. See also *The Remembered Present*, p. 186.

19. Edelman, *Bright Air, Brilliant Fire*, pp. 131–33. For the close similarity of this idea to that of George Herbert Mead, see chapter 10.

20. Edelman, *Bright Air, Brilliant Fire*, chap. 12.

21. Edelman may underestimate the schematic nature of memory. See Ulric Neisser, *Cognitive Psychology*, pp. 279–292. See also David Marr, *Vision: A Computational Investigation into the Human Representation and Processing of Visual Information* (San Francisco: W. H. Freeman, 1982).

22. Edelman, *The Remembered Present*, p. 9.

23. John Searle, *The Mystery of Consciousness* (New York: A New York Review Book, 1997), p. 48. Searle also maintains that the relationship between neural states and consciousness cannot be identity, but must be based on causality. But, on the other hand, he insists that life is not "caused" by the

molecular chemistry of an organism, but says rather that the organism is living. Why then, in his parlance, does he not see that consciousness is not "caused" by neural activity but that the organism, focused in the brain, has achieved the additionally higher level of consciousness?

24. Richard M. Restak, *The Modular Brain*, p. 133.

25. Searle, *The Mystery of Consciousness*, pp. 138 and 192. For an alternative view, see Hilary Putnam's *Reason, Truth and History* (New York: Cambridge University Press, 1981), particularly p. 92.

26. Jack Copeland, *Artificial Intelligence: A Philosophical Introduction* (Oxford and Cambridge, MA: Blackwell, 1993), p. 232.

27. Quoted in F.S. Beach, D.O. Jackson, C.T. Morgan, and H. W. Nissen, eds., *The Neuropsychology of Lashley* (New York: McGraw-Hill, 1960), p. 539. The on-and-off circuits suggested the use of a special mathematics, Boolean algebra, as the *lingua franca* of at least the first few generations of computers. What distortions this has created as computers mimic phenomena from thought to molecular processes are still being sorted out.

28. Francisco J. Varela, Evan Thompson, and Eleanor Rosch, *The Embodied Mind: Cognitive Science and Human Experience* (Cambridge, MA: M.I.T. Press, 1993). p. 86.

29. In genetics, Stuart A. Kauffman provides an example of just how much closer to biological processes a newer and more sophisticated kind of computer may be than the von Neumann variety. He writes, "In a genomic system, each gene responds to the various products of those genes whose products regulate its activity. All the different genes in the network may respond at the same time to the outputs of those genes which regulate them. In other words, the genes act in parallel. The network, insofar as it is like a computer program at all, is like a *parallel-processing network...*" *The Origins of Order*, p. 442. In this work, Kauffman indicates clearly how dependent his work is on computer modeling.

30. Howard Gardner, *The Mind's New Science: A History of the Cognitive Revolution* (New York: Basic Books, 1987), p. 319.

31. See *Ibid*, chaps. 6 and 10–14. For an attack on the similarity between computers and the human brain based on their differences in mechanism, see Jack Copeland, *Artificial Intelligence*, chap. 10.

32. John Searle, *Minds, Brains and Science* (Cambridge, MA: Harvard University Press, 1948), chap. 2, and John Searle, *The Mystery of Consciousness*, chap. 4. See also Edelman, *Neural Darwinism*, pp. 43–44; and Gardner, *The Mind's New Science*, chap. 13.

33. According to Alan Turing, if a trained researcher cannot distinguish a computer's decisions or its actions from those of humans, it can be considered to be "thinking." This procedure, called the "Turing test," proposed in the 1940s, is clearly based on a behavioristic hypothesis, which looks to the output of a system as sufficient evidence for any statement we may make about it.

34. Ray Kurzweil, *The Age of Spiritual Machines: When Computers Exceed Human Intelligence* (New York: Viking, 1999), p. 103. For an exuberant description of how computers will change our world, see Microsoft chairman Bill Gates's *Business @ The Speed of Thought: Succeeding in the Digital Economy* (New York: Warner Books, 1999).

35. Kurzweil writes: "Computation is the essence of order. It provides the ability for a technology to respond in a variable and appropriate manner to its environment to carry out its mission. Thus computational technology is also an evolutionary process, and also builds on its own progress." *The Age of Spiritual Machine*, p. 33.

36. *Ibid.*, p. 24.

37. *Ibid.*, p. 129.

38. John Rennie, "Introduction: The Uncertainties of Technological Innovation," in *Key Technologies for the 21st Century, a Special Issue of Scientific American* (New York: W.H. Freeman, 1996), p. xi. One area in which computers have flourished is strategic intelligence. See, for example, the chapter, "TECHINT: The NSA, the NRO, and NIMA," by Robert Dreyfuss, in *National Insecurity: U.S. Intelligence After the Cold War*, edited by Craig Eisendrath (Philadelphia: Temple University Press, 2000). Computers have also been used increasingly in weapons systems. In the recent wars in Afghanistan and Iraq, computer-identified targets and computer-guided weapons were prominent features, as they are in current outer space weapons research.

39. See Steven Ley, *Artificial Life: A Report from the Frontier Where Computers Meet Biology* (New York: Vintage Books, 1993).

40. Kurzweil, *The Age of Spiritual Machines*, chap. 7.

41. *Ibid.*, p. 153.

42. *Philadelphia Inquirer*, March 7, 2000.

Chapter 10. TOWARD A HUMAN PARADIGM

1. William James, *Pragmatism* (London, Bombay, and Calcutta: Longmans, Green and Co., 1912), pp. 256–57.

2. Adam Smith, *An Enquiry into the Nature and Causes of the Wealth of Nations* (New York: Modern Library, 1937).

3. Richard J. Herrnstein and Charles Murray, *The Bell Curve: The Reshaping of American Life by Difference in Intelligence* (New York: Free Press, 1994). For a critique of intelligence tests, see Stephen Jay Gould, *The MisMeasure Mismeasure of Man*, revised and expanded (New York and London: W.W. Norton & Company, 1996). Gould writes that his book is a critique of "the abstraction of intelligence as a single entity, its location within the brain, its quantification as one number for each individual, and the use of these numbers to rank people in a single series of worthiness, invariably to find that oppressed and disadvantaged groups—races, classes, or sexes—are innately inferior and deserve their status. In short, this book is about the Mismeasure of Man." p. 21. See also *Measured Lies: The Bell Curve Examined*, edited by Joe C. Kincheloe, Shirley R. Steinberg, and Aaron D. Gresson III (New York: St. Martin's Press, 1996).

4. Ironically, Smith was already beginning to peek around Locke's system to espouse something like a developmental psychology. In his *The Theory of Moral Sentiments* (New Rochelle, NY: Arlington House, 1969), he writes of the growing ability of human beings to put themselves in the place of others, and to observe that others are similarly empathic. In this way, human beings see themselves as others see them. When this notion is generalized, it becomes, for Smith, the "impartial spectator," the forerunner, we will find, of George Herbert Mead's "generalized other" and of the entire line of thought which sees human nature in a developmental process in relation to society and the natural world.

5. For a compendium of his work, see *The Portable Nietzsche*, edited by the great Nietzsche scholar Walter Kaufman (New York: The Viking Press, 1954).

6. From Isaiah Berlin, "My Intellectual Path," in the *New York Review of Books*, May 14, 1998.

7. See *George Herbert Mead on Social Psychology*, edited by Anselm Strauss (Chicago and London: The University of Chicago Press, 1977). The book contains Mead's central work, *Mind, Self and Society*, first published in 1934, and a number of Mead's key essays.

8. *Ibid.*, p. 140.

9. *Ibid.*, p. 158.

10. For example, in the reporting of scientific experiments, in addition to removing idiosyncratic meanings from language, the researcher must also remove special elements of the research situation which particularize his or

her report. Thus, a scientist conducting an experiment may be color-blind and observe an effect at 20,000 feet. The scientist's role is to translate the experiment's findings so they make sense for a generalized group of scientists who are assumed to have normal vision and work at sea level.

11. *Ibid.*, p. 202–03.

12. See Thomas S. Kuhn, *The Structure of Scientific Revolutions* (Chicago: The University of Chicago Press, 1962)

13. *Ibid.*, p. 334.

14. *Ibid.*, p. 338.

15. While Whitehead and Mead would agree on Mead's description of a changing prehensive view of the past, Whitehead, I suspect, was too much of a physicist to doubt that a moment in the past was an objective event occurring in space and time, and so approachable by "modernist" methods of historical research.

16. Dewey's language is the common speech of the American of his day, colloquial and non-academic, with sometimes just a hint of the after-dinner speaker. A beautiful work awaits its author in distilling a social history of their times from the styles and specific examples which appear in the work of Dewey, Mead, and Harry Stack Sullivan. One cannot read these writers today without the nostalgic thought that their America is as lost to us at the beginning of this new century, as is the England of Jane Austin or the Gawain poet.

17. John Dewey, *Experience & Nature*, first edition 1925 (Chicago and LaSalle: Open Court Publishing Company, 1997), pp. 9–10. For a fascinating comparison of Dewey with the contemporary German philosopher Jürgen Habermas, see Alan Ryan, "The Power of Positive Thinking," in *New York Review of Books*, January 16, 2003.

18. Dewey, *Experience & Nature*, pp. 273–74.

19. In Hegel's version of Kant's epistemology, which Dewey absorbed as a philosophy student, phenomenological existence is all that there is. The Kantian *noumenon*, or thing-in-itself, recedes into being a mere theoretical construct. See Robert B. Westbrook's *John Dewey and American Democracy* (Ithaca, NY, and London: Cornell University Press, 1991), pp. 13–32.

20. Dewey, *Logic: The Theory of Inquiry*, p. 25.

21. Dewey, *Experience & Nature*, p. 122.

22. The position that the class characteristics or essences are the true realities was called *realism*.

23. John Dewey, *Logic: The Theory of Inquiry* (New York: Henry Holt and Company, Inc., 1938), pp. 112–13. Dewey is clear that inquiry may alter the

environment it is studying, just as Werner Heisenberg is clear that experimentation may alter the path of the electron.

24. William James, *Pragmatism*, p. 133.

25. Dewey, *Logic: The Theory of Inquiry*, pp. 459–60.

26. Thus, Dewey can say, "It is as much a part of the real being of atoms that they give rise in time, under increasing complication of relationships, to qualities of blue and sweet, pain and beauty, as that they have at a cross-section of time extension, mass, or weight." *Experience & Nature*, p. 92; see also pp. 218–19.

27. *Ibid.*, pp. 147–48.

28. Dewey flirts dangerously, as does J.T. Fraser, with the idea that a society may actually experience, rather than the notion that experience is ultimately that of individuals in society.

29. *Experience & Nature*, p. 26.

30. *Ibid.*, p. 241.

31. See, in particular, Sigmund Freud, *The Interpretation of Dreams*, first published in 1900, contained in *The Basic Writings of Sigmund Freud* (New York: The Modern Library, 1938).

32. As part of this theory, Freud held views of "normality" which were a fairly rigid translation of the social mores of contemporary (circa 1900) Viennese upper-middle class morality, including its highly sexist view of women. Behavior which might be seen as within the spectrum of acceptance today was seen then as perverse or neurotic. Freud also attributed to this morality a universal truth which was oblivious of differences even within sectors of his own contemporary culture, and between different societies.

33. Freud often denied that the incest actually took place. Rather, he maintained, in these cases, that the child, due to his or her sexual attraction to the parent, "constructed," or imagined, the incestuous events. This disclaimer by Freud has come under recent criticism.

34. See Sigmund Freud, *The Ego and the Id* (New York: W.W. Norton, 1960); *The Problem of Anxiety* (New York: W.W. Norton, original copyright, 1936); *Civilization and Its Discontents* (New York: W.W. Norton, 1961), and Peter Gay, *Freud: A Life for Our Time* (Replica Books, 1988).

35. See, particularly, Ruth Benedict, *Patterns of Culture* (Boston: Houghton Mifflin Co., 1934.)

36. Harry Stack Sullivan, *The Interpersonal Theory of Psychiatry*, edited by Helen Swick Perry and Mary Ladd Gawell, copyright 1953 (New York: W.W. Norton & Company, Inc., 1997).

37. Sullivan states that his purpose is to show how "from birth onward, a very capable animal becomes a person...through the influence of other people, and solely for the purpose of living with other people in some sort of social organization." *Ibid.*, p. 5.

38. *Ibid.*, p. 39.

39. Sullivan writes, "A sign is a particular pattern in the experience of events which is differentiated from or within the general flux of experience . . ; and this differentiation occurs in terms of recall and foresight of a particular frequent sequence of satisfaction or of increasing distress [in the case of anxiety]." *Ibid.*, p. 77.

40. *Ibid.*, p. 78. See also *Ibid.*, p. 81.

41. *Ibid.*, pp. 63–64. This "end station" is what Whitehead would call the "locus of a field."

42. "The infant's personification of the good mother is the prehended pattern of her participation in recurrent nursing situations and integrations of other needful sorts which have been resolved by satisfaction." *Ibid.*, p. 111.

43. Sullivan writes, "The relatively invariant coincidence of felt need, foresight of satisfaction by adequate and appropriate activity, and independence of cooperation by an at least dimly prehended other person [that is, the "mothering one"] in securing the anticipated satisfaction—all these will come presently to be an important part of a master pattern of experience to which reference is made by the use of the word 'my,' and more particularly 'my body,' and, by the sophisticated, 'my mind' or even 'my soul.'" *Ibid.*, p. 139.

44. *Ibid.*, pp. 110–111.

45. *Ibid.*, pp. 161–62.

46. Sullivan tends to base socialized learning more on the avoidance of anxiety, and less on positive gratification, than I think is accurate. His idea that anxiety communicates inexplicably by induction seems mystical, and his separation of anxiety from somatic insecurity or fear, based on pain or unfulfilled needs, often appears artificial. Nevertheless, Sullivan, by overemphasizing anxiety, can provide extraordinary insight into how it operates, just as Freud, analogously preoccupied with sexuality, at the expense of other forces in the psyche, is particularly insightful regarding its operation.

47. See Jane Loevinger, *Ego Development* (San Francisco and London: Jossey-Bass Publishers, 1987).

48. Loevinger writes, "If one person is the ancestor of our concept, it is Harry Stack Sullivan." *Ibid.*, p. 69. Loevinger's stages of ego development are also more or less foreshadowed by Jean Piaget's work in cognitive development,

by Erik Erikson's work in psycho-sexual stages of identity formation, and by Abraham H. Maslow's description of the individual's progressive stages toward self-actualization. Loevinger's scheme of ego development is also somewhat parallel to Lawrence Kohlberg's stages of moral development. See Jean Piaget, *The Moral Development of the Child*, translated by Marjorie Gabain (New York: The Free Press, 1965) and H.G. Furth, *Piaget and Knowledge: Theoretical Foundations* (Englewood Cliffs, NJ: Prentice-Hall, 1973). For the relation to Erik Erikson, see *Childhood and Society*, 2nd edition (New York: Norton, 1963); *Identity and the Life Cycle* (New York and London: W.W. Norton & Company, 1959), "The Problem of Ego Identity," *Journal of the American Psychoanalytic Association*, 1956, 4, 56–121; and *Insight and Responsibility* (New York: Norton, 1964). For the parallels with Abraham H. Maslow, see *Motivation and Personality* (New York: Harper & Row, 1954) and *Toward a Psychology of Being* (New York: Van Nostrand, 1962). For an alternative scheme, see Lawrence Kohlberg, *The Philosophy of Moral Development: Moral Stages and the Idea of Justice* (San Francisco: Harper & Row, 1981). Loevinger, however, believes her stages include more elements of the personality and that her psychometrics are more open to new data than are Kohlberg's. See Loevinger, *Ego Development*, p. 433.

49. *Ibid.*, pp. 73–74. Loevinger adds, "What is lacking in his exposition is ego-development as an abstraction; his choice of titles for the stages, always in age-specific terms, proves that."

50. *Ibid.*, pp. 15–26. Loevinger does not seem to clearly distinguish between "stage" and "level."

51. See Augusto Blasi's chapter "Concept of Development in Personality Theory" in *Ibid*, p. 35.

52. *Ibid.*, pp. 308–9, 311–12, and 427.

53. See "Ego Development in Children and Adolescents: Another Side of the Impulsive, Self-Protective, and Conformist Ego Levels," in *Personality Development: Theoretical, Empirical, and Clinical Investigations of Loevinger's Conception of Ego Development*, edited by P. Michiel Westenberg, Augusto Blasi, and Lawrence D. Cohn (Mahwah, NJ, and London: Lawrence Erlbaum Associates, Publishers, 1998). Westenberg and coworkers make clear that even in Holland, a country whose culture is relatively close to that of the United States, in comparison to many other parts of the world, respondents score with statistically significant differences from their American counterparts on Loevinger's sentence completion test.

54. Loevinger, *Ego Development*, p. 447.

Chapter 11. IN THIS MOMENT

1. I have used the King James version here because of its familiarity.

2. A good review of the history of the twentieth century is contained in Eric Hobsbaum's *The Age of Extremes: A History of the World, 1914–1991* (New York: Pantheon Books, 1994).

3. *The State of the World 1999: A Worldwatch Institute Report on Progress Toward a Sustainable Society*, edited by Lester R. Brown, Christopher Flavin, and Hilary French (New York and London: W. W. Norton & Company, 1999) reports, "Three times as many people fell victim to war in our century than in all the wars from the first century A.D. until 1899.... World War II, however, dwarfed World War I in scale. It signaled a new era of warfare—total war, waged not just against military forces, but mercilessly against a country's economy, infrastructure, and civilian population." p. 153. These annual reports detail problems and solutions in a wide variety areas, such as international relations, population, ecology, and pollution.

4. Global military spending at the height of the cold war was $1.3 trillion a year, as large as during World War II. After going down for a decade, the United States massively increased its military and intelligence budget following the September 11, 2001, attacks.

5. Before September 11, 2001, recent American presidents had devoted less and less time to informing the public about the state of the world. For example, President Clinton in his last "state of the union" address, a speech not noted for its brevity, spent less than two minutes on foreign affairs.

6. Warnings of such developments abounded even before the September 11 attacks. See, for example, the study of Physicians for Social Responsibility, reported in the *New York Times*, April 30, 1998, indicating the danger of nuclear sales in the former Soviet Union. Agitation for greater control of nuclear weapons and materials in the former Soviet Union has continued until the present.

7. As of this writing, North Korea and Iran are moving toward or have achieved nuclear capacity, and other states, such as Japan, are considering the acquisition of nuclear weapons.

8. *State of the World 2003*, p. 5. For the role of scarce resources in promoting wars, see Michael T. Klare, *Resource Wars: The New Landscape of Global Conflict* (New York: Henry Holt and Company, 2002).

9. See, also, *State of the World 2000*, particularly chap. 4.

10. See Robert D. Kaplan's *The Ends of the Earth: A Journey at the Dawn of the*

21st Century (New York: Random House, 1996). Kaplan, focusing on West Africa, writes of a coming anarchy with a total breakdown of government services, with crime, disease, overpopulation, private armies, drug cartels, and other horrors running rampant.

11. See *The Evolution of U.N. Peacekeeping*, ed. by William J. Durch (New York: St. Martin's Press, 1993). For a short survey of UN history and the particular problems created by U.S. hegemony, see former UN Undersecretary General Brian Urquhart's "Looking for the Sheriff," in the *New York Review of Books*, July 16, 1998. For a study of the foundational work of former Secretary General Dag Hammarskjold's efforts in creating UN peacekeeping machinery, see Urquhart's *Hammarskjold* (New York and London: W.W. Norton & Company, 1972). For a review of U.S. peacekeeping, see William Shawcross, *Deliver Us from Evil: Peacekeepers, Warlords and a World of Endless Conflict* (New York: Simon & Schuster, 2000).

12. While, after September 11, the United States paid its UN dues, it continued not supporting either a UN-ready deployment force or the formation of an International Criminal Court, and has generally not supported multilateral arms control, as exemplified by its withdrawal from the Anti-Ballistic Missile Treaty in December 2001, and its refusal to sign the Comprehensive Test Ban Treaty and to adhere to pacts to limit biological weapons, small arms, and land mines. For a useful discussion of the role of the United States in today's complex world, see Joseph S. Nye Jr., *The Paradox of American Power: Why the World's Only Superpower Can't Go It Alone* (New York: Oxford University Press, 2002).

13. The first position is argued by Anthony Giddens in *The Consequences of Modernity* (Stanford, CA: Stanford University Press, 1990). The second position, argued by Stephen J. Kobrin, is perhaps best represented in his "Back to the Future: Neomedievalism and Postmodern Digital World Economy," in *Journal of International Affairs*, Spring 1998, 51, no. 2.

14. See Jean Beaudrillard, *The Mirror of Production* (New York: Telos, 1975), p. 121.

15. Steven Connor, *Postmodernist Culture: An Introduction to Theories of the Contemporary*, second edition (Cambridge, MA: Blackwell Publishers Inc., 1997), p. 45.

16. See Alan Wilde, *Horizons of Assent: Modernism, Postmodernism and the Ironic Imagination* (Baltimore: Johns Hopkins University Press, 1981), p. 45.

17. These trends were picked up early by William H. Whyte, Jr., in his seminal *The Organization Man* (New York: Simon and Schuster, 1956). Stephen J. Kobrin cites as a current example the World Bank—an organization whose

authority overlaps that of its nation-state members—whose employees are "citizens of 100 countries who attended six universities." From "Back to the Future: Neomedievalism and Postmodern Digital World Economy."

18. During World War I, Vladimir Lenin maintained that capitalism would expand to include the entire world because compensation to workers, which did not reflect their contribution to the value of the product, created inadequate demand, and necessitated a frantic drive to create new markets. The logical end of this movement would be globalization and world revolution. See V.I. Lenin, *On Politics and Revolution: Selected Writings*, edited by James E. Connor (New York: Pegasus, 1968).

19. Joseph E. Stiglitz points out that transnational corporations endanger local producers in the Third World by pitting them against productive systems which use the most advanced technologies and which are able to absorb local losses until markets are secured. The risk, according to Stiglitz, is heightened by aggressive neoliberal financial policies, such as high interest rates, enforced privatization, and reduced governmental programs, imposed through the International Monetary Fund and other institutions, as well as tariffs and subsidies for their agricultural products imposed by developed countries discouraging Third World imports. The net effect has been to increase Third World poverty. See his *Globalization and Its Discontents* (New York: W.W. Norton, 2002).

20. See "For Richer: How the Permissive Capitalism of the Boom Destroyed American Equality," *New York Times Magazine*, October 20, 2002.

21. E. J. Dionne, Jr., *Why Americans Hate Politics* (New York: Simon & Schuster, 1992), p. 9. The national election of 2000, resulting in a minority president and the suspicion that certain groups were denied full representation, coupled with the unequal influence of wealth in both parties, further increased the political detachment of most voters, particularly the poor.

22. The coalition against a war in Iraq in 2003 had some of the look of the earlier coalition against the war in Vietnam, although it was more narrowly focused.

23. According to Dionne, the conservatives unite "upper-income groups whose main interest is in smaller government and lower taxes, and middle-to-lower income groups, who are culturally conservative but still support most of the New Deal and a lot of the Great Society." The liberals define their position "not by its support for energetic government intervention in the economy, but by its openness to cultural change and its opposition to American intervention abroad." *Ibid.*, pp. 12–13. Throughout his study, Dionne also em-

phasizes the fragmenting use of television spots, the increasing cynicism of political rhetoric, and the appeal to individuals, rather than to socio-economic groups.

24. U.S. Census Bureau, 2000.

25. Center for American Women and Politics.

26. See Charles Lewis, *The Buying of the Congress: How Special Interests Have Stolen Your Right to Life, Liberty, and the Pursuit of Happiness* (New York: Avon Books, 1998). The passage of a campaign finance reform law in 2002 promised only partial relief in changing the substantial control of the political system by monied interests. Its effectiveness was weakened by the administrative policies of the Federal Election Commission (FEC), and by judicial interpretation.

27. See Edward S. Herman and Noam Chomsky, *Manufacturing Consent: The Political Economy of the Mass Media* (New York: Pantheon Books, 1988), and Dionne, *Why Americans Hate Politics.*

28. Widespread recognition of this problem was heightened in 2002 by the scandal surrounding the Enron Corporation and other corporate entities.

29. Table 4a, U.S. Census Bureau, February 27, 2002.

30. Terry Eagleton, *Literary Theory: An Introduction,* second edition (Minneapolis: The University of Minnesota Press, 1996), pp. 27–29. See also Fredrick Jameson's *Postmodernism or The Cultural Logic of Late Capitalism* (Durham, NC: Duke University Press, 1991).

31. From *Structuralism and Since: From Levi Strauss to Derrida,* edited by John Sturrock (Oxford and New York: Oxford University Press, 1979), p. 85. See, also, the reception theory of Stanley Fish in *Is There a Text in This Class? The Authority of Interpretive Communities* (Cambridge, MA: Harvard University Press, 1980).

32. Jonathan Culler remarks, the "work of Barthes, Levi-Strauss, Foucault and Lacan...has called into question the notion of the self as subject or consciousness which might serve as a source of meaning and a principle of explanation.... [They] have made the subject something constituted by or resulting from the play of systems rather than a controlling consciousness which is the master and ultimate origin of systems." *Ibid.,* p. 174.

33. Roland Barthes, "The Death of the Author" in *The Rustle of Language,* translated by Richard Howard (Berkeley, CA, and Los Angeles: University of California Press, 1989), p. 55.

34. Heinz Kohut, *The Restoration of the Self* (New York: International Universities Press, 1977).

35. For an anticipation of the postmodernist argument, see the position of George Herbert Mead, described in chapter 10.

36. Gertrude Himmelfarb, "Postmodernist History," in her *On Looking Into the Abyss* (New York: Alfred A. Knopf, 1994), p. 134. While I have consistent difficulty with Himmelfarb's scornful dismissal of virtually every aspect of postmodernism, and her inaccurate rendering of Marxist criticism, her exposure of the weaknesses of deconstructionist historical criticism is often on target.

37. *Ibid.*, p. 135.

38. See Lyotard, *The Postmodern Condition.* The phrase, "language game," taken from the Austrian- and Cambridge-based philosopher Ludwig Wittgenstein, implies both arbitrariness and competitiveness. See his *Philosophical Investigations*, third edition, translated by G.E.M. Anscombe (Englewood Cliffs, NJ: Prentice Hall, initial copyright, 1953).

39. See Steven Weinberg, "The Revolution That Didn't Happen," in *New York Review of Books*, October 8, 1998.

40. John Rajchman describes the "world market of ideas" as being "like the Toyota of thought: produced and assembled in several different places and then sold everywhere." From "Postmodernism in a Nominalist Frame: The Emergence and Diffusion of a Cultural Category," *Flash Art* 137 (1987), p. 51, cited by Connor, *Postmodernist Culture*, p. 17.

41. See Harold Bloom's brilliant study, *The Western Canon: The Books and School of the Ages* (New York, San Diego, and London: Harcourt Brace & Company, 1994).

42. George Macaulay Trevelyan, *A Shortened History of England* (New York: Longmans, Green & Co., Inc., 1942).

43. Richard Rorty suggests that the alternative is a set of values which are at the core of our culture, which we uphold in solidarity as best as we can. What he dismisses is the possibility that such values can reflect any "objective" standard, a position which brings Rorty close to David Hume. See "Solidarity or Objectivity," in *Relativism: Interpretation and Confrontation*, edited by Michael Krausz (Notre Dame, IN: University of Notre Dame Press, 1989).

44. The widely influential work of Michel Foucault is thought of as political, as it is essentially a critique of the prevailing power of the ruling class to shape social ideas and institutions, such as crime and prisons, madness and asylums, and sexuality in all its manifestations. But his works seldom conclude with constructive social programs, and, indeed, Foucault himself only sporadically

engaged in political activity. See J. Miller, *The Passion of Michel Foucault* (New York: Doubleday, 1994); see also, for example, *Madness and Civilization: A History of Insanity in the Age of Reason*, translated by Richard Howard (New York: Vintage Books, 1973); or his *Politics, Philosophy and Culture: Interviews and Other Writings 1977–1984*, edited with an introduction by Lawrence D. Kritzman (New York and London: Routledge, 1988).

45. Eagleton, *Literary Theory*, p. 124. Thus, we find Derrida declaring, "As far as I can see what this name deconstruction covers, deconstruction is not a movement which one day can arrive at an accomplishment, something which can be achieved—there is not success for deconstruction, there is no goal which we have a hope of reaching, there is no *telos* for deconstruction." From "Interview," in *Art Papers* 10 (1), 1986, p. 34; cited by Argyros, *A Blessed Rage for Order*, p. 12. See also Derrida's *Writing and Difference* (Chicago: University of Chicago Press, 1978) and *Of Grammatology* (Baltimore and London: Johns Hopkins University Press, 1977).

46. Rorty, *Achieving Our Country*, pp. 36–37.

Chapter 12. TOWARD A NEW ACTIVISM

1. Whitehead, *Process and Reality*, p. 515.
2. Matthew 5:37.
3. Eagleton, *Literary Theory*, p. 127.
4. John Dewey, *The Public and Its Problems* (Athens, Ohio: Swallow Press, Ohio University Press, 1991, originally published in 1927, with afterword written in 1946), p. 33.
5. For decades preceding the 1917 revolution, there was a debate in socialist circles on the question of whether or not the revolution, by altering the economic and social conditions, would produce the "socialist man." Hegel had suggested that involvement in a progressive society would work to sensitize its citizens to higher social values, but only over time. In Russia, the ascendancy of Stalin and the totalitarian state left this hypothesis untested.
6. Since September 11, 2001, some of these rights, such as the rights of privacy or of fair judicial procedures, have been under attack.
7. By calling themselves "legal persons," powerful economic groups, particularly corporations, have appropriated the legal protection of persons to secure for themselves immunity from being considered as having a public character and so to be subject to political control. From a moral point of

Endnotes

view, the doctrine has defined a wide sphere of activity in which corporations, as well as their collective owners, the stockholders, feel little responsibility for the effects of their acts on others. They act because it is in the interest of their corporations, and hence, in their private interest, as well. The fact that actions are legally permissible reciprocally blinds the various affected publics to these actions' coerciveness, immorality, or lack of social responsibility. The tobacco companies, for example, enjoyed decades of virtual immunity from public control despite clear evidence that their products not only caused millions of deaths, but were wilfully misrepresented.

8. Dewey writes, "The same forces which have brought about the forms of democratic government...have also brought about conditions which halt the social and humane ideals that demand the utilization of government as the genuine instrumentality of an inclusive and fraternally associated public." *Ibid.*, p. 109. Although Dewey, writing in the 1920s, before the New Deal, saw the desired role of the state as primarily regulatory, his remarks apply even more strongly to a state which could also engage in significant social legislation.

9. Dewey defines the democratic ideal as each individual "having a responsible share according to capacity in forming and directing the activities of the groups to which one belongs..." *Ibid.*, p. 147.

10. See Alexis de Tocqueville, *Democracy in America*, translated by George Lawrence, edited by J.P. Mayer (New York: Harper & Row, 1966).

11. It is important to note that many non-governmental organizations are not benign, such as militia groups or racist organizations, and that many, even with good purposes, are less than democratically run. The possibility of organizing with others for special purposes is morally neutral until the purposes are defined. The need to insist on democratic controls is as imperative here as in government.

12. *State of the World 2003*, p. xvii.

13. Alfred North Whitehead, *Religion in the Making* (Cleveland and New York: The World Publishing Company, 1966, copyright 1926), pp. 38–39.

14. This argues against the adversarial model of Anglo-American law in favor of methods of reconciliation and settlement which bring disputants together by emphasizing residual common interests, rather than furthering distance or isolation by legally structured conflict.

15. John Dewey, *Democracy and Education* (New York: The Free Press, 1966, first published in 1916), p. 331.

16. In 1988–89, I chaired a year-long forty-three–member Commission on His-

tory, Citizenship and Values for Pennsylvania's Secretary of Education, and found depressingly few examples of such education, at least in one state. See "History and Citizenship in a Free Society: The Report of the Secretary of Education's Commission on History, Citizenship and Values," submitted to the Pennsylvania Department of Education by the Pennsylvania Humanities Council, June 30, 1989.

17. For a devastating critique of contemporary textbooks, see Alexander Stille's "The Betrayal of History," the *New York Review of Books*, June 11, 1998.

18. Dewey, by dismissing contemplation as an upper-class diversion, whether it be Greek or modern, often misses the point that vision is a crucial component of situational involvements.

19. See *An Embarrassment of Tyrannies: 25 Years of Index on Censorship*, edited by W. L. Webb & Rose Bell (New York: George Braziller, 1998).

20. In *Renoir, My Father*, translated by Randolph and Dorothy Weaver (Boston: Little, Brown, 1962), Jean Renoir, the filmmaker and son of the painter, Pierre August, relates how his famous father was frantically hand-painting plates in competition with plate-painting machines. Eventually, the painter was thrown out of work because the public preferred the uniformity of the machine as opposed to the artist's "crude" painting.

21. See John Dewey, *Art As Experience* (New York: The Berkeley Publishing Group, copyright 1934), pp. 6–7.

22. Argyros, *A Blessed Rage for Order*, p. 197.

23. From "The World Is Too Much With Us."

24. See Walter Benjamin, "The Work of Art in the Age of Mechanical Reproduction," in *Illuminations: Essays and Reflections*, edited and with an introduction by Hannah Arendt (New York: Schocken Books, 1969).

25. For an attempt to show how an evolutionary perspective, such as I am taking here, translates into personal experience, see Mihaly Csikszentmihalyi, *The Evolving Self: A Psychology for the Third Millennium* (New York: Harper Collins Publishers, 1993). Csikszentmihalyi's sees what he describes as "flow experiences" coming from the kind of situational involvements Dewey has emphasized. His description of complexity is also very close to Loevinger's, whose work he acknowledges.

INDEX

Index

nence complex, 99, 101–102; in modern thought and science, 55–57, 107, 109, 110, 114–118, 130–148, 150, 158, 197–198, 262 n3, 263 n9, n10, n12, and n13; in Whitehead, 122–129; in Dewey, 180–182, 184; and deconstructionism, 216–217; and permanence, 223; and new paradigm, 223, 237, 238

Neumann, John von (*see also* van Neurmann computer), 144, 162, 163, 269 n29

new paradigm, 168–169, 176–195, 223–243

neurophysiology (*see also* neuroscience, and neurology), 61, 110, 119–121, 148, 149–161, 162, 163

New Testament (*see also* Christian Gospels or Gospels), 3, 4, 41–54, 69–70, 93, 98; text, 250 n1; historicity, 251–252 n3, n5, n7

Newton, Isaac: 8, 56; and Sumerian thought, 245 n6; and Aristotle, 250 n18; Descartes, 60, 61; and Locke 65, 69; and Hume, 72, 73; and Kant, 81; and Hegel, 87, 90; and permanence complex, 101–102; and modern thought and science, 108, 115–116, 130, 133–135, 137, 138, 170, 172, 197; and mathematics, 118; and Whitehead, 125, 128; and Sullivan, 185; and Freud, 185; and deconstructionism, 216–217

Nietzsche, Friedrich, 5, 10, 171, 185

Pagels, Elaine, 50, 51–52
Passmore, John, 109

Peirce, Charles Sanders, 259 n6
Penrose, Roger, 136–137, 264 n17
permanence, 2 (*see also* religion); in Sumer, 3, 7–15; in Plato, 3; in Judaism, 16–25; in Greek thought, 26–40; in Christianity, 2, 4, 41–54; in Descartes, 57–63; in Locke, 63–71; in Kant, 79–87; in Hegel, 87–92; under attack, 106, 108; in Whitehead, 121–129; in modern thought and science, 132, 150, 160; and Dewey, 181; and Sullivan, 190; and modern history, 198; and deconstructionism, 212; and new paradigm, 223–225, 241–243

permanence complex (*see also* permanence), 93–103, 158–159, 223

phenomenology (*see also* subjectivism), 62, 101

Pinter, Harold, 206
Philo of Alexandria, 24, 248 n18
Piaget, Jean, 80, 99, 147, 191, 193–194; and new paradigm, 238
Plank, Max, 133
Plato, 2, 3, 26–34, 93; and Judaism, 24, 248 n18; and Christianity, 4, 26, 32–33, 52; and Aristotle 34–40; and Descartes, 58–60; and Locke, 63–65, 68, 70, 255 n18; and Hume, 72, 76; and Kant 80, 81, 82, 86; and Hegel, 88, 91; and permanence complex, 95, 96, 98, 99, 100, 101, 103; and mathematics, 117; and Whitehead, 122,123, 124, 126–129; and modern biology, 140–144, 147, 150, 151, 158; and modern physics, 138, 262 n9; and Mead, 177, 179; and Dewey, 181, 183; and Sullivan, 188, 190; and mod-

291

Books from Helios Press

Helios Press and Allworth Press are imprints of Allworth Communications, Inc.. Selected titles are listed below.

The Shape of Ancient Thought
by Thomas McEvilley (hardcover, 6¼ x 9¼, 752 pages, $35.00)

The Tragedy of Zionism: How Its Revolutionary Past Haunts Israeli Democracy
by Bernard Avishai (paperback, 6 x 9, 400 pages, $16.95)

Secrets of the Exodus: The Egyptian Origins of the Hebrew People
by Messod and Roger Sabbah (hardcover, 304 pages, $24.95)

The Psychology of War: Comprehending Its Mystique and Its Madness
by Lawrence LeShan, Ph.D. (paperback, 6 x 9, 192 pages, $16.95)

The Dilemma of Psychology: A Psychologist Looks at His Troubled Profession
by Lawrence LeShan, Ph.D. (paperback, 5½ x 8½, 224 pages, $16.95)

The Medium, the Mystic, and the Physicist: Toward a General Theory of the Paranormal
by Lawrence LeShan, Ph.D. (paperback, 5½ x 8½, 320 pages, $19.95)

The Inner Source: Exploring Hypnosis, Revised Edition
by Donald S. Connery (paperback, 5⅜ x 8½, 304 pages, $16.95)

How to Heal: A Guide for Caregivers
by Jeff Kane, M.D. (paperback, 5¼ x 8¼, 208 pages, $16.95)

Healing with Nature
by Susan S. Scott (paperback, 6 x 9, 224 pages, $16.95)

What Money Really Means
by Thomas Kostigen (paperback, 6 x 9, 240 pages, $19.95)